"Eschewing the traditional compulsion to cover the Bible/Old Testament in a single term, John Kaltner has crafted an introductory textbook that works from the principle that "less is more." By limiting his attention to six key themes—creation, covenant, liberation, being human, "the other," and social justice—and tracing them through the canon and beyond, Kaltner deftly exposes first-time readers to both the central ideas and major interpretive questions surrounding the biblical text. Breezy and readable, the book should prove useful to instructors who are looking for ways to make the academic study of the Hebrew Bible more accessible to introductory students."

—Chris Stanley
St. Bonaventure University

"*Reading the Old Testament Anew: Biblical Perspectives on Today's Issues* shows that John Kaltner is not only a skilled biblical scholar but also an accomplished teacher. While the contents of the book consist of the findings of reliable and current biblical scholarship, its uniqueness lies in its carefully structured pedagogical format. Kaltner does not simply suggest a method of learning the material; he demonstrates it as he leads the reader step-by-step through each chapter. This begins with personal experience of reading the text; then an overview of general information about it; followed by in-depth study; ending with contemporary implications of its meaning. *Reading the Old Testament Anew: Biblical Perspectives on Today's Issues* will serve as a valuable resource as well as a fine text for undergraduates."

—Dianne Bergant
Catholic Theological Union

"While introductory textbooks on the Old Testament are a dime a dozen, John Kaltner has succeeded in creating something fresh and new. Most textbooks provide broad summaries of biblical texts and the various scholarly theories developed to interpret them. But Kaltner, by contrast, provides a detailed close reading of selected texts, showing how and why scholarly approaches have grown organically out of the critical issues encountered in a detailed engagement with biblical narratives. Kaltner does not just tell the reader what scholars say about these ancient texts. He instead shows the reader why the scholars say what they do and why this is important for how we interpret these texts in our contemporary context. This book will go a long way towards getting students of the Bible to critically engage with the Old Testament literature rather than just learn information about it. I highly recommend it."

—Robert F. Shedinger
Luther College

Author Acknowledgments

I wish to express my thanks to Brad Harmon and Maura Hagarty of Anselm Academic for their assistance, encouragement, and support as they helped me conceive and develop this project. Paul Peterson is an outstanding editor whose suggestions and advice were invaluable to me at each step along the way. The anonymous reviewers who read and commented on the initial draft of the manuscript offered very useful feedback, and I appreciate very much their insights and critiques. The book undoubtedly has shortcomings and flaws despite the help of these people, and I take full responsibility for them. Linda Schearing and Ellen White wrote the bridge sections that are found after three of the chapters, and I thank them very much for these very fine contributions to the book. A final word of appreciation goes to my colleagues in the Religious Studies Department of Rhodes College, whose commitment to teaching and scholarship continues to inspire me.

Publisher Acknowledgments

Thank you to the following individual who reviewed this work in progress:

Pauline Viviano, *Loyola University of Chicago*

READING *the* OLD TESTAMENT ANEW

Biblical
Perspectives
on Today's Issues

JOHN KALTNER

ANSELM
ACADEMIC

DEDICATION

To my siblings, Karen, Pinky, and Dennis
in appreciation for their love, support, and friendship

⌇

Created by the publishing team of Anselm Academic.

Printed in the United States of America

7081

ISBN 978-11-59982-774-2

Contents

Preface

What This Book Is, and What It Is Not

As its subtitle indicates, this book provides an overview of the Old Testament's perspectives on a number of topics that are of interest to many of its modern readers. It does this by considering biblical passages that are related to each of the themes, and by explaining how scholars have attempted to understand and interpret those texts. The following six topics are treated in the book: creation, covenant, liberation, the human condition, the other, and social justice.

That selective list of themes means that the book is not meant to be a comprehensive introduction to the contents of the Old Testament. Many other topics are discussed in the biblical text, which contains additional literary genres and styles of writing that will not be considered here. In addition, this book does not present an exhaustive treatment of how scholars have studied the passages considered here. Rather, it attempts to lay out some of the views and interpretive approaches that have been most commonly accepted within the scholarly community.

How the Book Is Arranged

The introduction presents some general background information on the Old Testament—what it is, its contents, the contexts from which it emerged and to which it responded, and the various ways it has been read and interpreted. This is followed by six chapters that each treat one of the topics mentioned above. Those chapters are all organized in the same way. After a brief introduction to the theme, three sections follow that are titled "First Impressions," "Second Opinions," and "Implications and Applications."

The "First Impressions" section identifies the biblical passage(s) to be read, and it offers some thoughts on what a careful reading of the text might reveal. Some of the observations are literary in nature, while others are theological, ethical, or practical. In most cases, these comments are the result of a careful and attentive reading of the passage that does not require special training or in-depth familiarity with biblical scholarship. The part of each chapter identified as "Second Opinions" seeks to build on the previous section by explaining how Bible scholars have tried to address some of the issues and problems that the initial reading uncovered. As will become clear throughout the course of the book, scholars often disagree about the best way to interpret or understand certain aspects of a text, and so different theories and interpretive strategies sometimes exist side-by-side in relation to the same passage.

Each chapter concludes with a section titled "Implications and Applications," which provides a set of questions meant to facilitate reflection and discussion about the theme and how it is presented in the Old Testament. Other questions might have emerged in the course of reading the chapter, and students and instructors are encouraged to add them to the list as new ideas occur to them. Also meant to foster further thought and engagement are the questions in textboxes throughout each chapter; these questions relate to particular issues and themes that have been discussed in the surrounding text. A final feature of note is that each chapter includes a section that puts the biblical themes in conversation with either works of art or, in one case, an organization that is attempting to address a social concern. The works of art include paintings, songs, a film, and a television show. Three of these sections are brief (in chapters 2, 3, and 5), while the other three (in chapters 1, 4, and 6) are in the form of longer essays that have been written by Linda S. Schearing and Ellen White.

Why These Topics?

Any number of topics could be added to the six that are discussed in this volume. These have been chosen because of the book's intended purpose as a classroom resource for courses in religion or theology that have a biblical component in them. Syllabi from dozens of such courses were examined to determine which biblical texts and themes are commonly covered in them, and these six topics were far and away the most frequently found. Their regular inclusion in these courses indicates that these are among the most important issues that instructors seek to address in relation to the Bible in their religion and theology courses, and it is hoped that this book's treatment of them all together will be pedagogically convenient and useful.

How to Use This Book: To the Instructor

Students do not need to have prior familiarity with the biblical literature in order to understand and benefit from this book. Similarly, the book does not assume or require that the instructor be formally trained in biblical scholarship. It is essential that students read the assigned biblical passages before reading the sections in the book that discuss them. Because students are to read the passages on their own, the passages are not retold or summarized in any great detail, although sometimes portions of them are paraphrased and highlighted in order to call attention to important elements. Each chapter stands on its own, so the chapters can be read independently of one another in any order, depending on the design of the course. The textbox questions throughout each chapter can be used in different ways. For example, they might form the basis of out-of-class assignments that are then submitted to the instructor. Alternatively, they could serve as conversation starters meant to generate discussion and debate in the classroom. The same can be said about the list of questions in the "Implications and Applications" sections, as well as the material in the sections that use works of art to explore biblical themes, which might be used for in-class interaction, out-of-class work, or a combination of the two.

How to Use This Book: To the Student

Each chapter of this book focuses on a particular set of passages from the Old Testament that are relevant to the theme that is the topic of the chapter. You do not need to have prior familiarity with these passages or with the Bible in order to follow along and understand what is being said. In fact, previous knowledge of the biblical material can sometimes be a drawback to understanding because one might approach the reading with certain preconceptions that could make it difficult to be open to a new and unfamiliar interpretation. For this reason, the reader is urged to put aside prior views of the Bible, to the extent that it is possible to do so, and approach the material as if one were a first-time reader of the text. The biblical passages to be read are identified in the section of each chapter that is titled "First Impressions"; it is important to read those passages before reading the rest of the section. If these passages are not read first, much of the material presented in this book will not make sense. Throughout each chapter there are questions in textboxes; one should attempt to answer these questions while working through the chapter. The set of questions at or near the end of each chapter that is titled "Implications and Applications" is meant to give a look at the big picture and to encourage reflection about what has been learned about the topic and how it is treated in the Old Testament. Each chapter includes either a short explanation in a textbox or a long essay that attempts to provide an example of how the themes and issues discussed in this book continue to be addressed in various artistic and social contexts.

Introduction

What Is the Old Testament?

The Bible is likely one of the most deceptive books you will ever encounter. It looks and feels like any other book, but between its two covers (if you are reading a hard copy) are an incredible assortment of writings composed over a period of more than one thousand years that treat a wide range of themes and topics. It is a compilation of separate writings, rather than a single work, so in that sense reading the Bible is like reading the collected works of Shakespeare. But, in another sense, reading the Bible is not at all like reading the Bard's plays because the biblical books were written by many authors over an extended period of time rather than by one person over the course of a single lifetime.

The word *bible* contains a clue as to its true nature, for the Greek word on which it is based (*ta biblia*) is actually a plural noun that means "the scrolls." The choice of this word to refer to the biblical canon indicates an awareness of the composite nature of the collection of writings that it designates.

If your preferred version of the Bible is not of the hard copy variety, you likely have something akin to it literally within your reach. Today's e-readers have much in common with the Bible, which in some ways was their ancient equivalent. Think about what is on the typical Nook or Kindle. In all likelihood, it contains an eclectic and wide-ranging hodgepodge of works written by all kinds of people from different places and times. That is what the Bible is. The collected writings on reading devices are personal canons created of works that have meaning and importance for their owners. But they probably have very little in common beyond the fact that they have all been brought together to form a unique library. None of the authors wrote with the intention of someday being part of the group of other writers assembled on a single device. This was exactly the situation for the largely anonymous authors of the Old Testament. They all wrote separate, stand-alone works, and they certainly did not think their writings would one day be included in a collected volume that was still centuries away and would be called "the Bible." So the Bible has the look and feel of a book, but it is not your average or typical book.

Formation: How Did the Bible Take Shape?

The Bible exists because of a process known as canonization, which is to say that it is the result of people's choices and decisions. Without that human involvement, there would be no Bible. That is why one scholar has aptly described it as an "accidental book."[1]

Whenever an accident occurs, an investigation is in order. The first step is to survey the accident scene for clues to better understand what happened. In this case, we wish to understand how this accidental book came to be by inquiring about the way it developed and took shape. In particular, we will focus on that part of the book that is known as the Old Testament or Hebrew Bible. What were the circumstances and events that ultimately led to the existence of an Old Testament originally written on scrolls that we can now access with the flip of a switch and a tap on a pad?

Many people approach the Old Testament with questions of historicity— how many of the events described in the Old Testament actually took place? Do the stories accurately report things that really happened? Scholars continue to debate this question, and opinions vary widely. At one end of the spectrum are those who argue that the Old Testament presents a fictionalized or theologized account of the history of Israel that bears little or no resemblance to actual events. At the other end, some maintain that the biblical account is an accurate and reliable presentation of what occurred. Between these two extremes are others, probably the majority, who believe that in some places the Old Testament relates events that really took place, but it is impossible to know how accurately it recounts them. Within this last group there is much debate over the methods by which one can reach a decision regarding historicity and what conclusions can be reasonably drawn when those methods are employed. The matter is complicated by the fact that the people and events mentioned in the Old Testament are rarely mentioned in sources outside the Bible. This means we have to rely primarily on internal evidence from the Old Testament, which is not an ideal situation for addressing questions of historicity.

Most probably it is only with the appearance of Abraham in Genesis 12 that the Old Testament begins to relate traditions that might have some basis in real events. The first eleven chapters of Genesis, which contain the stories of creation, Adam and Eve, Cain and Abel, and Noah and the flood, are mythological in nature and are probably not meant to be taken literally.

The question of historicity has little direct impact on the attempt to understand the process by which "the accidental book"— the Old Testament—reached its present form. It is likely that many of the biblical traditions that were later

---

1. Timothy Beal, *The Rise and Fall of the Bible: The Unexpected History of an Accidental Book* (New York: Houghton Mifflin Harcourt, 2011).

written down originally circulated by word of mouth; this is known as the "oral tradition." This was often the case with other bodies of literature in antiquity, and there is no reason to doubt that at least some parts of the biblical canon were originally transmitted orally.

Composition

Once the traditions began to be written down they went through a number of steps before reaching the form in which we have them today. The three main stages of this development were composition, transmission, and translation. The first stage was the period during which the various works were composed and put in written form. It is common to refer to those who were responsible for this activity as the biblical "authors," but this term is somewhat misleading. Every written work must have an author in the sense of someone who commits it to writing, and there were undoubtedly many individuals who played such a role for the biblical literature. Nonetheless, it has become increasingly clear that much of the material in the Old Testament does not come directly from its original author but has been passed through other hands before reaching the reader. Those other hands often left their own marks on the text either by reworking what an earlier author had written or by combining it with other sources, or both. In other words, in most cases it is better to think of the individual books of the Old Testament as composite works rather than single-author compositions.

It is therefore preferable to describe those responsible for the biblical text that has come down to us as editors rather than authors. The technical term biblical scholars often use for an editor is *redactor*, and the activity associated with that role is called *redaction*. Many places in the Old Testament show evidence of redactors hard at work. In fact, redaction can be detected on the first pages of the Bible in the opening chapters of Genesis, which was one of the first texts scholars looked at when they began to approach the Bible in this way during the eighteenth century. The first three chapters of Genesis present the biblical account of creation, but careful analysis of this material indicates that it actually contains two different stories that describe how the world came into existence. The presence of some of the telltale signs of editorial activity—including repetition, inconsistencies, and different perspectives—allows us to conclude that the biblical "author" was actually a redactor who drew upon and put together two different, older accounts to tell the story of the origin of the world. A similar thing can be seen a few chapters later in Genesis 6–9, where the story of the flood is told by weaving together two versions into one combined account that is full of contradictions and duplications.

Some Old Testament books are very upfront and blunt about their use of sources, and they do not try to hide the fact that they are edited works. For example, the books of 1 and 2 Kings provide a record of the histories of the

The Dead Sea Scrolls, discovered in these caves in Qumran in Israel, do not all agree with the now-standard Masoretic Text of the Hebrew Bible, demonstrating that the form of the text was still fluid in the first century.

southern kingdom of Judah and the northern kingdom of Israel by describing the reigns of their various rulers. After the description of each king, a standard formula is used that is repeated like a refrain throughout the books: "The rest of the deeds of King X, are they not written of in the Book of the Annals of the Kings of Judah (or Israel)?"[2] In other words, "If you want more information beyond what I've provided here, please consult the sources I used in compiling my history." Similarly, other books in the Old Testament testify to their composite nature by naming the sources within them. Two of the best examples are the books of Psalms and Proverbs, which both mark off collections of material within the larger book by identifying where they come from or the people associated with them. A final example can be seen in the book of Isaiah, which contains material addressed to different audiences over a span of more than a century that has been brought together in one book by its redactor.

The period of composition likely went on for an extended period of time, as evidence from the famous Dead Sea Scrolls suggests. That collection of documents was discovered in 1947 at a place called Qumran, near the western coast of the Dead Sea in modern-day Israel, and some have hailed it as one of the most important archaeological finds of the twentieth century. It contains approximately one thousand texts, some entire manuscripts and others fragments, that come from the period between 150 BCE and 68 CE. Among them are scrolls from almost every Old Testament book, and the evidence they contain suggests that the texts of some books were not yet firmly established and not agreed upon by

---

2. Examples of this formula can be seen in 1 Kings 14:29; 15:31; 16:5; 22:45; 2 Kings 1:18; 10:34; 21:25.

all. For example, among the findings are several different versions of the book of Jeremiah. This indicates that even at this relatively late date compositional activity was still going on; the text of parts of the Old Testament was in a state of flux.

Transmission

Different manuscript traditions were circulating and competing at places like Qumran, but the canonization process settled things once and for all as one version was deemed official for each Old Testament book. This ushered in the second stage of transmission during which the accepted text was disseminated and further refined for use within the community.

One of the most significant contributions made to this part of the process was by a group of scholars known as the "Masoretes," a term that comes from a Hebrew word meaning "tradition." The Masoretes, who were active in the second half of the first century CE, were primarily concerned with making the text of the Old Testament as readable and unambiguous as possible. The earliest biblical manuscripts included only consonants and contained no vowels, a practice that has continued into the present day since Hebrew is normally written with consonants only.[3] As unusual as this may seem, it causes very few problems because if someone knows the Hebrew language well the words are easily and immediately recognizable in their consonantal form and there is no confusion. Nonetheless, in a small fraction of cases it is possible to read a word in more than one way. In order to make sure that there would be no mistakes in reading the Old Testament, the Masoretes devised a way of adding vowels to the text through a system of markings that indicate how to vocalize the consonants. They also added a set of notes in the margins of their manuscripts that provided information on the proper spelling and pronunciation of words that might be unclear or confusing. Their work, which created what scholars refer to as the "Masoretic Text" (often abbreviated as MT), became the accepted version and it played a major role in the standardization of the text of the Old Testament. The MT is the Hebrew text that is commonly used by Bible scholars in their work, and it has been the basis for many of the translations of the Old Testament into the present day.

Translation

Translation is the third stage in the growth and development of the text of the Old Testament. The Old Testament was originally written in Hebrew and

---

3. While a full system for writing Hebrew vowels did not develop until centuries later, the earliest Hebrew manuscripts often did provide some guidance about how a word should be vocalized through the use of what are called *matres lectionis* (Latin for "mothers of reading"). These are consonants that do double duty by sometimes functioning as vowels after other consonants. For example, the consonant "w/v" on occasion can also serve as the long vowel "u."

Aramaic, another Semitic language that is closely related to Hebrew. As time went on, fewer and fewer people were able to read the text in its original languages; this led to the need for translations. One reason for this was the spread of Judaism into other areas of the Mediterranean world. The earliest translation was that of the Septuagint, begun in the third century BCE to accommodate the needs of Jews living in Greek-speaking Egypt. The term *Septuagint* comes from the Latin word for "seventy," and it is often referred to using the Latin numerals for that number, LXX. It takes its name from a tradition that says seventy (or, according to some versions of the legend, seventy-two) Jewish scholars were asked by the Greek king to translate the Torah into Greek, and they each produced the same translation. In fact, the work of translating the Septuagint took several generations, and it was not completed until the second half of the second century BCE. By the time of Jesus, it was well-known throughout the Mediterranean world; when the New Testament, which was written in Greek, quotes the Old Testament, the quotations usually follow the Septuagint.

Another reason why translations became necessary was the emergence of Christianity, which originally began in the first century CE as a subgroup within Judaism. Despite its eventual separation from the Jewish faith, Christianity maintained close ties with it and accepted the Old Testament as part of its own set of canonical writings. As the Christian community spread to areas where Hebrew and Aramaic were not well known, its scriptures were translated into the languages that were familiar to the local populations. After the Septuagint, two of the most important translations of the Old Testament associated with Christianity are those into Syriac and Latin. The Syriac version, known as the *Peshitta* (a Syriac word that means "common" or "simple"), is the second oldest translation after the Septuagint. It was done in the first or second century CE, and it was the work of Syriac-speaking Christians who wanted to make the Old Testament available to speakers of their language, which is a form of Aramaic. The Latin translation was eventually standardized in a version known as the Vulgate (which means "common"); it was primarily the work of Saint Jerome in the late fourth century CE.[4]

The first translation of the Bible into English was made by the Englishman John Wycliffe and his associates in the late fourteenth century; it was based on the Vulgate. His countryman William Tyndale did the first English translation directly from the original Hebrew, Aramaic, and Greek, but he had not completed his work on the Old Testament when he was executed in 1536. The famous King James Bible, which was the work of a group of nearly fifty scholars, appeared in 1611; it would serve as the standard English Bible translation for nearly two hundred and fifty years. In modern times, translation of

---

4. For more information on these and other translations of the Bible, see Bruce M. Metzger, *The Bible in Translation: Ancient and English Versions* (Grand Rapids: Baker Academic, 2001).

the Bible has continued unabated, and the United Bible Societies organization estimates that translation projects are presently underway in almost five hundred languages.

Translations can vary considerably when they are compared to one another, and those differences are often due to different philosophies regarding how to translate. The two main approaches are referred to as "formal equivalence" and "dynamic equivalence." With formal equivalence, special attention is paid to the original language, and the translation is rendered in the target language in a way that tries to conform to the linguistic norms and features of the original. This can sometimes result in a translation that seems stilted and wooden. Dynamic equivalence looks in the other direction and focuses on the target language. With this approach, every effort is made to produce a translation that seems as natural as possible to the reader or hearer. There is a potential drawback with this method as well, in that the effort to create the most comfortable translation possible can lead to distortion of the meaning found in the original text.

This survey of how the Old Testament came to be highlights the fact that its development was a very lengthy and complicated process. There were many twists and turns in its long and winding journey from oral traditions that were passed along by word of mouth to the space it now occupies on your bookshelf or reading device. And that is just the macro-view. When one breaks things down further, the story of the Bible's formation becomes even more compelling and fascinating. Each book of the Old Testament, and each section of each book, had its own unique odyssey that set it on the path to its eventual inclusion in the biblical corpus alongside other similar wanderers. You might say that they were all parts of an accident that was waiting to happen.

What Does the Old Testament Contain?

The Old Testament—or, as it is commonly known in Judaism, the Hebrew Bible—is a collection of texts that are sacred for billions of Jews and Christians around the world, but they do not all agree on its precise contents. Sometimes there is variation in the order in which the writings are found, in other places the differences relate to how those writings are grouped, and elsewhere the disagreement extends to which books should be included in the collection. If you were to go to the Bible section of your local bookstore and inspect the table of contents of a copy you had randomly pulled from the shelf, the material would be organized in one of three ways depending on which, or whose, version of the Bible you had chosen. Those various configurations are associated with particular faith communities—one with Jews, another with Protestant Christians, and the third with Roman Catholics and Orthodox Christians. The different arrangements can be outlined as follows:

Jewish Canon	Protestant Canon	Catholic/Orthodox Canon
Torah	*Pentateuch*	*Pentateuch*
Genesis Exodus Leviticus Numbers Deuteronomy	Genesis Exodus Leviticus Numbers Deuteronomy	Genesis Exodus Leviticus Numbers Deuteronomy
Nevi'im	*Historical Books*	*Historical Books*

Former Prophets
Joshua
Judges
1-2 Samuel
1-2 Kings
 	
Latter Prophets
Isaiah
Jeremiah
Ezekiel
Book of the Twelve
   Hosea
   Joel
   Amos
   Obadiah
   Jonah
   Micah
   Nahum
   Habakkuk
   Zephaniah
   Haggai
   Zechariah
   Malachi
	Joshua
	Judges
	Ruth
	1 Samuel
	2 Samuel
	1 Kings
	2 Kings
	1 Chronicles
	2 Chronicles
	Ezra
	Nehemiah
	Esther
		Joshua
		Judges
		Ruth
		1 Samuel
		2 Samuel
		1 Kings
		2 Kings
		1 Chronicles
		2 Chronicles
		Ezra
		Nehemiah[5]
		Tobit
		Judith
		Esther
		1 Maccabees
		2 Maccabees[6]

	Poetic Books Job Psalms Proverbs Qohelet Song of Songs	*Poetic Books* Job Psalms[7] Proverbs Qohelet Song of Songs Wisdom of Solomon Sirach[8]

continued

continued

5. The Orthodox canon includes 1 Esdras and combines Ezra and Nehemiah as a single book called 2 Esdras.

6. The Orthodox canon includes 3 Maccabees (and sometimes 4 Maccabees as an appendix).

7. The Orthodox canon includes Psalm 151.

8. The Orthodox canon includes the Prayer of Manasseh.

continued

Jewish Canon	Protestant Canon	Catholic/Orthodox Canon
Ketuvim	*Prophets*	*Prophets*
Psalms	Isaiah	Isaiah
Proverbs	Jeremiah	Jeremiah
Job	Lamentations	Lamentations
Song of Songs	Ezekiel	Baruch
Ruth	Daniel	Letter of Jeremiah
Lamentations	Hosea	Ezekiel
	Joel	Daniel
Qohelet	Amos	Hosea
Esther	Obadiah	Joel
Daniel	Jonah	Amos
Ezra-Nehemiah	Micah	Obadiah
1–2 Chronicles	Nahum	Jonah
	Habakkuk	Micah
	Zephaniah	Nahum
	Haggai	Habakkuk
	Zechariah	Zephaniah
	Malachi	Haggai
		Zechariah
		Malachi

The multiple forms the Old Testament can take are due to two factors: (1) its role as a sacred text, and (2) the process by which the Bible and similar works, like the Qur'an in Islam, achieve that special standing. For Jews and Christians, the Bible is the word of God that communicates the divine will to humanity, but how did it come to be understood in this way? The simple fact is that some people consider the Bible to be divine revelation because certain other people long ago made the decision to view it that way. In other words, some books are more sacred than others because communities have designated them as such and therefore set them apart as distinct from other writings. The Bible is considered to be the word of God for many people, but it reached that lofty status with the help of the words of human beings.

The Jewish Canon

A collection of sacred writings like the Bible is often referred to as a "canon." This term comes from the Greek word for a reed, which was a common measuring device in antiquity not unlike the way yardsticks or rulers function today. With that original meaning in mind, it might be said that a canon is a set of writings that serve as a yardstick by which a community seeks to measure itself and determine who its members are, what they believe, and how they should conduct themselves. The process by which writings become part of a canon is known as canonization, and the precise way that process unfolded in the case of the Bible remains something of a mystery. To put the matter bluntly, we know where we are but we're not completely sure how we got here.

There is a longstanding tradition within Judaism that understands the canon to have been decided by a gathering of rabbis and other Jewish scholars who met in the Mediterranean town of Jamnia around the year 90 CE to decide which works would be included in the Bible. Although the idea of Jewish leaders meeting during a seaside retreat to hammer out the details of the canon may seem attractive and quaint, it is too simplistic a way to explain what was undoubtedly a very long and complex process. We can glimpse the general contours of that process in only vague terms, and it is unlikely that we will ever know with certainty exactly how the corpus of the Bible took shape.

One of the things we do know is that for Judaism the end result was a three-part canon that is commonly known by the acronym TNK, written *Tanakh*. The "T" is the *Torah* (a Hebrew word that means "instruction"), which is comprised of the first five books of the Bible: Genesis, Exodus, Leviticus, Numbers, and Deuteronomy. This section is also known as the Pentateuch, which is Greek for "five scrolls." Scholars generally agree that this was the first part of the Old Testament to be canonized, and it had likely achieved that status before the time of the legendary meeting of the rabbis at Jamnia mentioned above. Jews, and some Christians, have traditionally identified Moses as the author of the Torah, but for reasons that will become clear, most scholars have rejected this idea.

The "N" in *Tanakh* comes from *Nevi'im*, a Hebrew word that means "prophets." It is comprised of two sections, usually referred to as the "Former Prophets" and "Latter Prophets." The first section contains four books: Joshua, Judges, 1–2 Samuel, and 1–2 Kings.[9] These works describe an approximately six-hundred-year period in the history of the Israelite people that includes their entry into the Promised Land, the rise of the kingship under David and Solomon, the split of the kingdom into northern and southern entities, and the fall of those kingdoms at the hands of the Assyrians and the Babylonians.[10]

The section known as the Latter Prophets also includes four books: Isaiah, Jeremiah, Ezekiel, and the Book of the Twelve. The latter is actually a collection of twelve different works that are each associated with a particular prophet: Hosea, Joel, Amos, Obadiah, Jonah, Micah, Nahum, Habakkuk, Zephaniah, Haggai, Zechariah, and Malachi. Each of these twelve writings is considered to

---

9. Samuel and Kings are each divided into two separate books in Christian Bibles.

10. The purpose of these books is more theological than historical. That is, the events they describe are presented through the lens of certain theological ideas, like the importance of following the law that was revealed to Moses on Mount Sinai. Consequently, the historicity of these books is disputed in some places. This type of approach to retelling historical events was common in antiquity, so there is nothing unusual about the Old Testament in this regard.

be a separate book in Christian Bibles. The books in the Latter Prophets each address particular political and social contexts during the latter part of Israelite history from nearly two centuries after the kingdom was split into two until the Babylonian invasion that ushered in a period known as the exile, the displacement of the people of Israel.

The third part of the Jewish canon, the "K" in *Tanakh*, is the *Ketuvim*, a Hebrew word meaning "writings." It contains a set of eleven works that cover a wide range of genres and have very little in common. The types of writing found here include prayers (Psalms), life lessons (Proverbs), short story (Ruth), history (1–2 Chronicles, Ezra-Nehemiah), reflections on human existence (Lamentations, Job, and Qohelet, also known as Ecclesiastes), apocalyptic (Daniel), and erotica (Song of Songs). In addition to their wide-ranging topics and styles, these works also range in date over a period of several centuries. Scholars generally believe that some of these books were among the last works accepted into the Old Testament canon.

The Christian Canons

When we view the Old Testament canon from the perspective of Christianity things are more complicated. In addition to certain differences when compared to the Jewish arrangement of the books, Christian disagreement over which books should be included results in two different collections of writings. All three forms of the canon agree on the contents and ordering of the first five books, so the differences begin to emerge only when we consider the second part of the Jewish canon. Unlike the tripartite structure adopted by Judaism, both Christian canons have four parts that include, after the Pentateuch, the Historical Books, the Poetic Books, and the Prophets. The section known as the Historical Books contains all the works of the Former Prophets from the Jewish canon as well as a number of books listed under the Writings: Ruth, 1–2 Chronicles, Ezra, Nehemiah, and Esther. The Poetic Books section contains a set of five works that are also part of the Writings in the Jewish canon: Job, Psalms, Proverbs, Qohelet, and Song of Songs (also known as Song of Solomon). The works identified as the Prophets in the Christian canons include all those listed as Latter Prophets in Judaism in addition to Lamentations and Daniel, two books the Jewish canon lists among the Writings.

As the above outline of the three canons indicates, the Protestant Christian canon differs from the Jewish arrangement. The number of sections is greater (three in the Jewish version, and four in the Protestant one) and all of the books in the *Ketuvim* section are relocated elsewhere. Despite this organizational shift, however, the Jewish and Protestant canons are identical in content.

That is not the case with the Roman Catholic/Orthodox canon. In addition to the same reordering that occurs in the Protestant canon, the other Christian canon contains seven books that are not found in the other two: Tobit, Judith, 1–2 Maccabees, Wisdom of Solomon, Sirach, and Baruch. The reason for this is that these added works are included in the Greek translation of the Old Testament known as the Septuagint that was done in the third and second centuries BCE. Catholic and Orthodox Christians consider these additional works to be canonical, but they were never accepted in the Jewish canon, and the Protestant canon accepts as canonical only the books found in the Jewish canon. Beyond these additional seven works, Catholic and Orthodox Bibles also contain extra material in the books of Esther and Daniel that is present in the Septuagint but not found in the Hebrew text. To complete the picture, it should be noted that the Orthodox version of the Bible includes an extra Psalm that is not found in Catholic Bibles.[11] This means that, technically speaking, there are three different canons in Christianity, not two. All of these additional writings are sometimes included in Protestant Bibles in a section that is titled "Apocrypha" (a Greek word that means "hidden"), but Protestants do not consider them canonical.

© The Schøyen Collection, Oslo and London

The number of books accepted in the Old Testament varies from one Christian community to another. The Ethiopian Orthodox Church, uniquely, accepts the book of Enoch (shown here) as canonical scripture.

This discussion of the different canons is related to the question of how best to refer to this particular set of writings. It is common for Christians to refer to them as the "Old Testament" as a way of distinguishing between them and the canonical works they do not share with Jews, the "New Testament." But this designation can come across as insensitive or insulting to Jews, who do not accept the Christian writings as part of the canon. Moreover, the term "old" can have a pejorative connotation: "old" can suggest "outmoded" or "no longer valid." This has caused some to use "Hebrew Bible" as a preferred alternative to "Old Testament," but this designation is not without its problems. Some parts of the text, including a lengthy section of the book of Daniel, are written in Aramaic rather than Hebrew and, as noted, some of the books in the Catholic/Orthodox canon exist only in Greek versions. Other ways of designating the two parts of the Christian canon have been proposed, like "First Testament" and "Second Testament," but none of them have caught on.

---

11. See the canon table for additional differences between the Orthodox and Roman Catholic canons.

Biblical Groupings

There are other ways of understanding the structure and makeup of the Old Testament beyond the three- and four-part arrangements already mentioned. In some places, several books can be viewed together as blocks of texts that share certain features. As noted, Jews and Christians put the first five books together in a group identified as the Torah or Pentateuch. But this is a somewhat forced grouping because the last of those books, Deuteronomy, better serves as the introduction to what comes after it rather than the conclusion to what comes before it. The books that follow Deuteronomy are the Former Prophets in the Jewish canon and the Historical Books in the Christian ordering. As already noted, they purport to tell the history of the people from their entry into the land until the invasion of the Babylonians. That history is told from the vantage point of the book of Deuteronomy, which deals primary with the law and the importance of obeying it. The books that follow Deuteronomy present Israelite history from the perspective of obedience to the law—when good things happen it's because people are following the law, and when bad things happen it's due to their straying from it. The connection between the last book of the Pentateuch and the works that come after it is so strong that this section of the Bible—Joshua, Judges, 1–2 Samuel, and 1–2 Kings—is usually referred to as the "Deuteronomistic History."

Another natural grouping of biblical writings can be seen in a set of three works commonly called the "Wisdom Writings" that includes Job, Qohelet (also known as Ecclesiastes), and Proverbs. These books are the Bible's best examples of a genre common throughout the ancient Near East that drew upon common human experience to offer reflections and advice on how to live life. Both Job and Qohelet address key questions that everyone can relate to: the former ponders the mystery of innocent suffering, while the latter wrestles with the absurdity of human existence. As its name suggests, Proverbs contains a series of maxims and observations on humanity and its place in the world that are meant to provide a blueprint for how to negotiate the ups and down, the ins and outs of daily living.[12]

A final example that shows how biblical writings can be clustered with one another can be seen in the prophetic literature, which it is possible to categorize in several different ways. One is by the length of the book. Because they are the longest works, Isaiah, Jeremiah, and Ezekiel are referred to as the major prophets, while the shorter books are called the minor prophets. A second way is by geography, depending on where the prophet's audience is located. Jeremiah directs his message to the people of Judah, so he is a southern prophet, while Amos is a northern prophet because he speaks to those in the kingdom of Israel. Chronology is also a helpful tool for distinguishing the prophets, with the dividing line

---

12. Within the Catholic/Orthodox canon, the books of Sirach and Wisdom of Solomon are also considered to be wisdom writings.

commonly seen to be the start of the Babylonian exile in the early sixth century BCE. Amos lived in the time prior to the initial invasion of the Assyrians, so he is considered to be a pre-exilic prophet. On the other hand, Ezekiel lived among those who had been deported to Babylon, which makes him an exilic prophet. Each prophetic book can be identified according to its length, geography, and chronology, and they can be compared and contrasted with one another based on those categories.

These and other ways of categorizing its contents indicate that the Old Testament can be viewed from many different angles. Paying attention to perspectives, genres, themes, dates, and geography can reveal connections between the various writings that make up the rich and diverse set of writings that comprise the Old Testament. Despite those many options, however, it is important to keep in mind that our reading and interpretation always take place within the relatively restricted and tight confines of a human-made canon whose origin remains largely a mystery.

Contextualization: What Influenced the Development of the Old Testament?

A text is always the locus of a complex set of relationships that radiate out from it like the spokes from the hub of a wheel. There is first of all the relationship that exists between a text and any oral traditions upon which it might be based. Then there is the relationship between a text and its author as the one who initially gives it shape and definition. If it is a text that is composite in nature like the Old Testament, its editors or redactors have a special relationship with the final form the text takes. Readers have distinct relationships with texts as well, and each of their relationships is unique depending upon who the reader is and how he or she interprets the text. Sometimes groups of readers form relationships with texts, and this is especially the case with sacred writings like the Bible that influence the lives and beliefs of entire communities. The three stages in the development of the Old Testament listed above (composition, transmission, and translation) underscore how, as the history of a text unfolds, the relationships with it multiply and new spokes are added to the wheel.

In addition, a host of other factors can have a profound impact on the composition of texts and the meanings assigned to them. The term commonly used to refer to this additional web of relationships is "context," which for our present purposes describes the circumstances in which a text is written. Every text is the product of a particular context, and we ignore that fact at our peril. The focus here will be on the context(s) in which the Bible emerged and to which it responded. Without a firm grasp of this dimension of the biblical material we are unable to read and interpret the Old Testament properly.

Geographical Context

Three aspects of the Bible's context that are particularly important to keep in mind are geography, history, and culture. Most of the events described in the Old Testament take place within an area that corresponds more or less to the borders and dimensions of modern-day Israel. It was part of a region, sometimes identified as "Canaan" in the Bible, that was located along the eastern Mediterranean coast and presently includes the modern states of Israel, Palestine, Lebanon, and a portion of Syria. Canaan was in a part of the world now commonly referred to as the "ancient Near East," which encompassed an area that included the Fertile Crescent, a quarter-moon shaped section of land extending from the head of the Persian Gulf in the east through Canaan and into Egypt in North Africa. The Fertile Crescent's name is due to the major river systems that are found at its two extremes. In the east, the Tigris and Euphrates rivers provide water to an area known as *Mesopotamia* (Greek for "between the rivers"), which is located in the modern country of Iraq. At the other end of the Fertile Crescent flows Egypt's Nile River, which empties into the Mediterranean Sea. The central section of the Fertile Crescent also had its own sources of water, with the most well-known being Israel's Jordan River. The Jordan is tiny compared to the rivers of Mesopotamia and Egypt. It empties into the Dead Sea, which is the lowest point on the face of the earth.

About the same size as the state of Vermont, Israel was a very small part of the ancient Near East. Nonetheless, its topography was remarkably diverse with lush farmland on the coastal and northern plains, a range of central highlands, the low-lying Jordan rift valley in the east, and stark desert wilderness to the south. Many of the stories in the Old Testament are set in the highland area, where Jerusalem and other important towns were located.

Israel made up for its lack of size with its strategic location. It was situated on a narrow strip of inhabitable land that linked the great civilizations of Mesopotamia and Egypt. To its west was the Mediterranean Sea and to its east were the mountainous areas of Transjordan and the Arabian Desert, so the easiest and most efficient way to travel between the eastern and western portions of the Fertile Crescent was via the system of roads that ran through Israel and Canaan. The two most prominent routes were the Via Maris ("Way of the Sea") that hugged the Mediterranean coast before veering inland and the King's Highway on the eastern side of the Jordan valley, which both led to the major city of Damascus.

Historical Context

All of the events described in the Old Testament took place within this geographical context. The archaeological evidence suggests that the Israelites emerged as a people in the latter part of the Late Bronze Age (1550–1200 BCE); by that time major civilizations had already existed in Egypt and Mesopotamia for thousands of years. Because of its location, the area of Canaan had great strategic importance, and for much of its history Israel came under the authority of foreign powers who sought to control it for their own advantage. Even during those brief periods when Israel was independent and relatively strong, like during the reigns of David and Solomon (ca. 1000–930 BCE), foreign powers attempted to make their presence known.

For most of the second millennium BCE, Canaan was loosely under the control of Egypt. During this period prior to the emergence of Israel, there was no unifying political system and people were organized in city-states that often clashed with one another. Assistance and advice were often sought from Egypt to help settle these disputes.[13]

During the bulk of the first millennium BCE, Israel's Mesopotamian neighbors to the east exerted the most influence on the people and events described in the Old Testament. A series of empires rose and fell, and each one played a key role in how Israelite history unfolded. The northern kingdom of Israel became a vassal of the Neo-Assyrian Empire (934–609 BCE) in the ninth century BCE, and was eventually destroyed by Assyrian forces in 721 BCE. Many passages in prophetic books like Isaiah and Amos were written in response to the threat that Assyrian forces posed for the people of Israel. The period of Assyrian domination came to an end with the rise of the Neo-Babylonian Empire, which lasted until 539 BCE. The southern kingdom of Judah attempted to avoid the same fate as Israel by aligning itself with Egypt against Babylon, which had been exerting influence over Judah for some time, but this strategy failed and Judah eventually fell to the Babylonian army. Jerusalem was destroyed and its temple was razed by the invaders in 587, a catastrophe that began a period known as "the exile," when many of Judah's leading citizens were deported to Babylon. The Bible recounts these horrific events in the final section of 2 Kings. The Babylonian invasion is the background to sections of the book of Jeremiah, who was himself eventually taken to Egypt. The exilic period lasted less than fifty years because the Babylonians were supplanted by the Persian Empire, whose ruler Cyrus the Great allowed all conquered peoples to return to their homelands in 538 BCE. Several prophetic books, like Ezekiel and portions of Isaiah, are set in the exile and they convey in vivid imagery the desire to return to Judah, and the books of Ezra and Nehemiah describe the realization of that wish as the people come back to Jerusalem and the Temple is rebuilt.

---

13. A record of these exchanges exists in an important collection known as the Amarna Letters. This set of correspondences, from the fourteenth century BCE, provides much valuable information about the relationships between the local Canaanite rulers and the Egyptian royal court.

Some scholars believe that the time of the exile was a particularly important period for the Old Testament. They maintain that many sections of the text reached their final forms in an exilic context as Israelites who were now far from their homeland attempted to make sense of their new situation and come to terms with the social, cultural, and theological implications of their circumstances in a foreign place. One example of this can be seen in the opening chapter of Genesis, which describes the six days of creation followed by a day of rest. This creation story is generally held to be written from a priestly perspective, and it can likely be traced back to the exilic period. It is a highly structured and orderly account in which everything happens like clockwork, and it presents an image of God as a supreme authority who is completely in charge. God then takes the first Sabbath rest after putting in a work week, which is a clear indication of the priestly leanings of the text's author or redactor since references to cultic matters like the Sabbath are usually evidence of an origin in priestly circles. This presentation of an all-powerful God who has a divine plan that is realized without a hitch and creates the world in an orderly way would have been very comforting to a people living in exile, who might have been questioning God's power and existence. The message of Genesis 1 is that there is no need to doubt or fear; God is still in charge and is as powerful as ever. Many biblical passages can be read in the same way as responses to the crises caused by the exile.

The biblical community shared the stage with some of the most powerful civilizations the world has ever seen, and yet people and events described in the Old Testament are rarely mentioned in extra-biblical sources. Of the hundreds of individuals identified in the Bible, only a few are named in contemporary written records. In addition, some of the most prominent heroes of the text, like Abraham and Moses, are not mentioned outside the Bible. The same holds true for the events that are recounted. The Old Testament's most celebrated and dramatic episodes—like the Egyptian plagues and the Exodus—are not mentioned elsewhere.

This silence is striking because the Mesopotamians and the Egyptians were meticulous record-keepers, particularly when it came to political matters and interactions with foreign peoples, and their archives are well preserved. The lack of attestation regarding things mentioned in the Bible could be interpreted in a number of ways. One possibility is that many of the events and individuals mentioned in the Old Testament are fictional and lack historical basis. It could also be that their absence is related to the point made earlier about the relative insignificance of Israel. Perhaps the Israelites were such minor players that they did not merit any mention in the written record. Because the Old Testament is written by them and for them, the events and people it describes are blown out of proportion and given greater importance than they deserve. It could be that a combination of these and other factors explains why the biblical story gets short shrift outside its own pages. However one understands it, the lack of attention to it beyond the Bible itself raises interesting and provocative questions.

The lone mention of Israel as such[14] in an Egyptian text is found on a stele, or stone slab, that commemorates a military campaign of a Pharaoh named Merneptah who ruled from 1213 to 1203 BCE. This stele dates to approximately 1208 BCE, and it is important because it contains the earliest reference to Israel outside the Bible. Merneptah's campaign took him to Canaan, and the inscription lists the various enemies he encountered and defeated along the way. Among those listed is one referred to as "Israel," and what is particularly interesting is that the name is identified as a group of people and not, as the others on the list, a place. This tells us that by that time there was a population in Canaan that was known collectively as Israel. It sheds no light on how they got there or how long they had been there, but this Egyptian evidence provides the earliest clue we have that is related to the origin of the people who would go on to produce the Old Testament.

The following are the approximate dates[15] of some of the key events and individuals mentioned in the Old Testament:

1800 BCE – Abraham

1200 BCE – The Exodus

1000 BCE – King David

930 BCE – Death of Solomon /
the division of the kingdom

721 BCE – Destruction of the
northern kingdom (Israel)

587 BCE – Destruction of the
southern kingdom
(Judah) / beginning
of the exile

538 BCE – Return from exile

Pharaoh Merneptah (r. 1213-1203 BCE), in the stele shown here, boasts of having laid waste to a number of population groups then present in the land of Canaan; one of these defeated populations is "Israel."

---

14. Some specific place names within Israel, however, do receive occasional mention in Egyptian texts, most notably in conjunction with the military incursion into the region led by Pharaoh Shoshenq (probably the biblical "Shishak"; see 1 Kings 11:40; 14:25; 2 Chron. 12:2–9).

15. It should be noted, however, that the further back in time one goes, the more scholars question whether the biblical stories have a basis in actual events and thus whether they can be "dated" in any meaningful sense. This is particularly the case with regard to Abraham and the events of the Exodus.

Cultural Context

Culture is a third aspect of the biblical context that plays a significant role in how we read and interpret the Old Testament. Much of what we know about the cultural reality of ancient Israel is due to the work of archaeologists who have conducted excavations throughout the ancient Near East. Their efforts have uncovered valuable evidence and data about daily life in antiquity, and in many cases we now have a better understanding of the meanings of biblical passages thanks to their findings.

Archaeological results can sometimes confirm information that is found in the biblical text. Such is the case with the Lachish Letters, which were found in 1935 at a site in Judah that served as a military fort just prior to the Babylonian destruction of Jerusalem. One of the letters is from an officer stationed at the fort, who reports that he cannot see the signal fire at the fortress in nearby Azekah. The information in this letter confirms what is said in Jeremiah 34:7 about Lachish and Azekah being the only remaining fortified cities in the area. Elsewhere, the archaeological record can call into question the accuracy of something reported in the Old Testament. This can be seen in connection with Joshua 6 and the famous story of the walls of Jericho falling down. According to that passage, the Israelite forces were able to defeat the city because of a week-long march around Jericho that was led by priests who were carrying the Ark of the Covenant containing the tablets of the law that had been given to Moses on Mount Sinai. They circled Jericho once on each of the first six days and then marched seven times around the city on the seventh day, at which point the walls came down. The site of Jericho has been excavated and studied repeatedly since the nineteenth century, and there is no evidence that it had a wall during the time in which the invasion of the city in Joshua 6 is supposed to have occurred.

Written texts like the Lachish Letters and the Merneptah Stele are extremely helpful in providing cultural context for the Old Testament. The Mesopotamians and the Egyptians were among the first people to develop writing systems, and a wide assortment of different types of texts has come down to us from them. These include royal annals, personal correspondence, marriage contracts, business records, political treaties, literary works, legal codes, and religious texts. Mesopotamian texts are typically written in a style of writing called cuneiform (Latin for "wedge-shaped") that is done by pressing a stylus or writing utensil into a piece of soft clay to produce wedge-shaped markings. The clay is then baked in fire to produce a hard tablet that is extremely durable. The hieroglyphic (Greek for "sacred carving") writing system of the ancient Egyptians is better known to people in the western world, and it was a source of interest and curiosity even prior to its decipherment in the early nineteenth century. Mesopotamian and Egyptian texts have often been studied by Old Testament scholars. In general, the Mesopotamian ones have proven to be more relevant and important for biblical scholarship.

Many of the genres of writing present in the Old Testament can also be found within the corpus of ancient Near Eastern texts that have been unearthed and translated during the past couple of centuries. The Code of Hammurabi, who was a Babylonian king in the eighteenth century BCE, contains a set of 282 laws that has some intriguing connections to the legal material in the Old Testament. A number of texts have been discovered that lay out the terms of political treaties established between ancient Near Eastern rulers, and scholars have argued that these documents help to shed light on how the biblical concept of covenant was conceived and formulated. One Babylonian text contains echoes of the book of Job in its description of the trials and tribulations of a man who complains to his friends about the way the gods have mistreated him. These examples, and many others like them, help to contextualize the Old Testament writings within their larger literary and cultural milieu, and they demonstrate that the Israelites had much in common with their neighbors in the quest for justice, social stability, and meaning in their lives.

In some cases the similarities between Old Testament and extra-biblical texts are so close that it appears the biblical authors have borrowed from the Mesopotamians and Egyptians. The flood story recounted in Genesis 6–9 has many parallels with several ancient Near Eastern texts, including a portion of the Epic of Gilgamesh. Similarly, the opening chapter of Genesis describing the six days of creation has a number of features in common with a Mesopotamian creation story known as *Enuma Elish*. The clearest example of biblical borrowing can be seen in Proverbs 22:17–24:34, which is an adaptation of an Egyptian wisdom text from around 1100 BCE known as "The Instruction of Amenemope."

A final example of how familiarity with its wider cultural context can facilitate our understanding of the Old Testament is seen in Ugarit, an ancient port city north of Israel in modern-day Syria. The city was destroyed in the twelfth century BCE, and it was long forgotten until it was accidentally rediscovered in 1928. Among the findings was a trove of texts in many languages, including a previously unknown language now called Ugaritic that was written in cuneiform. Some of the texts are religious in nature, including many that contain myths about the gods who were worshipped in the area. Among those deities are some like Baal, El, and Asherah, who are mentioned in the Bible and often referred to as among the foreign gods the Israelites should not follow. Prior to the discovery of the texts at Ugarit we had no knowledge of who these divine figures were and what cultural roles they played, but because of the information the tablets contain we now have a much better understanding of the nature of Canaanite religion and the environment in which Israelite religion took shape.

When we read the Old Testament it is essential that we be aware of the geographical, historical, cultural, and other contexts that all played a role in the making of the text. Each is an important part of the network of relationships that combine to make the Old Testament what it is, and when we ignore even one of them we miss something valuable and our own relationship with the text is diminished.

Interpretation: What Does the Bible Mean?

Despite what many people claim, the Bible doesn't really "say" anything. It is a written work, and as such it has to be interpreted by a reader in order for it to have any meaning. A text has significance only because people read it, reflect on its contents, and then determine what it means for them. It goes without saying that every reader is unique and brings his or her own experiences and perspective to the task of interpretation, and that is why a text never has only one meaning. It means many different things, depending on who is doing the interpreting. The same thing can be seen with works of art, which are simply texts formed in other media. Perhaps you have had the experience of discussing a painting, sculpture, or film with a group of friends only to discover that each person in the conversation has a different understanding of what the work means. That is an inevitable outcome of the act of interpretation. Meaning is not something fixed that is passed along from a text to a passive reader or viewer. Rather, it is the result of the interpretive activity of an individual who is creatively engaged with a text. That is why one should always say, "This is what the Bible means to me," rather than, "This is what the Bible says."

Throughout the history of its interpretation, the Old Testament has meant many different things, depending on who the interpreter has been and what questions were being asked of the text. The process of canonization was a form of interpretation since it required that a group of people had to make decisions about which works were worthy of inclusion in the canon and which ones were not. Similarly, every time the Old Testament is translated it is being interpreted; every version of it you read conveys someone else's understanding of what the text means. The same can be said about the work of the countless individuals throughout the ages who have sought to derive meanings from individual passages and books of the Old Testament. Their efforts have contributed to the mountain of musings that have accumulated over the centuries, all attempting to answer one basic question: what does the Old Testament mean?

Early Forms of Interpretation

Some of the earliest Jewish interpretation of the Old Testament is of a type commonly termed *midrash* (from a Hebrew root meaning "to study"). Midrash traces its roots to the second century CE. The rabbis and other scholars engaged in this sort of study attempted to explain parts of the Old Testament that were confusing or hard to understand. Very often it fills in gaps in the text by providing information or details that are missing. The two main types of midrash are known as *halakah*, which treats the legal material in the Old Testament, and *haggadah*, which is interested in the non-legal, narrative portions of the text.

Another important Jewish source is the Mishnah, also called the "oral Torah," which contains a set of laws and teachings that traditional Jews believe God gave to Moses but were not preserved in the written Torah of the Old Testament. This work was formulated in the early third century CE,[16] and it provides a framework for interpreting the written Torah. Over the centuries rabbis studied and commented on the Mishnah, and their work was eventually combined with it to produce the Talmud. This is the primary text for rabbinic Judaism, and it provides instruction and commentary on many subjects mentioned in the Old Testament as well as others not covered in it. There are two versions of the Talmud, one from fourth-century Jerusalem and the other from seventh-century Babylon, with the latter being the more important and influential.

On the Christian side, a number of approaches to interpretation of the Old Testament were developed early on and maintained their popularity for centuries. One was *typology*, in which individuals, events, or themes from the Old Testament are considered to be "types" that prefigure or predict events and figures of the New Testament and aspects of the Christian faith. This approach can already be seen in the New Testament itself, indicating that early followers of Jesus were combing the Jewish Scriptures to validate and support their growing religious movement. For instance, the Gospels present Jonah's three-day stay in the belly of a giant fish as a prefiguring of Jesus' time in the tomb prior to his Resurrection (Matt. 12:38–42; Luke 11:29–32). Similarly, Adam is described by Paul in the letter to the Romans as a type of "the one who was to come," namely Jesus (Rom. 5:14). Many commentators used passages such as these as a basis and support for their own interpretations, arguing that people and events mentioned in the New Testament are also represented in the Old Testament. In its most extreme form, some who employ typology have claimed that the entire Old Testament is nothing but a preparation for and prefiguring of the New Testament.

Typology is a subcategory of a form of interpretation known as *allegory*, in which the Old Testament is read in a symbolic and nonliteral way. With this approach, the characters and events in a story represent other things. The main point behind allegorical interpretation is that the real meaning of the text of the Old Testament is hidden. Here, too, the New Testament provides the earliest

---

16. At that time the "oral Torah" was finally committed to writing.

examples in Christian writing. It can be seen in Paul's letter to the Galatians, where Abraham's relationships with Sarah and Hagar are allegorized and reinterpreted as referring to two different covenants established by God, one with the Jewish people and the other with the Christian community (4:21–31). One of the main early proponents of this approach was Origen (182–251), a prominent Christian theologian from Alexandria in Egypt, the main center of allegorical interpretation.[17]

The various methods of biblical interpretation developed in the early centuries of Christianity eventually resulted in the idea of the "four senses of scripture." According to this framework, any passage in the Bible can contain four different meanings: (1) the *historical sense*, or the literal meaning of the text; (2) the *allegorical sense*, or the symbolic meaning of the text; (3) the *tropological sense*, or the moral meaning of the text; and (4) the *anagogical sense*, or the mystical meaning of the text.

The differences among these four senses are seen in how the Garden of Eden can be interpreted in light of each one. Historically (for the ancient reader, at least), it refers to the environment created by God in which Adam and Eve resided. Allegorically, it can be seen as a portrayal of the perfect human-divine relationship in which God provides for all of humanity's needs. The tropological sense of the Garden of Eden underscores the importance of acting responsibly and being obedient to God's will. From the anagogical perspective, it refers to the heavenly reward that is in store for every person who does not give in to sin and remains faithful to God.

Two events that occurred in the pre-modern world had a significant impact on how the Bible was read and interpreted, and their influence is felt into our own day. In the mid-fifteenth century Johannes Gutenberg invented the moveable-type printing press, a device that revolutionized society and had a profound effect on who had access to the biblical text. For the first time in history, the Bible could be mass produced and made available to large numbers of people at a relatively low cost. Individuals could now own a copy of the scriptures and spend as much time as they liked reading its contents and reflecting on its meaning for their lives. Only those who were literate could avail themselves of this opportunity, but wider access to the text meant that study and interpretation of the Bible was no longer the exclusive domain of scholars and clergy. Gutenberg's genius set in motion a revolution that has continued unabated ever since. The phones and tablets on which we read the Bible today are the newest links in a chain of technological advancements that stretches back to his time.

Approximately seventy years later another German rocked the status quo, this time theologically rather than technologically. In 1517 Martin Luther nailed

---

17. Another famous practitioner of allegorical interpretation was Philo of Alexandria, a Jewish philosopher who lived ca. 25 BCE to ca. 50 CE.

The Metropolitan Museum of Art, New York, Gift of Robert Lehman, 1955

Martin Luther (1483-1546) and the other Protestant Reformers argued that only those books found in the Hebrew Bible should be included in the Old Testament. Protestant Bibles either place the apocryphal books in a separate section or omit them entirely.

his Ninety-Five Theses to a church door in Wittenberg and ushered in the Protestant Reformation. Luther (1483–1546) was a German priest and a harsh critic of certain practices of the Roman Church that he considered to be abuses of its power. Many people found his ideas appealing, particularly in northern Europe, and they eventually led to the establishment of the various denominations of Protestant Christianity. One of the rallying cries of the movement was *sola scriptura* (Latin for "by scripture alone"), which conveys the idea that the biblical text should be the sole authority for Christians. This view was in contrast to that of Roman Catholicism, which continues to maintain that both the Bible and Church teaching are authoritative, and the latter includes how to interpret the Bible. As they formulated and developed their ideas, Luther and his fellow Reformers devoted much time to careful study of the scriptures, and a similar focus on the Bible remains a hallmark of Protestant Christianity into the present day.

Later Forms of Interpretation

Critical study of the Bible began to emerge in the late seventeenth century. In this context, the term "critical" refers to a new way of thinking about and analyzing the Bible that took shape as scholars began to ask questions of the text that their predecessors had not considered, particularly regarding the Bible's origin. Issues like the sources the biblical authors might have used and the historical accuracy of the events described in the Bible began to be debated and discussed. Evidence was put forward for human involvement in the creation and shaping of the biblical corpus, a notion that directly challenged longstanding assumptions about the Bible as the direct word of God. This way of studying the biblical text had its roots in the Renaissance and Enlightenment, two European movements that challenged the authority of institutions like the Church and celebrated the individual as a rational subject free from external control. Those who adopted this line of thinking called for more objective and scientific ways of studying the Bible that were not bound by what they perceived to be the limitations of religion and tradition.

These developments eventually gave rise to an approach toward studying the Bible that is called the "historical-critical method," which has continued to be employed into the present day. Within the historical-critical method, a distinction has sometimes been made between lower criticism and higher criticism. This distinction is less commonly made today, but it is worth keeping in mind because it highlights the different aims of the historical-critical method. Lower criticism, also referred to as "textual criticism," is mainly interested in trying to determine the original wording of the text. Most people do not realize it, but the ancient manuscripts that are the basis for our modern Bible translations contain many discrepancies. What should one do when the readings in these manuscripts do not agree? Scholars compare the various readings and attempt to reconstruct what was most likely the original form of the text. This is the goal of lower criticism: to establish the wording of the text, rather than to determine its meaning.

Establishing the meaning of the text is the goal of higher criticism, and it attempts to do this by trying to uncover the origins of the biblical material. It pursues questions like the following: Who wrote the text? When was it written? Where was it written? How was it written? To whom was it written? For what purpose(s) was it written? Issues related to the authorship, dating, audience, location, motivation, and possible sources of a given text are explored and examined in an effort to reach a deeper understanding of the meaning of the text. As that list of questions suggests, the historical-critical approach is actually a set of different methods rather than a single way of studying the text. It might best be thought of as a toolbox containing a number of tools, or a palette with a range of colors on it. Depending on the job to be done, a hammer might be more useful than a screwdriver, or just the opposite. If the aim is to determine the audience of a particular biblical text, lower criticism will not be a very helpful tool, but other approaches within the historical-critical toolbox would come in handy.

Among those approaches, three have been frequently employed: source criticism, redaction criticism, and form criticism. As its name implies, source criticism is interested in the possible sources behind a given text. This can be done in a number of ways, but one of the most common is to look for literary clues that a particular passage is composite in nature. The presence of repetition, inconsistencies, or multiple viewpoints can often point to sources. A further indication of a possible source is the existence of another text outside the Bible that predates the biblical text and bears a striking resemblance to it.

Redaction is another word for editing, and redaction criticism is concerned with the process by which the various sources and elements of a text were brought together into a single unit. It pays attention to the seams and stitches within a text that point to the work of the redactor, or editor. This is similar to what happens when one listens to a piece of music and focuses on each of the instruments one-by-one to appreciate how they have all been harmonized to create the composition.

Form criticism is interested in how a text might have functioned within society, and one of its main premises is that the genre or form of a given text can tell us something about the role it played for its community. Familiarity with the various sociological contexts of the biblical world is necessary for this type of study, and form criticism has suggested interesting connections between certain parts of the Bible and dimensions of social life in antiquity like the royal court, the family, religious practice, and the legal system.

Each of these methods can be illustrated in reference to Genesis 1–3, the opening chapters of the Bible that describe the creation of the world. This section is one of the clearest examples of the use of sources in the entire Bible. These chapters contain two distinct versions of creation that exhibit some of the tell-tale signs mentioned above, particularly inconsistences and multiple viewpoints. This can be demonstrated by paying attention to how God is presented in the chapters. In the first story (Gen. 1:1–2:4a) the deity is identified by the Hebrew term *'elohim*, which is usually translated as "God," but the second story (Gen. 2:4b–24) consistently uses *yahweh 'elohim*, which is rendered "Lord God" in the NRSV translation of the Bible. Similarly, the image of the deity is markedly different in the two accounts. As noted earlier, in the first story God is in complete charge as he calls into existence everything in creation in an orderly fashion in six days. This is different from the second story, where things are not created in the same order (or as orderly) as in the first. The Lord God has to make some adjustments as things unfold, and the relationship between the deity and humanity is more personal; God and human beings have conversations, something that is missing in the first account. In addition, source critics have identified intriguing similarities between the first creation story in Genesis and another ancient Near Eastern creation story, mentioned above, titled *Enuma Elish*, which is much older than the biblical tradition. The connections between the two have led many to conclude that the biblical author was familiar with the earlier work and likely borrowed elements from it.

Employing the method of redaction criticism, it can be noted how these two different creation accounts are found one right after another with no attempt to integrate or combine them. It might seem strange that the first one ends in the first half of verse 4 of chapter 2 in Genesis, and the second one begins in the second half of the verse. The chapter and verse divisions are a later addition to the Bible and often, like here, they do not correspond to the real divisions in the text, and can even obscure its meaning. In Genesis 1–3 it is easy to differentiate the sources because they are left more or less intact and one is appended to the other. But elsewhere sorting them out is a more complicated process because they have been mixed together. A good example of this is seen in the flood story, told in Genesis 6–9. In those chapters, two sources, probably the same two that are found in Genesis 1–3, have been blended so that they appear to be one story containing much repetition and many inconsistencies. For example, in one source Noah is told to bring one pair of each animal into the ark while the other source identifies the number of pairs as seven, and both numbers are present in the text.[18]

Form criticism's attention to the genre and style of a written work can sometimes shed light on the social context in which a text emerged or to which it was responding, and this can be seen with the first creation story in Genesis. This account culminates with God resting on the seventh day after a six-day work week, and therefore serves as an explanation for and endorsement of the practice of resting on the Sabbath, an important practice in Judaism. The text's concern with legitimating the weekly day of rest, as well as other evidence related to the story's structure and vocabulary, have led scholars to conclude that this account was written from a priestly perspective and its author(s) was probably someone affiliated with the religious leadership who was trying to justify the practices and beliefs that were important to that group.

In recent times, some interesting new approaches to reading and interpreting the Bible have been developed that have challenged the longstanding supremacy of the historical-critical method because they are less interested in issues related to the origins and formation of the text. Some of them study the text as we have it, and so do not ask questions regarding its possible sources or how it came about. Others use methods that were first developed in other disciplines to approach the Bible from fresh new perspectives. Elsewhere it is the reader's social location that is the determining factor in the quest to determine what the biblical text means.

Some methods that study the text as we have it are literary in their orientation and examine the Bible as a work of literature. Narrative criticism is interested in the various elements that comprise a story, including the plot, narrator, characters, setting, and related literary features. Rhetorical criticism explores the devices a text employs in the hope of having a particular effect on its readers. Reader-response criticism takes seriously the role of the reader in giving meaning to the text, and so it examines closely the ways individual readers respond to the Bible. Semiotic criticism sees the biblical text as a collection of signs that need to be interpreted and mean much more than just what the words on the page say.

Other approaches draw upon the insights of scholars working in other fields and introduce them into biblical studies. The disciplines in the social sciences have proven to be particularly valuable resources in this area. Sociology, anthropology, and cultural studies have helped to uncover and reveal aspects of the

---

18. Noah is ordered to bring one pair of animals onto the ark in Gen. 6:19–20, but seven pairs in Gen. 7:2–3.

social world of the Bible that were previously unacknowledged or understudied. By drawing upon work in areas like economics, class criticism, Marxist analysis, and postcolonial studies, some Bible scholars have reached important and provocative conclusions about the roles politics, class, and power played in the formation and development of the Bible. In a similar way, work being done in psychology and trauma studies has increasingly informed the research of Bible scholars, leading to a greater appreciation of how the human psyche has been engaged in or affected by the composition, contents, and interpretation of the Bible.

Finally, a host of other approaches have emerged in recent years that take as their starting point the social location of the reader, interpreting the biblical material through that lens. These are sometimes referred to as "perspectival" interpretations because they are informed by the personal perspective of the reader or they adopt a particular perspective from which to interpret the text. These approaches take many forms, but they all agree that one's personal experiences and the viewpoint from which he or she reads the Bible is the determining factor in what a text means. Such interpretations study the Bible through lenses such as gender, race, ethnicity, nationality, sexuality, and religious affiliation. Among the types of biblical criticism that have developed from this way of reading are the following: Feminist criticism, Womanist criticism, African-American criticism, Latino criticism, Chinese criticism, Queer criticism, Reform Jewish criticism, and Evangelical criticism.

The previous paragraphs contain just a sampling of the many ways of reading the Bible that have come on the scene recently, further enlarging the toolbox/palette the interpreter has at his or her disposal. A more complete picture can be seen in the recently published *Oxford Encyclopedia of Biblical Interpretation*, a two-volume work with almost 120 entries that treat different ways of reading the Bible. Many of the articles in the encyclopedia discuss approaches that have been around for a long time, but approximately one-half of them are of recent vintage and have been developed since the 1960s. A result of that explosion of interpretive approaches is a corresponding expansion in our understanding of what the Bible means. Although the text has remained unchanged in the many centuries since it was canonized, its significance has evolved and morphed countless times since then and will continue to do so as long as there are people around to read it. Can you think of another work that has had that kind of longevity and elasticity? That's what makes the Bible a one-of-a-kind read—it's ever old, ever new.

Perspectives on Creation

The first three chapters of Genesis might be the best-known section of the entire Bible. Most people who have grown up in the United States are familiar with the story of Adam and Eve, the garden of Eden, and the creation of the world in six days. Even those who don't read the Bible or have never set foot in a church or synagogue are often familiar with these stories, and if they were asked to jot down an outline of what takes place in Genesis 1–3 they would be able to come up with a fairly accurate account of the events described there. A recent book by Linda S. Schearing and Valarie H. Ziegler, *Enticed by Eden: How Western Culture Uses, Confuses (and Sometimes Abuses) Adam and Eve*, explores how the garden of Eden story has influenced and infiltrated various dimensions of modern life, ranging from humor and advertising to online dating.

The technical term for a text like Genesis 1–3 is *cosmogony*, which is a combination of two Greek words that mean "world" and "birth." Part of the reason why the Bible's cosmogony is so familiar to people, even to those who do not usually read it, is that it treats many of life's "big questions" and tackles some slippery issues that human beings have been wrestling with ever since we first began to wonder what it's all about. How did the world begin? How did we get here? What is our relationship to the animals and the rest of the nonhuman world we inhabit? How and why are men and women different? Why do we die? These and many other topics are explored in the opening pages of the book of Genesis. Even though it is only one of countless attempts through the ages to deal with those questions, this particular set of answers has had a profound influence on shaping the views and understanding of many people throughout history and into our own day.

The role it has played in supporting certain views about the nature and purpose of humanity requires that we examine and reflect upon what this opening section of the Bible has to say. These chapters address important questions, many of which have no clear-cut answers, in order to create a sense of identity and meaning for people, both individually and collectively. A reexamination of these well-known stories can uncover nuances and shades of meaning that have often gone unnoticed. Whether we like it or not, we live in a world that has been profoundly shaped by the biblical view of origins as articulated in Genesis

1–3, and so familiarity with the text is essential. For this reason, this chapter will begin "in the beginning" by taking a look at the Bible's account of creation.

First Impressions

It has long been recognized that there are actually two different creation stories in Genesis 1–3. This part of the Bible provided some of the earliest clues to scholars that there are multiple sources behind the biblical texts. One obvious difference between the sources behind Genesis 1–3 that was mentioned in the introduction is that each story has its own way of referring to God, with the first one using "God" (*'elohim* in Hebrew) and the second using "LORD God" (*yahweh 'elohim*). While this is an important distinction between the two sections, other differences are equally significant and point to the likelihood that Genesis 1–3 is a composite work.

The break between the two accounts occurs in the middle of the fourth verse of chapter 2. We will look at each story in turn, and we will do so by engaging in what is often called a "close reading" of the text. This is a style of reading that pays careful attention to the details of a written work and monitors the impact of those details on the reading experience with particular interest in what questions or issues the text raises in the reader's mind. This approach is not always as easy as it sounds. As mentioned above, many people are quite familiar with the contents of Genesis 1–3 because of the prevalent role it has played in society. This familiarity can sometimes make a close reading difficult because people believe they already know these stories. Consequently, readers tend to rush and miss important details. Those who consider these texts to be sacred are particularly susceptible to this mistake because they have read and heard the stories countless times in synagogues and churches and generally assume that they know exactly what is in them.

> Before reading Genesis 1-3, jot down some of your thoughts on what you believe the Bible's account of creation contains.

The First Story

READ: Genesis 1:1–2:4a

It is immediately apparent that the first creation story really isn't much of a story. Things happen and events unfold, but there is hardly any dialogue and some of the classic components of a plot are missing. It describes the creation of the world in a six-day period, but there is only one actor and speaker: God. Everything and everyone else in the story is, quite literally, *acted upon* as the text describes how they are brought into existence by God. The action, such as it is, is described rather woodenly, repeating the same basic formula and outline: God creates X, God sees that X is good, and there is evening and morning, day Y. Sometimes a bit of additional information is provided, but for the most part each day's creation repeats the same pattern.

The close reader will notice that the pattern is broken on days three and six, when there are in fact two acts of creation and the text says twice that God saw that it was good. After God gathers the waters so that the dry land can appear and God sees that it is good, readers expect the familiar refrain, "And there was evening and there was morning, the third day." Instead, that first act is immediately followed by the creation of vegetation and trees before the concluding formula (1:9–13). Similarly, the announcement of evening and morning on day six does not come after the creation of the cattle and other living creatures, as anticipated, but is delayed until the creation

Like most readers of the Bible, the artist who created this manuscript illustration has failed to distinguish the two creation accounts in Genesis. The six days of creation combine with Eve's creation from Adam's rib.

of humanity (1:24–31). Might the text have originally described an eight-day period of creation that was shortened to six days? Be that as it may, there is a symmetrical structure to the present arrangement, with the second three days of creation mirroring the first three:

Day One Creation of light and separation from darkness	Day Four Creation of sun, moon, and stars
Day Two Creation of sky and separation from waters	Day Five Creation of fish and birds
Day Three Creation of dry land Creation of vegetation and trees	Day Six Creation of animals Creation of humans

The two halves complement each other because what is created on the left side of the chart matches up with its corresponding day on the right side: the sun and moon of day four have a close connection with the light and darkness of day one; the fish and birds of day five occupy the sky and waters created on day two; and the animals and humans of day six occupy the dry land created on day three. Beyond that, there is a connection between the additional things created on days three and six: the vegetation and trees (day three) are given to humanity and animals as food (day six, 1:29–30).

Digging Deeper: Questions to Consider

A close reading of the text raises some important questions. In places, the first story conflicts with the findings of science and the modern understanding of the natural world. For example, how could light be created before the sun? Similarly, how could God create vegetation, plants, and trees on the third day, when the sun was not created until the following day? The idea that the sky is a protective dome that holds back waters that would otherwise flood the earth and return it to a state of chaos is another element of the text that does not agree with the modern understanding of the natural order. Finally, the description of a separate creation of human beings, distinct from the creation of animals, goes against the basic premise of evolutionary theory. These contradictions with the physical laws and facts of nature demonstrate that the story reflects a pre-scientific worldview and is the product of a context different from our own.

Several things about the creation of humanity raise additional questions. Perhaps the most intriguing is the reference to humanity being created in God's "image," which is mentioned three times (1:26–27). No other part of creation is made in God's image, so this appears to give humans a special status in the world. But the text never explains what it means to be created in God's image. Is it meant to be taken literally, that humans somehow look like God? Or should it be read symbolically or metaphorically? It could be that other information in the passage provides a clue about what being created in God's image means. Verse 26 reads, "Let us make humankind in our image, according to our likeness; and let them have dominion over the fish of the sea, and over the birds of the air, and over the cattle, and over all the wild animals of the earth, and over every creeping thing that creeps upon the earth." The reference to human dominion over the other living creatures comes immediately after the mention of being created in God's image, so perhaps that is humankind's unique role. Just as God has dominion over all of creation, including humans, they in turn have dominion over the rest of creation.

Verse 27, which mentions creation in God's image twice, offers another possible way of understanding what it means: "So God created humankind in his image, in the image of God he created them; male and female he created them." In this verse the relationship of human beings with God is stressed, rather than

> What do you think humanity being created in God's image means?

In this illumination from the Moutier-Grandval Bible (ca. 830), the artist has depicted God, Adam, and Eve with a strong family resemblance to convey the idea that human-kind was created "in the image of God."

their relationship with the rest of creation as in the previous verse. The comment that humans are created both male and female comes right after the double reference to being created in God's image, and maybe this provides the key to interpretation. Perhaps it is only in its totality, as expressed in the complementarity and diversity of the genders, that humanity is created in God's image.

There is no doubt that the first story supports a simultaneous creation of male and female, and not the two-step process that will be described in the second story. Men and women came into existence at the same time according to this version, and both are in the image of God. It is worth noting that the Hebrew term translated here as "humankind" is *'adam*, the same word that will identify the male member of the first couple in the second story. But there is no way that Genesis 1 is referring only to the creation of human males because the text explicitly states, "Male and female he created them."

There might be another subtle allusion to the special role of humanity in 1:31 where the sixth and final use of the refrain reads, "God saw everything that he had made, and indeed, it was very good." This is the only time the word "very" is used in this repeated formula. Perhaps it is simply an acknowledgement of divine contentment and approval of all that has been brought into existence. After a busy six days, God surveys the results and takes pleasure in a job well done. But there could be a suggestion here that only with the creation of humanity is the work truly complete and satisfactory. We are the culmination of creation and now things are not just good, but very good.

> Why do you think God sees that things are "very good" on the sixth day?

Does the special status of humanity mean that it is superior to the rest of creation? The reference in verse 26 to humankind having dominion over the other living creatures could point in this direction, and God's words in verse 28 seem to take things a step further: "Be fruitful and multiply, and fill the earth and subdue it; and have dominion over the fish of the sea and over the birds of the air and over every living thing that moves upon the earth." The earth is to be subdued by human beings, under whose dominion the animals will live. On an initial reading, this passage appears to endorse humanity's superiority over all of creation, and it has sometimes been used to justify human control and domination over the natural world. According to this reading, people can use and consume animals, forests, and other natural resources as they wish because they have a divine mandate to do so. As noted below, there are problems with this interpretation and a careful study of the vocabulary used in the passage indicates that those who use Genesis 1 to support irresponsible human exploitation of the natural environment are on shaky ground. In fact, an attentive reading of the first creation story reveals a fascinating aspect of our original nature that will undoubtedly be unpalatable for some: in this story, people were created to be vegetarians. "See, I have given you every plant yielding seed that is upon the face of all the earth, and every tree with seed in its fruit; you shall have them for food" (1:29).

> What are some of the main qualities of God in the first story?

A Double Focus: Cosmology and Theology

As a cosmogony, the primary purpose of the first creation story is to provide an account of the origin of the world. It accomplishes this goal, but in a way that devotes as much attention to the creator as to what is created. The reader learns about how the various elements of the natural world came into existence, but in the process also learns a great deal about the one responsible for causing them to be. Therefore, another aim of this text is to present a particular portrayal of God; the text shapes the reader's understanding of the deity. In other words, the first creation story is not just a cosmological text but a theological one as well.

God has supreme power and authority in this story and everything proceeds as directed, unfolding according to the divine plan without a hitch. The orderly structure and repeated pattern of the day-by-day process of creation helps to reinforce the sense of everything being overseen by God, and by the third day the reader can almost anticipate what will happen next. This is a God in charge, and nowhere is that more apparent than in the way things are created. Not having to bother with the physical labor and exertion that goes into building or constructing something, God simply speaks and is able to call things into existence. By divine command and the utterance of a word, matter forms and objects appear in an impressive display of creative skill beyond the capability of the most powerful human being.

This is also a God who acts alone. There is no indication that God has any help or assistance in creating the world, and so the story is a monotheistic one involving a single creator deity. This idea appears to be challenged in the first part of verse 26, with its use of the first person plural in the comment, "Let us make humankind in our image, according to our likeness." Most commentators think this statement reflects a belief in a heavenly divine council comprised of other supernatural beings, something that was found in the religious systems of other ancient Near Eastern cultures and is referred to in other biblical passages. The first two chapters of the book of Job, for example, refer to a figure known as "the Satan" who functions as a member of the divine council. If that is the case here and God is speaking to the other members of the heavenly court, there is still no indication in the text that any of them are involved in the work of creation.

The overall impression left by the end of the first story is one of an all-powerful God whose plan of creation is flawlessly executed. The cyclical nature of the six-day process establishes in the reader's mind the notion that order and structure are built into the very fabric of creation and that God is the ultimate authority who will prevent things from reverting to chaos.

The Second Story

READ: Genesis 2:4b–3:24

The second creation story is markedly different from the first, and at times the differences between the two are difficult to reconcile. In the first place, it has more of the features and characteristics that are associated with a typical story, including a well-developed plot, fuller characters, extended dialogue, and narrative detail. For example, unlike the first story this one has other actors besides God: Adam, Eve, and the serpent. Each character has its own personality and role to play. The story also has a specific setting, the garden of Eden, which locates the action in a particular place on earth. (Where does the first story take place? That's a tough question to answer.) It covers some of the same ground as the first account, particularly the creation of humanity, but it quickly introduces additional elements that kick-start the plot and draw the reader into the world of the text.

God's first words to the first human in this story take the form of a command that declares part of the garden to be off limits: "You may freely eat of every tree of the garden; but of the tree of the knowledge of good and evil you shall not eat, for in the day that you eat of it you shall die" (Gen. 2:15–16). This immediately creates narrative tension around the figure of the human, the *sine qua non* of any good story: will he or won't he eat of the tree? Before that question can be answered the other characters are brought into the story to complicate the plot and increase the tension. That tension is resolved somewhat when Adam does eat of the tree, but this only leads to another question that draws the reader in further: when will Adam die? As it turns out, he will hang in there

> Do you agree that the second creation account is a more effective story than the first one? Why or why not?

for quite some time, and doesn't die until chapter 5 of Genesis. But his eating of the fruit leads to a different kind of death since the rest of the text describes the breakdown of his and his mate's relationship with God and their growing alienation from their creator. It's a riches-to-rags story that has all the features of a great tale, which is why most people find the second creation account to be a more compelling and engaging read than the first one.

Playing with Words

An interesting feature of this text goes unnoticed by almost everyone because they read the Bible in translation. The original Hebrew text of the garden of Eden story contains a number of wordplays and puns that are very difficult to reproduce. The word "Adam" ('adam in Hebrew) is actually not a personal name, but a more general term that refers to a human being. As noted earlier, it is found in the first chapter of Genesis to describe humanity at large, and it is still used in modern Hebrew to designate an individual person. The human's creation is described in 2:7, where it says that "the Lord God formed man from the dust of the ground." The Hebrew word translated "ground" is 'adamah, identical to 'adam except for the addition of the final syllable. The 'adam is taken from the 'adamah, and the original Hebrew-speaking audience would have been struck by the similarity between the two words. There is an echo of this wordplay in 3:19, when God tells Adam, "You shall eat bread until you return to the ground."

Another wordplay can be seen in Genesis 2:23, when Adam responds to the creation of Eve with the comment, "This at last is bone of my bones and flesh of my flesh; this one shall be called Woman, for out of Man this one was taken." Here, too, there is a phonetic similarity between two words since the Hebrew word for "woman" is 'ishshah and the term for "man" (in the sense of "male") is 'ish. Just as the human being ('adam) is taken from the ground ('adamah), so too the woman ('ishshah) is taken from the man ('ish). While we are on the subject of Eve, it should be noted that Genesis identifies her name as another example of wordplay or, to use the technical term, paronomasia. "The man named his wife Eve, because she was the mother of all living" (3:20). Her name in Hebrew is havvah, which bears a close resemblance to the word for "living." A final instance of word punning in this story can be seen at the end of chapter 2 and the beginning of chapter 3, where the Hebrew terms for "naked" and "crafty" are almost identical and are separated by only six words. "And the man and his wife were both naked, and were not ashamed. Now the serpent was more crafty than any other wild animal that the LORD God had made." Similar wordplay is a fairly common phenomenon elsewhere in the Hebrew Bible, and awareness of its existence helps us to better appreciate the creativity and humor that was part of the writing process.

> Why do you think an author would use wordplay in a narrative?

Invading the Garden: The Devil and Other Intruders

A close reading of the garden of Eden story can lead to some unexpected discoveries, not so much about what's in the text as what's *not* in it. Take the character responsible for the couple's problems, for example. The serpent is first introduced in the passage cited above from the beginning of chapter 3, and is mentioned several times throughout the rest of the chapter. In each case the same Hebrew term is used for it (*nahash*), and it is a well-known word found elsewhere in the Bible to describe a snake.

So why is it that so many people think the devil made them do it? It is often claimed that Satan was responsible for what happened in the garden, but there isn't a shred of evidence in the text to support this idea. The term "Satan" is found in the Hebrew Bible in a number of places, like in the beginning of the book of Job as mentioned above, but nowhere does it refer to a devil-like figure who is the personification of evil. That was a much later development in Israelite religion. By the time of Jesus, the notion of the devil was well established in Jewish thought, but there is no devil in Genesis 3.

So how did he come to play such a prominent role in the garden of Eden story? If you visit the medieval Europe collection of any major museum you will find paintings of the Adam and Eve story with a serpent that bears a striking resemblance to the devil. In all likelihood, this is a Christian reinterpretation of the story that reconceives it as a battle between God and Satan to see which one the humans will choose. Such an idea did not come out of thin air, but was probably based on later passages that equate the devil with the serpent of Genesis 3. One is found in the Wisdom of Solomon, an apocryphal book that was likely written in the late first century BCE or the early first century CE and makes a reference to the garden of Eden story: "For God created us for incorruption, and made us in the image of his own eternity, but through the devil's envy death entered the world, and those who belong to his company experience it" (2:23–24). Similarly, the New Testament equates the serpent with Satan in the book of Revelation: "The great dragon was thrown down, that ancient serpent, who is called the Devil and Satan, the deceiver of the whole world—he was thrown down to the earth, and his angels were thrown down with him" (12:9; cf. 20:2).

Another part of the story that underwent a similar transformation is the fruit that the couple ate, which most people would identify as an apple. Apples are mentioned a few times in the Bible, but not in the garden of Eden story. The Hebrew word that is used there is *peri*, which is the generic term for fruit; it does not specify a particular type. Throughout history all sorts of fruit have been put forward as the likely candidate, from the fig to the pomegranate, but they are all conjectures. The apple floated to the top, at least in the western world, probably because of the

> Did you think the devil is present in the Garden Story? How does the story change if he is not?

fact that in Latin the words for "apple" and "evil" are practically identical and the opportunity for wordplay was, you could say, too tempting to pass up.[1]

Another way this story is sometimes interpreted that is not supported by its content concerns its outcome. "Original sin" is a term that is used by some to describe the cause of humanity's fallen nature after Adam and Eve ate of the fruit. According to this concept, all people are born in a state of sin that can be traced back to the events that occurred in the garden of Eden. The belief that the actions of the first couple had long-term negative consequences for their offspring in perpetuity is held by many Christian denominations. While this doctrine has a long and venerable history, it is important to keep in mind that Genesis 3, and indeed the entire Old Testament, offers little support for it.[2]

The person most closely associated with the idea is Augustine of Hippo (d. 430). He interpreted the second creation story in light of Paul's teachings in the New Testament, and in the process he gave it a meaning that, in the view of many scholars, is not well supported by the details of the text.[3] The words "sin" and "fall" are not found in the garden of Eden story, and the text does not indicate that Adam's offspring will forever be ontologically evil. Adam and Eve do disobey God's prohibition against eating the fruit of the tree and their relationship with the deity and with each other is changed as a result, but not in the way that the Christian concept of original sin teaches. Rather, at the end of Genesis 3, all three of the characters are punished for their

As in this carving from Notre Dame Cathedral in Paris, medieval artists sometimes depicted the serpent with female characteristics, thereby emphasizing the woman as temptress and responsible for the Fall. Such interpretations do violence to the text of Genesis.

Jebulon / Temptation Adam Eva.jpg / Wikimedia / CC0 1.0

---

1. The term for "apple" in Latin is *malus*, and the word for "evil" is *malum*.

2. Original sin is not a tenet of Judaism, and so Jews do not interpret Gen. 2–3 as describing the fall of humanity. See Steven Kepnes, "'Turn Us to You and We Shall Return': Original Sin, Atonement, and Redemption in Jewish Terms," in *Christianity in Jewish Terms*, ed. Tikva Freymer-Kensky et al. (Boulder, CO: Westview, 2000), 293–304.

3. A key verse for the doctrine of original sin is Rom. 5:12, but many New Testament scholars believe Augustine's interpretation does not accurately reflect what Paul is saying in that passage. The matter is complicated by the fact that the text's wording is ambiguous in places, and so it lends itself to multiple interpretations. For a discussion of this verse and how it has been read through history, see Joseph A. Fitzmeyer, *Romans* (New York: Doubleday, 1992), 411–17.

transgressions in ways that make their existence more difficult going forward: the serpent is forced to crawl on its belly, Eve will experience pain in childbirth, and Adam will have to sweat and toil to work the land. All those conditions still apply to snakes and people, and they might represent a "fall" of sorts, but they do not carry the stigma and stain that the notion of original sin does.

It is therefore an interesting fact that three of the things most closely identified with the garden of Eden story—Satan, the apple, and the fall of humanity—lack explicit textual support in the book of Genesis. The technical term for this phenomenon is *eisegesis*, a term from Greek that describes the act of reading into a text something that is not actually there.

> What is your view of the concepts of "the fall of humanity" and original sin?

Creative Tension: Comparing the Two Stories

When the second creation story is compared with the first one, quite a number of differences are immediately obvious. First of all, there are differences in the sequences in which things are created. In the first story, human beings are created last, after all the vegetation, animals, birds, and fish have been brought into existence. But in the second story the first human is created before all the other living things (2:5a), and the animals do not come along until sometime later (2:19). It is difficult to reconcile those two sequences.

The Divine Character

As already noted, each account has its own way of referring to God, and this was one of the first clues that caused scholars to entertain the possibility that there are separate sources behind Genesis 1–3. But much more interesting than God's different names are the different ways the divine character acts in the two stories. The all-powerful, majestic figure of the first story, who is in complete control and calls everything into being just by speaking, is nowhere to be found in the second story. In his place is a God who is not transcendent and otherworldly, but one that is easier to relate to and identify with. This is a God with decidedly human qualities, including some that many would consider to be flaws.

The technical term for the ascription of a human-like quality to a non-human is *anthropomorphism*, and the garden of Eden story's depiction of God is arguably the most anthropomorphic depiction of God in the entire Bible. In the creation of the first human being, God appears as an artisan who is intimately engaged in the creative act: "Then the LORD God formed man from the dust of the ground, and breathed into his nostrils

> Do you find the image of God in the first story or the second story more appealing?

the breath of life; and the man became a living being" (2:7). The Hebrew verb translated as "formed" is used elsewhere in the Bible to refer to the act of molding or shaping a vessel, and so God is presented here as a divine potter who takes a very hands-on approach to the act of creation. In addition, the reference to breathing into the nostrils of the human is a clear anthropomorphism that highlights the close relationship that exists between the creator and what is created.

This same image of a deity who acts like a human being continues in the very next verse when it says that the Lord God planted a garden in Eden (2:8). It carries over into chapter 3, which contains two of the most stunning examples of anthropomorphism. The explanation for why Adam and Eve run for cover after eating the fruit describes God engaged in an activity that has been a time-honored tradition among people for ages: going for a sunset stroll. "They heard the sound of the Lord God walking in the garden at the time of the evening breeze, and the man and his wife hid themselves from the presence of the Lord God among the trees of the garden" (3:8). This scene presents God as an authority figure they seek to avoid at all costs, an image that softens somewhat later in the chapter when the deity takes on a more parental air by providing attire for Adam and Eve: "And the Lord God made garments of skins for the man and for his wife, and clothed them" (3:21). The divine potter is now busy with handiwork of a different sort, and this anthropomorphism has prompted one modern commentator to characterize God as a seamstress.[4]

For the most part, these anthropomorphisms have an appealing and endearing quality that makes God more accessible and bridges the divide between divinity and humanity. What's not to like about a deity who gardens, has an artistic side, is into fashion, and enjoys a little fresh air? At the same time, though, there are other aspects of God's character in the garden of Eden story that give us pause. For one thing, this is not a deity who has a well-thought-out plan for creation that is flawlessly executed as in the first story. In contrast to Genesis 1, where humanity is created male and female, here God creates only a single human and then realizes something is missing (2:18). While this might be dismissed as a relatively minor design flaw that is easily fixed, what happens next comes as a surprise. God creates all the animals and birds and parades them before the man in order to find him a suitable mate. Only after all of them have been rejected by Adam does God come up with plan B and create a woman. Unlike his counterpart in chapter 1, this is a God who is learning as things unfold and has to think on his feet.

> What do you think of the use of anthropomorphisms to depict God?

---

4. Phyllis Trible, "Depatriarchalizing in Biblical Interpretation," *Journal of the American Academy of Religion* 41 (March, 1973): 33.

The reader is left with the same impression throughout the conversation God has with the couple after they eat the fruit. In the course of that exchange God asks four questions, the first three to Adam and the fourth to Eve:

1. "Where are you?" (3:9)
2. "Who told you that you were naked?" (3:11)
3. "Have you eaten from the tree of which I commanded you not to eat?" (3:11)
4. "What is this that you have done?" (3:13)

On one level, these might simply be rhetorical questions meant to put Adam and Eve on the spot and force them to come clean about what they have done. But if we keep in mind the seeming lack of foreknowledge and omniscience on God's part when trying to find a mate for Adam, perhaps the questions here are actually attempts to fill in the missing pieces and make sense of what has happened. If so, the anthropomorphic dimension of the story extends beyond God's actions to include God's knowledge and presents a divine character who is even more like us.

> Do the questions to Adam and Eve reflect a lack of knowledge on God's part?

The way the story ends suggests that this may be the case, and that God's lack of knowledge is an important part of the plot. With the three punishments mentioned earlier—the snake is forced to crawl on its belly, the woman experiences pain in childbirth, and the man has to work the land by the sweat of his brow—these parts of creation are now different from what God created them to be. This same idea is dramatically portrayed in the expulsion scene, when Adam and Eve are forced from the garden of Eden and banned from ever returning to the place God built for them to inhabit, a work-free environment where childbirth would be painless and snakes would have feet. Things have changed and creation is not the harmonious whole it was intended to be. As God looks around and surveys the damage, he comes to a different conclusion from that reached in the first creation story—he sees that it is *not* very good, and he knows what he did not know before.

The Human Characters

When considering how humanity is portrayed in the two accounts, readers are struck by similar differences in detail and focus. The first story tells a fair amount about humans—they were created in God's image, they come in two forms (male and female), they are to exercise dominion over the earth, they will reproduce, and they are vegetarians—but all this is conveyed in a span of just four verses in a creation account that is thirty-five verses long. In the second account humanity makes its appearance in the fourth verse and, except for a brief five-verse interlude about the rivers that flow from the garden of Eden (2:10–14), it is referred to or spoken to in virtually all of the remaining forty-three verses of the story. Thus the second story is concerned more with human beings than with any other element of creation.

The garden of Eden story lacks a reference to humanity being created in God's image, but the several anthropomorphisms it contains might hint at this same idea. Because God behaves and thinks much like people do, there is a sense in which humanity is somehow an imperfect mirror image of the deity. The garden story also does not state that humanity is to exercise dominion over the non-human elements of creation like in the

Do the anthropomorphisms suggest that we are created in God's image or that God is created in our image?

first account, but it does call attention to humanity's close relationship to a particular portion of the earth: "The LORD God took the man and put him in the garden of Eden to till it and keep it" (2:15). The vocabulary of the two texts is noteworthy because the image of exercising dominion over the earth and subduing it in the first story is somewhat in tension with the idea of tilling and keeping the land in the garden of Eden story, a point that will be discussed later in this chapter.

It is important to note that God first describes the relationship that Eve will have with Adam in positive terms: "Then the LORD God said, 'It is not good that the man should be alone; I will make him a helper as his partner'" (2:18). God envisions another being who will share Adam's nature. After all the animals fail to fit the bill, that helper and partner is created from some part of Adam, an indication of the powerful bond of closeness between the two. That body part is commonly understood to be one of Adam's ribs, but there are some problems with that identification. Whatever part of him she may have come from, Adam immediately recognizes their common nature and exclaims, "This at last is bone of my bones and flesh of my flesh" (2:23a). From the very beginning, then, both God and Adam consider the relationship between the couple to be egalitarian.

The scene that describes the conversation between the serpent and Eve is significant not only because it leads to her fateful decision to eat the fruit, but it also contrasts her character with Adam's in a subtle but important way. When the serpent exercises its God-given craftiness and persuades Eve to take and eat, she doesn't jump in with both feet: "So when the woman saw that the tree was good for food, and that it was a delight to the eyes, and that the tree was to be desired to make one wise, she took of its fruit and ate; and she also gave some to her husband, who was with her, and he ate" (3:6). Eve's eating is not the thoughtless and impetuous act of someone who has been tricked and doesn't know any better. It is a measured and thoughtful response by one who has exercised her power of reason and has made a reasoned choice—she examines the tree and considers its nutritional value, she marvels at its beauty, she reflects on what it has to offer her, and only then does she reach out and pick its fruit. It is a rational act that is the result of careful thought and deliberation. In light of the divine prohibition against eating it she might be faulted for the decision she reaches, but it cannot be criticized as an impulsive or hasty act.

But that assessment would fit Adam to a T. Her silent, passive mate exhibits none of the thoughtful mental reflection that preceded Eve's decision to partake of the fruit. She gives and he eats, from hand to mouth with no input from the brain. The text says Adam "was with her," suggesting that he was present during the conversation between the serpent and Eve about God's initial prohibition against eating the fruit. If that is the case, then Adam's silence is especially appalling and incriminating because Eve had not been created yet when God told him not to eat from the tree of the knowledge of good and evil. The serpent was therefore quizzing Eve about something that happened before she was even around, but Adam, who *had* been present for God's prohibition, does not step in to offer his perspective.

The next scene describes God's four-question conversation with the couple that was mentioned earlier, and Adam and Eve are both true to form here. When God asks Adam if he has eaten from the tree he replies, "The woman whom you gave to be with me, she gave me fruit from the tree, and I ate" (3:12). What Adam says here is technically the truth, but he is clearly trying to absolve himself of all blame by finger-pointing with both hands. His first defense is to say it's all Eve's fault because she gave him the fruit and he was simply in the wrong place at the wrong time. But he also indirectly accuses God by referring to Eve as "the woman whom you gave to be with me." In other words, "If you hadn't created her in the first place, we wouldn't be in this mess right now." The reference to Eve as the woman "with me" echoes the description of Adam as "with her" during the eating scene and highlights a key difference between their two characters.

> What is your reaction to the way that Adam and Eve are portrayed in the story?

Eve, on the other hand, owns up and accepts responsibility for her actions. When God asks her what she has done she replies, "The serpent tricked me, and I ate" (3:13). While she does fault the serpent, she could well have pointed the finger at Adam too, but does not do so. Unlike Adam, Eve was not yet created when God gave the prohibition against eating the fruit, and so she might have tried to reduce her punishment by appealing to that fact. Similarly, she could have faulted Adam for not coming to her defense, but she did not.

As already mentioned, God's response to the eating of the fruit is immediate, as the serpent, Eve, and Adam are each admonished in turn. These are sometimes referred to as "curses," but in fact of the three only the serpent is literally cursed by God (3:14). The ground is also cursed, and this will make it more difficult for Adam to work it (3:17), but neither of the two humans is directly cursed by the deity. Increased labor, both in giving birth and cultivating the land, is part of the price humanity must pay for its disobedience, but God's words also signal a change in the relationship between Eve and Adam. After being informed about how childbirth will now be more difficult she is told, "Yet your desire will be for your husband, and he shall rule over you" (3:16). This is the first reference in the text to inequality or imbalance in the relationship between men and women, but it is important to note that it occurs only after the couple's offense and it goes against the way God intended things to be.

A final aspect of this story that can be easily missed by readers relates to how the human characters are identified. It is standard practice for us to refer to them as "Adam" and "Eve," just as has been done throughout this discussion of the garden of Eden story. But using these names is somewhat misleading since it does not reflect the language and content of the text. As explained earlier, "Adam" is not a personal name but a noun that means "human being." In almost every place in the Hebrew text where it is found it takes the definite article, so that it literally means "the human" (in Hebrew *ha'adam*). The only place it lacks the definite article is in 3:17, in the section on the punishments, where it says, "And to *'adam* he [God] said, . . ."[5] Most English translations avoid the use of "Adam" and render the Hebrew as "the human," "the man," or something like that. In some translations, though, at a certain point in the story the generic term "human" becomes the personal name "Adam," and that shift often occurs somewhere near the scene in which God brings the animals before him. This is what happens in the King James Bible that was translated in 1611 and became the most commonly used English language version of the text for centuries. Its popularity and influence undoubtedly played a role in transforming "the man" into "Adam" in our minds and language.

> What effect would it have if Adam and Eve were referred to as "the man" and "the woman" throughout the story?

The situation with Eve is a bit different. She remains nameless, like Adam, for much of the story, but acquires a name toward the end of the account. "The man named his wife Eve, because she was the mother of all living" (3:20). Prior to this point, she is referred to in a way similar to Adam and is always "the woman" (*ha'ishshah* in Hebrew).

The opening chapters of Genesis provide two distinct creation accounts. They do not line up on the details but do agree on some fundamental points. The most important point is theological: God is responsible for bringing all things into existence. The theological dimension is more to the fore in the first story, with its formulaic and orderly telling in which the elements of the natural world are created to demonstrate God's power and

> Do your own close reading of Genesis 1:1-3:24. Can you identify any other interesting or unusual features of the stories that were not treated here? How do they affect your understanding of the text?

---

5. Author's translation.

authority. This same theme is also present in the garden of Eden story, but its more narrative-like structure in which Adam and Eve play a central role shifts the focus so that humanity shares the stage with God and the human response to divine authority is explored as a central theme.

Second Opinions

At several points the introductory chapter's section on interpretation discussed how Genesis 1–3 played an important role in the rise of critical biblical scholarship. Scholars commonly cited the creation stories to help illustrate and support some of the emerging trends and methods that were taking shape at the time, like source, redaction, and form criticisms. The differences and inconsistencies between the two stories that we have noted here, and others like them, were studied and analyzed to help bring about a new way of conceiving the origin and transmission of the biblical material. The long-held view that Moses was the author of the Pentateuch is no longer tenable for many, and it has been replaced with a more complex understanding of how the Old Testament came about.

Sources and Audiences: Created from What and for Whom?

The alternative model that came to be most widely accepted and the one that has dominated critical biblical scholarship for centuries is called the "Documentary Hypothesis." There are a number of versions of this theory, but they all agree that the Pentateuch is a composite text that shows evidence of reliance upon multiple sources or documents and is not the work of a single author. The Documentary Hypothesis identifies four different sources in the first five books of the Bible; these sources are commonly referred to as J, E, D, and P after their initial letters: Jawhist,[6] Elohist, Deuteronomist, and Priestly. The first two take their names from the term for God that is typically used in each: Yahweh and Elohim, respectively. The Deuteronomist source is so called because it shows clear affinities with the vocabulary and ideas found in the book of Deuteronomy, and some scholars think the source's author(s) might be responsible for parts of Deuteronomy. As explained in the introductory chapter, the Priestly source is marked by frequent references to subjects like ritual practice that would be of particular interest to priests.[7]

---

6. The hypothesis was first formulated in Germany, where "Yahwist" was spelled with a "J": "Jahwist."

7. The development and influence of the Documentary Hypothesis is discussed in Ernest Nicholson, *The Pentateuch in the Twentieth Century: The Legacy of Julius Wellhausen* (New York: Oxford University Press, 1998). For an alternative approach to the formation of the Pentateuch that is critical of the Documentary Hypothesis, see Antony F. Campbell, SJ, and Mark A. O'Brien, OP, *Rethinking the Pentateuch: Prolegomena to the Theology of Ancient Israel* (Louisville: Westminster John Knox, 2005).

As scholarship on the Pentateuch has developed, the Documentary Hypothesis has been modified and tweaked, especially in recent times. Some have gone so far as to say that it is no longer a viable theory and it should be replaced entirely. In particular, the Elohist source has often been questioned, with many arguing that there is not enough evidence to justify its existence. Similarly, some have claimed that the Deuteronomist source should be abandoned and that the idea of a Pentateuch should be replaced with that of a Tetrateuch that would group together the Bible's first four books. This has been suggested because the book of Deuteronomy appears to have a closer connection to the books that follow it rather than to those that precede it.[8] However these debates eventually play out, the basic premise of the Documentary Hypothesis is on solid ground and can be validated by a careful reading of Genesis 1–3: strong evidence supports the idea that the Pentateuch is the work of multiple hands.

> What is your initial impression of the Documentary Hypothesis?

In some passages in the Pentateuch, such as the flood story (Genesis 6–9), the sources have been spliced together in such a way that each one covers only a sentence or a couple of verses before giving way to another source. That is not the case with the creation stories, which are preserved as two intact stories, recounted one after the other. The first story about the six days of creation comes from the Priestly source, which is generally held to be from a late date during the exilic period of the sixth century BCE. Its location at the beginning of Genesis is an important warning against drawing chronological conclusions based on where a text is found in the Bible. Just because something comes first doesn't mean it's earlier. In this case, the second creation story is actually older than the first one.

> What is your reaction to the idea that there are sources behind the Pentateuch?

Similarly, we cannot base our view on which source a text comes from solely on vocabulary. As already mentioned, the first creation story uses the term *'elohim* to refer to God, so one might be tempted to think that it comes from the Elohist

---

8. The books in question are referred to as the "Former Prophets" in the Jewish canon and are among the "Historical Books" in the Christian canon. They include the books of Joshua, Judges, 1 and 2 Samuel, and 1 and 2 Kings, which provide a history of the Israelite people from the entry into Canaan in the twelfth century BCE until the Babylonian invasion of Judah that began the exile in the sixth century BCE. Scholars commonly term those six books the "Deuteronomistic History" because they present a highly theologized account of Israelite history that is told from the perspective of the book of Deuteronomy. In particular, Deuteronomy's focus on the law becomes the lens through which Israel's history is recounted. When the Israelites prosper and are at peace, it is because they are observing the law. On the other hand, their lack of obedience to the law is the cause of the hardships and suffering they experience. The Deuteronomistic History was first proposed by the German scholar Martin Noth in 1943, and an English translation of his seminal work is available in Martin Noth, *The Deuteronomistic History* (Sheffield: Sheffield Academic Press, 2002). An overview of issues related to the Deuteronomistic History is available in Thomas Römer, *The So-Called Deuteronomistic History: A Sociological, Historical and Literary Introduction* (London: T&T Clark, 2007).

source. But that would be a mistake. The Priestly source also frequently uses *'elo-him*. Other elements of the story are characteristic of P, so that source is its likely origin. The prime example of a P-related theme in the first story is the rest that God takes on the seventh day that is described using a Hebrew term related to the word "Sabbath," something that would be of obvious interest to a priestly writer.[9]

The Documentary Hypothesis assigns the second creation story to the Jahwist source. The story usually refers to God as *yahweh 'elohim*, an interesting blending of the two words for the deity in the J and E/P sources that is not commonly found elsewhere in the Old Testament. Here, too, it could be argued that this way of naming God reflects the use of more than one source, but that would also be a mistake, since other characteristics of the story clearly identify it as a J text. Paramount among these is the heavy use of anthropomorphisms to describe God, which are a hallmark of the Jahwist material.

While scholars disagree on the precise dating of the Jahwist material, there is less debate about the exilic origin of the Priestly source. When we keep that context in mind, the literary structure and theological message of the first creation story make a great deal of sense. The exile (587–539 BCE) was a time of tremendous upheaval and confusion for the people of Judah, many of whom now found themselves living in Babylon.

Far from their native land, the Israelites were confronted with a host of challenges and issues as they adjusted to life in their new environment. Among these concerns were questions about the religious significance of their changed circumstances. When the Babylonians destroyed the temple in Jerusalem, what did that mean for the relationship God had established with the people of Israel? Had God been defeated? Now that they were living in a foreign land, did their relationship with God continue, or should they now follow the local gods of Babylon? Was the destruction of Jerusalem and the exile their own fault? Was it an indication that God had abandoned them for something they had done? Was God dead? Perhaps God was not as powerful and in control as they had thought.

The first creation story was written for a community that was grappling with questions like these, and it attempted to put their minds at ease and to encourage them to maintain their faith and trust in God. It reminded them that their God was the creator of all that exists, and that everything was brought into being in an orderly and systematic way that unfolded over six days exactly as God intended. Such a message would have been a tremendous comfort to a people whose lives had been turned upside down and who may have been filled with doubt about the power and authority of their God. Even the Sabbath rest was built into the order of things from the beginning of time, and so it should be practiced whether one is in Jerusalem or in Babylon. The story's theology and literary structure work hand-in-hand to address the concerns of its audience and alleviate their fears.

---

9. This issue will be treated in more detail later in this chapter.

The First Story: A Babylonian Counterpart

A Babylonian origin for the first story is supported by some interesting similarities between it and a creation story from Babylon known by its first two words, *Enuma Elish*.[10] This text of approximately one thousand lines, discovered on seven clay tablets in the mid-nineteenth century, is centuries older than the Jahwist account. Its opening lines read as follows:

> When on high the heaven had not been named,
> firm ground below had not been called by name,
> there was nothing but primordial Apsu, their begetter,
> and Mummu-Tiamat, she who bore them all,
> their waters commingling as a single body;
> no reed hut had been matted, nor marsh land had appeared,
> when no gods whatever had been brought into being
> uncalled by name, their destinies undetermined—
> then it was that the gods were formed within them.

One of the most interesting similarities between *Enuma Elish* and the first creation account is a grammatical one that affects how the first sentence of the latter text should be translated. Although "In the beginning" is one of the best known phrases in English from the Bible, it does not accurately translate the likely original Hebrew text. Like the opening of *Enuma Elish*, the first words of Genesis are a temporal clause that is better rendered as, "When God began to create the heavens and earth—the earth being formless and empty with darkness over the surface of the deep and a divine wind sweeping over the surface of the water—then God said, 'Let there be light.'" With its initial phrase taking the form of a temporal clause, the Bible is following a formula found in *Enuma Elish* and other ancient Near Eastern creation accounts: "When on high the heaven had not been named, . . . then it was that the gods were formed."

After describing the births of the gods, the Babylonian text recounts a conflict between the primordial goddess, Tiamat, and the younger gods. Marduk, the leader of the younger generation of gods, overcomes Tiamat in a battle and cuts her corpse in two, using one-half of her to make the sky and the other half to create the earth. Once the rest of the cosmos is established, Marduk forms humans out of the blood of a wayward god so

Does the alternative translation of the opening words of Genesis affect the meaning of the text?

---

10. A translation of *Enuma Elish*, along with background information on its origin and use in Babylonian ritual, can be found in Stephanie Dalley, trans., *Myths from Mesopotamia: Creation, The Flood, Gilgamesh, and Others* (New York: Oxford University Press, 2009), 228–77. The translation used here is that of E. A. Speiser in James B. Pritchard, ed., *Ancient Near Eastern Texts Relating to the Old Testament* (Princeton: Princeton University Press, 1969).

Marduk battles Tiamat in this bas-relief. Genesis 1 shares important details with the Babylonian creation myth, but lacks the conflict motif: the Lord creates by his word, alone and unopposed.

The British Library Board, Add MS 10546

that they can do the work of the gods. The text concludes with the gods celebrating Marduk as their ruler and enthroning him in Babylon.

In the first creation story, the word for "deep" in Genesis 1:2 (*tehom*) is generally thought to be the Hebrew form of the Babylonian word *Tiamat*, the name of the sea goddess. Similarly, the biblical view of the sky as a dome over the earth that holds back water relates to the Mesopotamian idea of the cosmos being made up of the two halves of Tiamat's (watery) body.[11] Another intriguing connection between the two texts is the fact that the elements of the created world are brought into existence in the same order in both: light, sky, land, lights in the sky, and humanity. Finally, God's rest after the six days of creation can be compared to the gods celebrating at the conclusion of *Enuma Elish*.

The parallels between the two works are striking, but there are key differences as well. Most important among these are the different theologies—Genesis is a monotheistic text, while *Enuma Elish* is polytheistic—and the different modes of creation whereby God in the Bible does not create by building or by defeating a rival god, as in the Babylonian account, but mostly by speaking. Some scholars have suggested that the Priestly author(s) of Genesis 1:1–2:4a resided in Babylon and knew *Enuma Elish*, and if so perhaps the first Genesis story was written to offer an alternative to the Babylonian theology.

The first creation story, then, may have been written in response to and in dialogue with the context in which it was composed. It was directed to an

---

11. In fact, both Enuma Elish and Genesis 1 describe the waters being *divided* in two so that half of them might be placed above the sky.

audience in exile that needed reassurance that their God was still in control despite the destruction of the Temple and their banishment to a distant land. Its message is clear and unambiguous—God is the creator of all that exists and they should maintain faith and confidence in the face of their difficulties and hardships. At the same time, the story offered an implicit critique of the Babylonian cosmogony by drawing upon some of its elements to present a different theological take on how the world came about.

> How should we interpret the parallels between the first creation story and *Enuma Elish*?

The Second Story as Etiology: Where Did *That* Come From?

The identity of the audience to whom the second story is addressed is less certain, but the purpose of the text is nonetheless quite apparent. A notable feature of the garden of Eden story is its high number of etiologies, or explanations of where things come from. An etiology can explain the origin of any number of things, including objects, locations, practices, or names. The Bible contains many examples of etiologies, and the second creation story has one of the highest concentrations of them. By its very nature, of course, any cosmogony is etiological since it attempts to explain how the world was created. So the first story, with its orderly six-day account of creation, is another example of an etiology. But the etiological dimension of the second story is more pronounced since it provides explanations for a number of specific things whose origins people in antiquity were likely quite curious about.

A good example of an etiology is seen in 2:19–20, which explains where the names of animals come from. In the quest to find his partner, Adam names each of the animals that God brings to him: "And whatever the man called every living creature, that was its name." In the ancient world, to name something was to exercise a degree of control and ownership over it, so this scene is related to the reference in the first story to humanity having dominion over creation (1:26–28). It also has an obvious connection to Adam's naming of Eve in 3:20, and that passage is sometimes cited to support a hierarchical view of the relationship between male and female in which the former is superior to the latter. But it should be noted that Adam does not name Eve until after they eat of the fruit and God punishes them for that infraction, so even if the naming does imply Eve's subordination to Adam, that is not the type of relationship God originally intended the couple to have.

The garden of Eden story also attempts to answer the question, "Why do we wear clothes?" According to 3:7, immediately after eating the fruit, "Then the eyes of both were opened, and they knew that they were naked; and they sewed fig leaves together and made loincloths for themselves." The Hebrew word translated "loincloths" occurs in several other places in the Old Testament where it is used to describe both a belt and a girdle-like object, and so the author likely envisions something that covers the private parts from the waist down. As already noted, later in the chapter God will upgrade their wardrobe before expelling them from the garden: "And the LORD God made garments of skins for the man and for his wife, and clothed them" (3:21). The Hebrew word for "garments" typically refers to a loosely fitting article of clothing that covers the body, and the reference to their being made of skins is an interesting detail. Where did the skins come from? Is there a suggestion here that God the seamstress is also God the hunter? Hidden behind the mention of animal skins might be an allusion to the first death(s) in the Bible, which would be an interesting plot twist in light of Adam and Eve being created as vegetarians. Here, too, the text makes it clear that clothing was not part of God's original plan for humanity, but it was an add-on that became necessary after the couple's fateful decision to eat from the tree.

An additional set of etiologies is the trio of punishments directed at the serpent, Eve, and Adam that have already been discussed (3:14–19). Each of these is meant to explain the origin of something associated with one of the three figures. Snakes do not have legs, women experience pain in childbirth, and working the land is tiresome, not just because that is the way things are, but because their roots can be traced back to the beginning of time and the events that occurred in the garden.

> Can you find any other etiologies in the Garden Story?

That is the way etiologies typically work. Sometimes they just provide the explanation for why someplace has a certain name, like a particular land formation called "Hill of the Foreskins" (Joshua 5:2–7). But at other times they attempt to address questions that are unanswerable, and they therefore create a sense of meaning and order. That is precisely what the etiologies in the garden of Eden story try to do. Who knows why a cat is not called a dog, or vice-versa? Why can't children be born painlessly? These and other mysteries of life have no clear-cut answers, but when they are explained by a well-crafted etiology we are better able to accept our lot and embrace the mystery. And that acceptance comes a lot easier when there is a theological dimension to etiologies, with God as the one ultimately responsible for the status quo. That is one of the reasons why the Bible's cosmogonies continue to be meaningful for so many people; they offer the comforting message that, no matter how absurd or incomprehensible life may seem, there is a God who brings order out of chaos and provides for humanity.

> How does the heavy presence of etiologies in it change your view of the second creation story?

Even in our own modern, technologically advanced world we still have all kinds of questions about why things are the way they are, and we occasionally resort to etiologies to try to make sense of them. Ask long-suffering Chicago Cubs fans why it took their baseball team more than a century to finally win a World Series in 2016, and they will likely attribute it to the "curse of the Billy Goat." During a World Series game in 1945, a bar owner named Billy Sianis was kicked out of Wrigley Field because other fans couldn't stand the odor emanating from his pet goat, and on his way out he declared that the Cubs would never again win the World Series. They went on to lose that series and didn't make it back to one until 2016. Etiologies can help make life's uncertainties more tolerable, whether they are traced back to God or a goat.

The strong etiological nature of Genesis 1–3 is one reason why many scholars prefer to label these texts as *myths*. Myths can serve a variety of purposes. Very often a myth attempts to establish a common identity for a group of people by giving them a shared origin, even if it is not completely based on historical facts. In American culture, the story of the Pilgrims and the first Thanksgiving functions in this way. It is an etiology for

> What are some of the key differences between a myth and a text based on scientific knowledge? How does this have an impact on your understanding of the Bible's creation stories?

an annual ritual that plays a powerful role in shaping American identity—who they are as a people—even though the events might not have happened exactly the way the myth says they did. Creation accounts like the ones in Genesis try to do a similar thing. They create a sense of meaning and order by providing a way of understanding mysteries like where the world came from and how human beings were created. Along the way, myths also typically explain the origins of different things in the world, like the names of animals, pain in childbirth, and clothing. Obviously, there are significant differences between a mythological text and one that is based on science and factual knowledge.

Beyond the Garden: New Meanings for Old Stories

In recent times, biblical scholars have begun to read and interpret the creation stories in some interesting new ways. As alternative methods of engaging in the study of the Bible have emerged and gained wider acceptance, the text has been approached from novel perspectives that can open up new horizons of interpretation and meaning.[12] Many scholars are now raising questions about the Bible that their predecessors did not dream of asking because they tended to focus on issues related to "the world behind the text"—like its possible sources and historical background. More and more readers now attempt to put the Bible in conversation with scholarship being done in other fields or with some of the big

---

12. A volume that discusses some of these new methods is Steven L. McKenzie and John Kaltner, eds., *New Meanings for Ancient Texts: Recent Approaches to Biblical Criticisms and Their Applications* (Louisville: Westminster John Knox, 2013).

social and cultural issues of our time. A few examples of these new developments will now be briefly considered.

Feminist Interpretation

The opening chapters of Genesis have played a pivotal role throughout history in shaping attitudes and behaviors surrounding gender relations, and very often they have been interpreted in ways that support a patriarchal view of the world that marginalizes and alienates women. This is especially the case with the garden of Eden story since the first creation account is more egalitarian in its understanding of male-female relations. Certain aspects of the second story, like the circumstances of Eve's creation, her eating of the fruit, and God's punishment of her for that act, are often cited as evidence that she is inferior to Adam and she is the one responsible for "the Fall." This way of reading the text has been challenged of late as an increasing number of scholars have employed feminist criticism to propose new ways of interpreting it.[13]

It has sometimes been argued that God's reference to Eve as a "helper" (2:18) is meant to put her in a subordinate position in relation to Adam, and that she is created as his servant rather than his equal.[14] But this is to ignore the fact that the same Hebrew word is found in a number of places elsewhere in the Bible to describe God's relationship to humanity, especially in the Psalms (see Ps. 115:9–11; 121:2; 124:8; 146:5). The term therefore cannot be used to support the notion that Eve is somehow inferior to Adam. In a similar manner, some have suggested that Eve's being created second from something that was taken from Adam's body implies she was a derivative afterthought and therefore not as important as he was.[15] But nothing in the text supports this idea, and if the same negative connotation of being created from something were extended to Adam, where would that leave him? He was created from the ground; does that make him inferior to it? Again, there is nothing in the text to support this interpretation.

---

13. For an anthology of interpretations and commentaries on Genesis 2–3 throughout history that focus on the role of gender in the text, see Kristen E. Kvam, Linda S. Schearing, and Valarie H. Ziegler, eds., *Eve and Adam: Jewish, Christian, and Muslim Readings on Genesis and Gender* (Bloomington, IN: Indiana University Press, 1999).

14. An overview of the various ways the term "helper" has been understood is presented in Michael L. Rosenzweig, "A Helper Equal to Him," *Judaism* 35, no. 3 (1986): 277–80. Phyllis Trible adopts an egalitarian view of the relationship between the man and woman in her *God and the Rhetoric of Sexuality* (Philadelphia: Fortress, 1978), 90. Trible was a pioneer in feminist biblical scholarship, and her work has been enormously influential since the 1970s. She presents a reading of the Garden Story from this perspective in "Eve and Adam: Genesis 2–3 Reread," *Andover Newton Quarterly* 13 (1972–1973): 251–58. Much of the discussion in this part of the chapter relies upon her work.

15. Jerome Gellman argues for Adam's, and therefore the male's, superiority from the beginning in his article "Gender and Sexuality in the Garden of Eden," *Theology and Sexuality* 12, no. 3 (2006): 319–36.

Another part of the garden of Eden story that has been used to support notions of female inferiority is the scene in which the serpent convinces Eve to eat of the fruit. It is sometimes interpreted as evidence of her lack of intelligence because she is so easily duped by the serpent to go against God's command due to her pride.[16] But as noted earlier, this argument doesn't really hold water because Eve eats only after using her powers of observation and reason. It is the act of a rational person who exercises her free will to make an informed decision, and not a hasty, knee-jerk reaction by someone who doesn't know any better.

That would be a better description of Adam's role in the scene, and if anyone should be labeled as dimwitted in this story, he is the better candidate. When Eve is confronted by God about what she had done, she owns up to her error ("The serpent tricked me, and I ate") and she takes the fall, and so Augustine and his successors unfairly pinned the Fall on her by portraying her as the one who led Adam and the rest of us astray. In fact, as an intelligent human being who takes responsibility for her actions, Eve comes across as the kind of person one should strive to be.

God's words to Eve in 3:16 are also commonly cited as proof that the second creation story endorses male superiority: "I will greatly increase your pangs in childbearing; in pain you shall bring forth children, yet your desire shall be for your husband, and he shall rule over you." There is no doubt that this is the first reference in the text to an imbalance in gender relations, particularly in the last phrase's statement about the male ruling over the female. But, as noted above, it is important to keep in mind that this comes about only after the couple has eaten of the fruit; it does not describe the ideal state of the relationship between men and women as God intended it to be. This has important implications for any lessons that might be drawn from the story for our own day and age.

The Hebrew word that is translated as "desire" in 3:16 is a relatively rare one that appears only three times in the Bible (the other two places are in Genesis 4:7 and Song of Songs 7:10). Some commentators have considered it to be an etiology meant to explain the origin of the female sex drive, which they sometimes then go on to discuss in negative or derogatory terms. Evidence from nonbiblical sources and the history of interpretation suggests that a better translation of the term would be "return" and that the verse is expressing the idea that, despite the increased pain of childbirth, Eve would actively seek to return

> What is your reaction to a feminist reading of the garden of Eden story?

to Adam. If this alternative way of translating the word is adopted, then a nice connection is established with God's words to Adam a few verses later where he is told, "By the sweat of your face you shall eat bread until you return to the

---

16. Thomas Aquinas considers Eve's sin to be more serious than Adam's for this reason; see question 163 of part 2-2 in his *Summa Theologiae.* This passage is quoted in Kvam, et al., eds., *Eve and Adam,* 234–35.

ground, for out of it you were taken; you are dust, and to dust you shall return"
(3:19). Both members of the couple must now experience more hardship—she
in childbirth, and he in working the land—and each will return to the place he
or she came from, the 'ishshah to the 'ish and the 'adam to the 'adamah.[17] Alternative interpretations like the ones considered here demonstrate how a reading
informed by feminist criticism can allow for a less hierarchical understanding of
gender relations in the Bible's creation stories.

Psychological Interpretation

Another field that Bible scholars have increasingly utilized in their inter-
pretative work is psychology.[18] Concepts and methods that have been developed by psychologists have sometimes proven valuable in efforts to understand
the biblical material, including Genesis 1–3. One scholar has reread the garden
of Eden story through the lens of developmental psychology; she suggests that
the story traces the various stages through which an individual passes on the
way from infancy through adolescence
and into adulthood.[19] The tree of the
knowledge of good and evil represents
the intellectual, emotional, and spiritual
experiences and information the per-

> What are some possible criticisms
> of the use of psychological theory in
> biblical interpretation?

son will attain on the path to maturity. The prohibition against eating from
the tree signals the passage into childhood, which is marked by many similar
restrictions. Adam's naming of the animals parallels the acquisition of language
and the ability to differentiate oneself from others. Eve's creation corresponds
to a person's increased awareness of gender distinctions, and the couple's being
together symbolizes one's ability to interact with others. In this reading, Eve's
encounter with the serpent represents the attainment of wisdom, which is both
life-affirming and life-threatening. By eating the fruit, Adam and Eve reach
adolescence, and their awareness of their nakedness reflects their growing vul-
nerability and self-awareness. The references to pregnancy and physical labor
in God's final words to the couple mark the stage of adulthood. When they
are barred from reentering the garden it is a reminder that, once adulthood is
reached, one cannot return to childhood.

---

17. This proposal is found in Joel N. Lohr, "Sexual Desire? Eve, Genesis 3:16, and *teshuqa*," *Journal of Biblical Literature* 130, no. 2 (2011): 227–46, which presents a thorough overview of how this
verse, particularly the Hebrew word translated "desire," has been interpreted through the ages.

18. See, for example, D. Andrew Kille, *Psychological Biblical Criticism* (Minneapolis: Fortress,
2001), and Wayne G. Rollins and D. Andrew Kille, eds., *Psychological Insight into the Bible: Texts and
Readings* (Grand Rapids: Eerdmans, 2007.)

19. Lyn Bechtel, "Developmental Psychology in Biblical Studies," in *Psychology and the Bible:
A New Way to Read the Scriptures*, ed. J. Harold Ellens and Wayne G. Rollins (Westport, CT:
Greenwood-Praeger, 2004), 122–27.

Many will find this reading of Genesis 2–3 strange because it proposes an allegorical meaning for the garden of Eden story; the characters and events represent things outside the world of the story. Regardless of what one thinks of this interpretation, it is a good example of an approach that draws on the terminology and methodology of another discipline, in this case psychology, to establish what the text means. It allows one to see how the method used has an impact upon the questions one asks of the text, and it shows how meaning is something that a reader creates in the course of interacting with the text rather than something the text communicates to the reader. The author(s) of the garden of Eden story did not compose it with developmental psychology in mind—terms that would have meant nothing back then—but a text that is now more than two thousand years old can still "make sense" within the context of that relatively new field of study. Many newer approaches to reading the Bible exhibit the same capacity to make connections and build bridges between ancient texts and the modern world.[20]

Ecological Interpretation

A final example to consider comes from the relatively recent field of biblical studies known as ecological criticism, which approaches the study of the Bible from an environmental or earth-centered perspective. It can take a variety of different forms, and the creation stories have proven to be of particular interest to ecological critics. This is so because these texts have played a key role in shaping views about what humanity's relationship to the natural world should be, and they have been used to support both a harmonious and a hostile understanding of that relationship.[21]

An important passage related to the environment that has generated much discussion among scholars is Genesis 1:26–28, which was considered earlier in this chapter.

> Then God said, "Let us make humankind in our image, according to our likeness; and let them have dominion over the fish of the sea, and over the birds of the air, and over the cattle, and over all the wild animals of the earth, and over every creeping thing that creeps upon

---

20. See, for example, the essays in McKenzie and Kaltner, eds., *New Meanings for Ancient Texts*.

21. In 1967 Lynn White Jr. published a very influential article in which he argued that the modern ecological crisis is primarily due to Christians who have interpreted texts like Genesis 1 to support their exploitation of the natural world. See Lynn White Jr., "The Historical Roots of Our Ecological Crisis," *Science* 155 (1967): 1203–7. In recent years, it has become increasingly more common to read the Bible with ecological concerns in mind. This approach can be seen in works like Norman C. Habel and Peter Trudinger, eds., *Exploring Ecological Hermeneutics* (Atlanta: Society of Biblical Literature, 2008); Arthur Walker-Jones, *The Green Psalter: Resources for an Ecological Spirituality* (Minneapolis: Fortress, 2009); and the many publications of The Earth Bible Project, *http://www.webofcreation.org/Earthbible/earthbible.html*.

the earth." So God created humankind in his image; in the image of God he created them; male and female he created them. God blessed them, and God said to them, "Be fruitful and multiply, and fill the earth and subdue it; and have dominion over the fish of the sea and over the birds of the air and over every living thing that moves upon the earth."

The most commented-upon words in this passage are the two Hebrew verbs that are here translated as "have dominion" (*radah*) and "subdue" (*kabash*). They are fairly common in the Old Testament, with the first verb appearing twenty-four times and the second fourteen times. The basic meaning of the verb *radah* is "to rule," while *kabash* conveys the idea of subjugating someone or something to oneself. Because both these terms sometimes appear in contexts that describe a forceful, even violent, imposition of control over another, some scholars have suggested that the first creation story teaches that humanity is to exercise mastery and dominance over everything else that exists.[22] For some, this terminology reflects the anthropocentric bias of the biblical literature, which views everything through a lens that privileges humanity and holds it up as the pinnacle of creation. In a way similar to what feminist readers do with patriarchal passages, they argue that the anthropocentrism of the text must be exposed so that the nonhuman elements of the created world can become more apparent.

Others attempt to interpret the passage in ways that present a more positive image of human/nonhuman relations.[23] For example, the language of ruling and exercising dominion is clearly associated with the royal court, and so some scholars have argued that the text is best understood by appealing to Israelite notions of kingship that, in its ideal form at least, was concerned with equity and justice rather than domination and power. According to this reading, humans are to care for and tend the earth in the same way that good rulers provide for those in their charge. Along the same lines, others insist that the account in Genesis 1 must be interpreted and understood in light of the second creation story, which presents a different picture of humanity's bond with nonhuman creation. In particular, the reference in 2:15 to God taking Adam and putting him in the garden of Eden to work it and guard it helps to balance things out and illustrates the

---

22. This view was commonly held in the early centuries of Christianity, as outlined in Morwenna Ludlow, "Power and Dominion: Patristic Interpretations of Genesis 1," in *Ecological Hermeneutics: Biblical, Historical, and Theological Perspectives*, ed. David G. Horrell et al. (London: T&T Clark, 2010), 140–53.

23. See Donald B. Sharp, "A Biblical Foundation for an Environmental Theology: A New Perspective on Genesis 1:26–28 and 6:11–13," *Science et Esprit* 47, no. 3 (1995): 305–13; Norman C. Habel, "Playing God or Playing Earth? An Ecological Reading of Genesis 1.26–28," in *"And God Saw That It Was Good": Essays on Creation and God in Honor of Terence Fretheim*, ed. Frederick Gaiser and Mark Throntveit (St. Paul: Luther Seminary, 2006), 33–41.

relationship of interdependence at the heart of the biblical view of creation. This has led some to refer to humans as the stewards of creation.[24]

Widening our field of vision to include the entirety of the primeval history found in Genesis 1–11, the first creation story can be seen as a critique of the present-day status quo rather than a mandate for human exploitation of the environment. When Noah and his family exit the ark after the waters of the flood subside, God tells them, "The fear and dread of you shall rest on every animal of the earth, and on every bird of the air, on everything that creeps on the ground, and on all the fish of the sea; into your hand they are delivered. Every moving thing that lives shall be food for you; and just as I gave you the green plants, I give you everything" (9:2–3). The flood is an eye-opening experience for God, as only now does the deity come to realize that "the human heart is evil from youth" and will remain that way (8:21). The deluge was meant to destroy human wickedness, wipe the slate clean, and move things in a new direction, but it accomplished nothing. Human beings remain the same flawed creatures they were before the first drop of rain hit the ground, and the rainbow represents God's coming to terms with that situation.

Humanity's relationship with non-human creatures also undergoes a change after the flood. They are now terrified of human beings, who will hunt them, catch them, and trap them so they can eat them. They have become fair game. From the other side of the flood, the events of Genesis 1 are seen in a new light. The first creation story describes the way things were supposed to be, a time when animals and humans lived in harmony and not in fear of one another. However we choose to translate the terms *radah* and *kabash*, those concepts helped set the terms of the relationship and established the framework for a peaceful world whose inhabitants all got along. Viewed from this perspective, the creation story is not an etiology that explains how the uneasy relationship that exists between humans and non-humans came to be, but a painful reminder of what might have been.

> Can you think of other fields besides feminist, psychological, and ecological criticisms that might contribute new ways of reading the creation stories in Genesis?

Feminist criticism, psychology, and environmental studies are just three of the many fields from which Bible scholars now sometimes draw in order to better understand the biblical literature and propose new meanings for it. They all have their limitations and some are more beneficial than others, but when used carefully and properly, these disciplines have the potential to open up new ways of interpreting the Bible and allowing it to speak to the lives and concerns of modern readers.

---

24. This is a theme discussed, for example, in Richard Bauckham, *The Bible and Ecology: Rediscovering the Community of Creation* (Waco, TX: Baylor University Press, 2010), 1–36.

Implications and Applications

1. How has your understanding of the Bible changed after reading this chapter?

2. How has your understanding of the creation stories changed after reading this chapter?

3. Is there a place in the modern world for cosmogonies like this one?

4. Do you feel that the Genesis creation stories have had a positive effect on people? If so, what are some examples? Conversely, do you feel that these stories have had a negative effect? Again, what are some examples?

5. How is God presented in Genesis 1–3? Identify the main qualities and features of the deity in these chapters and explain how they contribute to the portrait of God that emerges from the text.

6. How is humanity presented in Genesis 1–3? Identify the main qualities and features of human beings in these chapters and explain what they suggest about the human condition.

7. How are gender differences understood in Genesis 1–3? How does the text understand the relationship between men and women, and what are the implications for us today?

8. How is the relationship between humanity and the rest of creation presented in Genesis 1–3? What role do human beings play in the world according to the text, and what are the implications for us today?

9. The Genesis creation stories put forth a vision of how the world began that is at odds with modern, scientific explanations of the way things originated. Nonetheless, people continue to derive meaning from the stories, and they maintain there is a certain truth in them. In your estimation, what is "true" in Genesis 1–3? What is "false"?

10. Consider these stories in light of your own understanding of the world. Have they played a role in shaping your views about creation, humanity, and God? If so, how? If not, why not?

Images of Adam and Eve

Linda S. Schearing*

John Kaltner discusses techniques of critical reading and methodolgy useful when discerning what is and what is not present in a biblical text. In Genesis 2–3 there is no "apple" on the tree of knowledge, nor is Satan even mentioned as a character in these chapters. People familiar with cultural depictions of the story, however, assume their presence. The same is true when one analyzes a *visualization* of a biblical text. While a critical reading of a text pays close attention to the literary devices used by the author, a critical "reading" of a painting is attentive to the artistic devices used (such as placement of subjects and use of color). Thus learning to read critically a written text can help us learn to read critically a visual one. Why is this important? Today people are surrounded by images, whether it be traditional media (television, movies), internet media (Instagram, Facebook, and Twitter), or print (advertisements). Artists, as interpreters, add to a written text when they create a visual depiction. When artists depict scenes from religious texts, such as the Bible, they often communicate theological messages, which can have cultural consequences. Examples of this type of visual interpretation can be found in artistic depictions of the snake as female in Genesis 3. Such depictions are significant since, as Kaltner notes, Genesis 1–3 has played a pivotal role in shaping attitudes and behaviors concerning gender. As a result, their interpretation often reflects patriarchal values that have marginalized women.

Kaltner calls Genesis 1–3 the "best known section of the entire Bible." Of the two creation stories in Genesis 1–3, however, it is the second one (Gen. 2:4b–3:24) that has achieved iconic status in people's memories. The story of the first man and woman in a garden setting with one prohibition (not to eat from a certain tree) is well known even to those who have never studied the Bible. The same is true of its presence in the visual world. This is not surprising, given its easily recognizable symbolic elements: a man, a woman, a snake, and a fruit tree. But *how* these elements are visualized is important to the cultural and theological message received by viewers.

Two examples of such visualization are found in *The Fall of Adam* by Hugo van der Goes (ca. 1468)[25] and *Adam, Eve* by Ewing Paddock (2012).[26]

continued

---

* Linda S. Schearing is professor of Hebrew Bible at Gonzaga University, Spokane, Washington.

25. Van der Goes (ca. 1430/1440–1482) was a Flemish painter and, in his later years, a monk.

26. Paddock is a contemporary English painter.

Images of Adam and Eve   *continued*

- What about the foreground and background?
- How are the characters being depicted (remember that biblical texts rarely include physical description of characters)?
- How do all the parts work together?
- What messages are being conveyed (both theological and cultural)?

Below the Surface

The *Fall of Adam* is the left panel of a diptych. The right panel (not shown above) is entitled *Lamentation* and shows Christ being carried to the grave.[28] Knowing this allows us to realize that Goes sees Genesis 3 through the lens of the New Testament, in which Jesus is often seen as a kind of "second Adam."

A close reading of either a text or a picture draws attention to what is actually in the object being analyzed and how various elements function. As one gazes at Goes's painting, the viewer's eye is immediately drawn to the figure of the naked women in the center of the picture. Note how her placement at the center and brightly lit coloring serve to accent her presence. Both serve to highlight her prominence in the action being imaged. A strategically placed lavender flower functions to conceal her genitals—while at the same time drawing attention to them. Her distended abdomen presents the possibility that she is pregnant. In her right hand she holds a piece of fruit (apple?) with a bite out of it, while her left hand is extended in the act of picking a second piece of fruit. To her right (the viewer's left) stands a man with darker coloring, possibly meant to deemphasize his prominence. His right hand covers his genitals while his left hand extends in readiness to receive the fruit the woman is picking. Both man and woman gaze without emotion into the distance. The backdrop of the picture is filled with vegetation but devoid of animal life. The one exception to this is the figure to the woman's left (viewer's right). Here we have a creature with four appendages and a long tail. It has a human head with female facial features and is holding onto the tree while gazing at the woman.

continued

---

28. "The Lamentation of Christ," *Art and the Bible, http://www.artbible.info/art/large/797.html.* Often, however, viewers do not realize this about Goes as they see only the one panel focusing on Genesis 3. Readers of sacred texts often fall into this quandary of not knowing the context of a work as well. Thus Christian readers may be unaware in their reading of the Old Testament of the influence of New Treatment passages (as well as the writings of early church leaders), while Jewish readers are often influenced by Rabbinic writings and midrashim. In this way, readers sometimes base their interpretations not on the text itself but on what subsequent readers in their tradition have said.

Images of Adam and Eve *continued*

Both paintings provide examples of how artists interpret biblical texts. When biblical texts are depicted visually, artists make decisions about what scene to depict, how to flesh out the characters, and what point of view to take.

Van der Goes's *Fall of Adam*

Public Domain

Hugo Van der Goes, *The Fall of Adam* (1479)

As you gaze at this image, consider the following questions:

- What part of Genesis 2–3 is being imaged?
- What story elements can you identify in the picture?
- How are they arranged?
- What do colors[27] and shading add to the images?

continued

---

27. A full-color version of *Fall of Adam* is accessible at "*http://www.artbible.info/art/large/291.html.*"

Images of Adam and Eve *continued*

That we are in a scene from Genesis 3 is clear even if one did not have access to the painting's title, *The Fall of Adam*. Here we have a man, a woman, a fruit tree, a serpent—all elements of the iconic symbol system that has made Genesis 3 so easily recognizable. But how has the artist represented the written text and what messages are being communicated to viewers? First of all, note that both the man and the woman are present at the fruit tree. Like readers, some painters, when imaging this scene "see" only the woman, tree, and serpent. This tends to emphasize the *woman* as the one solely responsible in the disobedience. Yet a close reading of the biblical text specifically states that the man "was with her."[29] Moreover, in Goes's painting the man does not look *forced* to eat the fruit; rather he seems in full compliance with its acceptance. There is no resistance or hesitation on his part. While some commentators would "fill in the gap" in the story by suggesting that Eve did something to make Adam eat, Goes's painting—like the biblical text—does not give that impression. The absence of the animals in the background, or much detail about the surrounding foliage, allows the viewer's attention to focus entirely on the action being depicted. But the most striking character in the painting is the creature. That it has legs may be a reference to the fact that, after the disobedience, the snake is cursed to slither on the ground.[30] This seems to imply, as the picture suggests, that prior to the disobedience, the snake did *not* slither on the ground, but had legs. That it is depicted with a human head might be a nod to the fact that, in the text, it speaks. While some artists depicted the snake as male, others, like Goes, made it female. Making the snake female, however, has both cultural and theological consequences.

Perspectives and Theological Reflections

Just as readers often get different messages from a text, so viewers sometimes see different things when they "read" a painting. What do they see when they look at *The Fall of Adam* by Hugo van der Goes?

Melissa Huang, who received her BFA in Fine Arts Studio from Rochester Institute of Technology and works as a gallery assistant in the Rochester, New York, area, points out that, in the Hebrew text, the snake is referred to with male, not female, pronouns. Since Goes depicts the snake as female, Huang suggests that he is identifying the "knowledge" derived from the forbidden tree as *carnal* knowledge and sees the serpent is a visual metaphor for women's sexuality. Such identification sends the message that once Eve

continued

29. Gen. 3:6.
30. Gen. 3:14.

Images of Adam and Eve *continued*

becomes sexually aware, she can use that awareness to tempt Adam. Huang argues that Goes's depiction of the snake as female is a result of the patriarchal culture of the Renaissance period in Europe.[31] One of its cultural messages is that Eve, as temptress, represents the essential nature of all women, and thus the dangers that feminine sexuality presents for males.

Janet How Gaines, English professor at the University of New Mexico, has a different interpretation:

> Eve, meet Lilith. Lilith–depicted with a woman's face and a serpentine body–assaults Adam and Eve beneath the Tree of Knowledge in Hugo van der Goes' *Fall of Adam and Eve* (c. 1470), from the Kunsthistorisches Museum, in Vienna. According to medieval Jewish apocryphal tradition, which attempts to reconcile the two Creation stories presented in Genesis, Lilith was Adam's first wife. In Genesis 1:27, God creates man and woman simultaneously from the earth. In Genesis 2:7, however, Adam is created by himself from the earth; Eve is produced later, from Adam's rib (Genesis 2:21-22). In Jewish legend, the name Lilith was attached to the woman who was created at the same time as Adam.[32]

Gaines, drawing on rabbinic tradition, sees the female serpent not so much as every woman but as a specific character: Lilith. Some Jewish readers, just like later historical critical scholars, realized that there were problems reconciling the differences between the two creation stories found in Genesis 1-3. As Kaltner describes, modern scholars would explain the differences by reference to the Documentary Hypothesis, the theory that posited various written sources (JEDP) that were combined to form Genesis-Deuteronomy. One Jewish tradition, however, resolved the tension between Genesis 1:1-2:4a and Genesis 2:4b-3:24 by saying that they represented two different creations.[33] Understanding the female serpent in Goes's painting as Lilith, however, results in a double shaming of women. *She* (Eve) is the first to eat and *she* (Lilith) is the one who precipitates the action of disobedience. Such a reading leaves the male (later called "Adam") remarkably free of any responsibility for the disobedience.

continued

---

31. Melissa Huang, "The Sexualization of Eve and the Fall of Woman," *http://www.melissa huang.com/2012/03/09/sexualization-eve/*.

32. Janet How Gaines, "Lilith: Seductress, Heroine or Murderer?" Bible History Daily, *http://www.biblicalarchaeology.org/daily/people-cultures-in-the-bible/people-in-the-bible/lilith/*.

33. Kristen E. Kvam, Linda S. Schearing, and Valarie H. Ziegler, *Eve and Adam: Jewish, Christian, and Muslim readings on Genesis and Gender* (Bloomington, IN: Indiana University Press, 1999), 161–63.

Images of Adam and Eve *continued*

Paddock's *Adam, Eve*

Ewing Paddock, *Adam, Eve* (2012)

As you gaze at this image, consider the following questions:

- What part of Genesis 2-3 is being imaged?
- What story elements can you identify in the picture?
- How are they arranged?
- What do colors[34] and shading add to the images?
- What about the foreground and background?
- How are the characters being depicted (remember that biblical texts rarely include physical description of characters)?
- How do all the parts work together?
- What messages are being conveyed (both theological and cultural)?

continued

---

34. A full-color version of *Adam, Eve* is accessible at "Ewing Paddock—Contemporary Commuter Art," *Redbird*, *http://redbirdreview.com/exhibitions-1-1/*.

Images of Adam and Eve *continued*

Below the Surface

Paddock's *Adam, Eve* is a part of a series of twenty-five paintings, which he explains as follows:

> In June 2009 I began a personal project of making paintings of people in the London Underground. In the last few decades London has become one of the most diverse places on earth and this is even more true of the Underground–the whole world is down there, all squashed up together. I've tried to reflect that in my paintings.[35]

Paddock created a subway set in his studio and approached various "ordinary" folk to model for him. While most of his paintings seemed to "invent themselves" two, he notes, were "deliberate constructions."[36] The painting entitled *Adam, Eve* is one of those two. Perhaps this intentionality can be explained by his terse description of the painting on his website: "An old, old story, deep underground."[37]

Paddock's painting is both strikingly different from Goes's *The Fall of Adam* while at the same time containing some similar messages. In Paddock's painting the images are more spread out on the canvas. If anything approximates the "center" it is the laptop. Once again we have a man and woman, but they are clothed and not as distinct from each other as we saw in Goes's painting. Here they have their arms around each other and their legs intertwined. What they do, they do *together*; they are partners. Gone is the foliage backdrop, replaced now by a subway sign saying "Garden," though the concept of vegetation remains in the decoration of the woman's dress. The "serpent" is not merely human-like but fully human, with a shirt with a snake decoration and snake-colored tights. There is no tree, but a pole, which the snake-surrogate is holding. At the base of the pole is a black bag that echoes her black shoes. Since there is no tree from which the fruit/laptop is to be plucked, perhaps the bag is its source and is a laptop carrier. If so, does it have a rather strange (even sinister?) visage embedded in its folds? Since the black bag echoes the blackness of

continued

---

35. Ewing Paddock, "Painting London Underground," *http://ewingpaddock.com/painting-London -underground*.

36. "Ewing Paddock—Contemporary Commuter Art," *Redbird, http://redbirdreview.com /exhibitions-1-1/*.

37. Paddock, "Painting London Underground."

Images of Adam and Eve *continued*

the snake-surrogate's shoes, one wonders if it is *her* bag and perhaps *her* computer that they are using. If that is the case, then once again the fruit is linked to a woman/snake.

On the man and woman's laps we have an Apple computer with its famous apple-with-a-bite-out-of-it logo. Of course there is no apple in Genesis 3; this is a later understanding of the Garden's fruit. And, interestingly, there was originally no bite out of Apple's logo. Early ads utilized the story of Sir Isaac Newton and the apple (a whole apple), not Genesis 3.[38] In Genesis the Hebrew word translated "knowledge" can indicate either carnal or intellectual knowledge. In Goes's painting the knowledge implied is sexual. In Paddock's painting, however, there is room for both definitions–laptop/intellectual and snake/voluptuous female/sexual. The female character standing to the left of the couple (the viewer's right) in Paddock's painting introduces a more sensual element into the picture with exposed highly decorated legs, etc., that reinforces the older identification of the "forbidden" knowledge as carnal knowledge.

Perspectives and Theological Reflections

Relationships and their fragmentation are an important issue in Genesis 2-3. By including the Apple computer, the artist adds nuance to his visual representation of the "forbidden knowledge" by associating it with contemporary technology. Notice that in Paddock's subway scenario, the man and woman are entwined but not talking to each other. It looks as if their gaze is fixed on the screen in front of them. If this is the case then it is reminiscent of a scene that is common today, although the object of one's gaze is more often a smart phone than a laptop. Thus, while fragmentation of relationship is a consequence of "knowledge" gained by the disobedience in Genesis 3, Paddock's picture might also imply an unintended

continued

---

38. Linda S. Schearing and Valarie H. Ziegler, *Enticed by Eden: How Western Culture Uses, Confuses, (and Sometimes Abuses) Adam and Eve* (Waco, TX: Baylor University Press, 2013), 123–25. By using the Apple computer in his painting, Paddock references another type of imaging of sacred texts that we have not yet mentioned: commercial use. What happens when an image of a biblical text is recycled for purposes far from its original author's intent? Googling "Adam and Eve ads" will lead one to a host of such recycling (not to mention a premier adult products site). One can even purchase a tie on the internet that has Goes's *The Fall of Adam* on it. Just as the product of contemporary recycling in no way guarantees that the end product will resemble the use of the former, the same is true when biblical texts get recycled for commercial purposes.

Images of Adam and Eve *continued*

consequence of contemporary technological advances. Another interpretation, however, is possible. While the woman's gaze is on the screen in her lap, the line of the man's gaze might not be directed toward the screen but toward the standing woman's body. If this is the case, then the man is "checking out" the woman and thus the image represents both types of knowledge—technological and sexual. If that is the case, the fragmentation reflects the different kinds of knowledge being pursued. Such fragmentation might be reflected in the painting's title, which is *Adam, Eve*, not "Adam *and* Eve."

While Paddock's painting plays off of both kinds of knowledge—technological and carnal—the snake on the woman's tee shirt and the snake-like coloring of the woman's tights once again evokes the association of serpent/female/temptation. In spite of the cultural advances of women, it is a reminder that modern culture persists in seeing women as dangerous temptresses.

Why It Matters

That Genesis 2–3 is alive and well in the twenty-first century is not surprising. As a story of origins, the issues facing the ancients are, in some ways, the same ones confronting people today. Who are we? What should be our relationship to God, to each other, and to our environment? The account in Genesis 2 emphasizes a sense of mutuality between humans, animals, and the ecosphere. This mutuality is a far cry from the original author's lived reality as it is from our reality in the twenty-first century. Genesis 3, with its fragmentation and dysfunction, characterizes both the original author's world as well as our own. The ancient, biblical writers critiqued their own relationships by explaining them as an aberration of God's intention for creation. Carefully and critically reading the text allows readers this realization. In Genesis 2, the vision of mutuality between genders, humans, and their ecosphere conveys a message for today, a goal to pursue. It is somewhat ironic that visualizations of Genesis 3 often perpetuate rather than challenge the fragmentation people experience today. Nevertheless, Kaltner notes that contemporary feminist and ecological critical approaches to these Genesis chapters try to recover the critique inherent in the Bible by rereading the text and reclaiming a more positive way of understanding our relationship to each other and to our ecosphere.

continued

Images of Adam and Eve *continued*

Further Exploration[39]

While our analysis has looked at the visual depictions of the snake as female, other elements of the story draw the attention of artists. For example, look up the painting *The Search for Adam and Eve* by Braldt Bralds.[40] How does race and ethnicity enter into the visual depiction of biblical texts?

Keep in mind that a close reading of any visual text representing the Bible involves consideration of the following questions:

- What part of Genesis 2–3 is being imaged?
- What story elements can you identify in the picture?
- How are they arranged?
- What do colors and shading add to the images?
- What about the foreground and background?
- How are the characters being depicted (remember that biblical texts rarely include physical description of characters)?
- How do all the parts work together?
- What messages are being conveyed (both theological and cultural)?

Now—what would you say if you were told that the picture was originally commissioned as cover art for an issue of *Newsweek* magazine?[41]

---

39. Additional help in analyzing visual rhetoric can be found online at sites like the Owl Purdue Online Writing Lab. See *https://owl.english.purdue.edu/owl/section/1/7/* and *https://owl.english.purdue.edu/owl/resource/725/01/*.

40. Bralds describes its commission in Itabari Njeri, "COLORISM: In American Society, Are Lighter-Skinned Blacks Better Off?" *Los Angeles Times* (April 24, 1988). The drawing was cover art for *Newsweek* (Jan. 11, 1988).

41. The article it represented was J. Tierney, "The Search for Adam and Eve: Scientists Explore a Controversial Theory about Man's Origins," *Newsweek* 111 (Jan. 11, 1988): 46–52.

2

Perspectives on Covenant

Much of the Hebrew Bible is concerned with telling the story of a particular group of people, the Israelites. But the first eleven chapters of the book of Genesis are more general in scope as they recount events that have an impact on humanity as a whole, like creation (chapters 1–3), the flood that destroys everyone but Noah's family (chapters 6–9), and the Tower of Babel episode (chapter 11). This first part of Genesis is sometimes referred to as the "Primeval History." Beginning with chapter 12, the focus narrows and attention is directed at a single individual, the ancestor to whom all Israelites trace their roots. That person is Abraham; he takes center stage in Genesis 12, and his lineage comes to dominate the rest of the biblical story.

At the heart of the Old Testament, then, is a family story. It recounts the comings and goings, the ups and downs, of an extended group of people who are kinfolk. Families are about relationships, and by their very nature relationships are messy and complicated, so it should be no surprise that biblical families sometimes come across as dysfunctional and flawed (see the description of Abraham's family dynamics in Genesis 16, for example). In other words, they often look like our own families.

As important as familial ties and connections are to the biblical story, another relationship dominates the text and looms large on practically every page. This is the relationship between God and humanity, particularly the Israelite people. Israel's relationship with God is a central theme in many of the stories in the Old Testament, and much of the non-narrative portion of the text is also concerned with that bond by either commenting on it or interpreting it. For example, many of the writings of the prophets attempt to warn the people about the disastrous consequences that await them unless they improve their relationship with God. The Psalms also often have the divine/human relationship as their central theme, sometimes celebrating it and elsewhere lamenting its shortcomings and pleading that it be improved.

The term most commonly used in the Bible to refer to God's relationship with Israel is "covenant," a concept that will be the focus of this chapter. The Hebrew word that is used to convey the idea of covenant is *berit*, which can be used to describe a number of different types of relationships. Covenant is also connected to some other notions that are central to the Bible's understanding of God's relationship to the Israelites—like election, law, and obedience—and so it is an extremely important concept that merits careful attention and study. Some have gone so far as to say that covenant is the central theological idea of the entire Hebrew Bible and that one cannot truly understand the text without a solid grasp of it.[1]

First Impressions

The Hebrew word *berit* is one that many non-Jews have seen before in contexts outside the Bible, often with a variant spelling. For example, there is a well-known philanthropic organization of Jewish men found in many large cities known as "B'nai B'rith," which translates as "sons (or children) of the covenant." It is also seen in the word *bris*, the Yiddish[2] version of *berit*, referring to the act of circumcising a male baby eight days after he is born, in accordance with God's command to Abraham in Genesis 17. The etymology of the word *berit* is not known, but various ideas have been proposed about its source, including its derivation from roots in Hebrew and other Semitic languages that have to do with eating, deciding, bonding, and setting apart.[3] Whatever its precise origin, in the Bible the word *berit* is used to describe a relationship or arrangement between two or more parties that has a binding status. It is sometimes found in texts that discuss such a relationship between humans, but our focus here will be on those passages that describe a *berit* between God and an individual or group.

The Covenant with Noah

READ: Genesis 6–9

The word *berit* first appears in the flood story, which is found in Genesis 6–9. Prior to the deluge, God provides Noah with a blueprint for how to build the ark and then tells him, "But I will establish my covenant (*berit*) with you; and you shall come into the ark, you, your sons, your wife, and your sons' wives with you" (Gen. 6:18). After riding out the storm in the safety of their vessel, Noah and

---

1. This can be seen in the first volume of Walther Eichrodt's influential work on the theology of the Old Testament, first published in German, in which the titles of all but one of the book's chapters contain the word "covenant." See Walther Eichrodt, *Theology of the Old Testament* (Philadelphia: Westminster John Knox, 1967).

2. The Yiddish language, a combination of Hebrew and German, developed among the Jews of central and eastern Europe. The word "Yiddish" means "Jewish" in the Yiddish language.

3. An excellent overview of the term *berit* can be found in Moshe Weinfeld, "ברית berith," in *Theological Dictionary of the Old Testament*, ed. G. Johannes Botterweck and Helmer Ringgren (Grand Rapids: Eerdmans, 1975), 2:253–79.

his family are once again back on dry land when God returns to the topic in a speech that mentions the covenant seven times.

> Then God said to Noah and to his sons with him, "As for me, I am establishing my covenant with you and your descendants after you, and with every living creature that is with you, the birds, the domestic animals, and every animal of the earth with you, as many as came out of the ark. I establish my covenant with you, that never again shall all flesh be cut off by the waters of a flood, and never again shall there be a flood to destroy the earth." God said, "This is the sign of the covenant that I make between me and you and every living creature that is with you, for all future generations: I have set my bow in the clouds, and it shall be a sign of the covenant between me and the earth. When I bring clouds over the earth and the bow is seen in the clouds, I will remember my covenant that is between me and you and every living creature of all flesh; and the waters shall never again become a flood to destroy all flesh. When the bow is in the clouds, I will see it and remember the everlasting covenant between God and every living creature of all flesh that is on the earth." God said to Noah, "This is the sign of the covenant that I have established between me and all flesh that is on the earth." (Gen. 9:8–17)

As in other texts to be examined later in this chapter, God takes the initiative here by establishing the covenant and informing Noah and his family about its existence. Covenants in the Old Testament are typically presented in this way, with God being the one who sets the terms and the human party having no input in the matter. Of course, humans can always choose to not live up to their end of the bargain and violate the terms of the covenant, and this becomes a frequent theme later in the biblical story. But the humans involved do not initiate a covenant, nor do they determine its precise nature. This underscores an important dimension of divine/human covenants in the Hebrew Bible: the parties are not of equal status, as God clearly plays a superior and dominant role.[4]

> What does the fact that covenants in the Old Testament are divinely initiated say about the biblical understanding of God?

A Universal Covenant

An interesting aspect of this passage is that God does not just establish this covenant with humans. God establishes this relationship with all living creatures,

---

4. The unequal nature of the biblical idea of covenant is reflected in the words used to translate *berit* into Greek and Latin in the ancient versions of the Bible: *diathēkē* and *testamentum*, respectively. These two terms describe agreements in which only one of the parties dictates the terms.

and this point is stressed repeatedly in the passage. In fact, of the eight verses in which God speaks, only three do not mention that the covenant affects all living things (vv.9, 11, 14). God's relationship with the entire world, not just human beings, is the focus here.

The flood story is related only a few chapters after the creation story, and the two sections share a number of terms and phrases that establish a clear link between them. For example, the reference to the birds, animals, and creeping things, all "according to their kinds" (6:20), recalls the creation of these same categories of animals in 1:20–25. The description of the windows of the heavens opening and releasing rain (7:11) calls to mind the creation of the dome in the sky that holds back the waters in 1:6–8. As the waters of the flood subside, God makes a wind blow over the earth (8:1), just as a wind from God sweeps over the waters at creation (1:2). The statement that humans were created in God's image (9:6) was made earlier in 1:27. Finally, the divine command to Noah and his family to be fruitful and multiply (9:1, 7) is identical to what God tells humanity in 1:28. All of these echoes suggest that the flood story can be read and interpreted in light of the creation story. The flood story is, in a sense, a re-creation story; God's relationship with the entire world is reestablished after the destruction caused by the flood. This is why Genesis 9:8–17 stresses repeatedly that God's covenant is with all of creation, not just humanity.

> Is humanity's importance relativized in the covenant with Noah because it is made with all creatures?

As will be seen in other biblical covenants, a *berit* is commonly reciprocal in that there is a shared responsibility by both parties. Each side has certain obligations or duties that must be met in order for the covenant to remain effective and in place. Marriage is an example of a human relationship often associated with a covenant, and this is a helpful analogy by which to consider the reciprocity inherent in bonds of this sort.

An important feature of the covenant with Noah is that there does not seem to be a clearly defined obligation or expectation on the human side. The divine duties are laid out, but Genesis 9:8–17 does not say anything about what Noah and other people are asked to do in return. It might be that the verses just prior to this are meant to play such a role and delineate what is expected of the human parties in the covenant.

> Does the comparison of a covenant to a marriage seem like a good one to you? Are there any important differences between the two?

God blessed Noah and his sons, and said to them, "Be fruitful and multiply, and fill the earth. The fear and dread of you shall rest on every animal of the earth, and on every bird of the air, on everything that creeps on the ground, and on all the fish of the sea; into your hand they are delivered. Every moving thing that lives shall be food for you; and just as I gave you the green plants, I give you everything. Only, you shall not eat flesh with its life, that is, its blood. For your own lifeblood I will surely require a reckoning: from every animal I will require it and from human beings, each one for the blood of another, I will require a reckoning for human life. Whoever sheds the blood of a human, by a human shall that person's blood be shed; for in his own image God made humankind." (Gen. 9:1–6)

This section contains clear guidelines on what humans can and cannot do. In the first place, they are no longer vegetarians, as God gives them permission to eat the other animals (vv. 1–3). But there are some limitations as well. The prohibition against eating flesh with its life, or blood (v. 4), is the basis for the Jewish dietary law that meat must be drained of all blood prior to being prepared in order to be kosher. In addition, the approval that humans may shed blood does not extend to their own species, since God explicitly forbids taking the life of another person (vv. 5–6). It could be that these conditions placed on humans are their covenantal obligations, and so what appears to be missing later in the chapter is actually present here. If they are not a part of the covenant-making scene, then this is an example of a one-sided covenant in which the duties of one party remain unexpressed.

The simultaneous permission to take animal life while forbidding the taking of human life may be tied to the passage just prior to this one, in which God comes to a realization: "I will never again curse the ground because of humankind, for the inclination of the human heart is evil from youth; nor will I ever again destroy every living creature as I have done" (8:21b). Perhaps the consent to shed animal blood is really a concession on God's part that acknowledges a violent tendency in humanity that, if left unchecked, would escalate into aggression and hostility toward fellow human beings. However one understands God's comment here, it should be noted that it is uttered as a result of one of the best examples of anthropomorphism found in the Bible. Noah's first act upon leaving the ark is to build an altar and offer animal sacrifices, and God's comment about the human heart's propensity toward evil is in response to the aroma of the cooking meat reaching the divine nostrils: "And when the LORD smelled the pleasing odor, the LORD said in his heart . . ." (Gen 8:21a).

Do you think God's permission to kill animals might be a concession that acknowledges humanity's violent nature?

An Uneasy Relationship

God's statement that "the inclination of the human heart is evil from youth" is a broad condemnation of humanity in general, and it raises some important questions about the deity and the flood story. The verse is almost a restatement of what God says prior to opening the floodgates in 6:5. "The LORD saw that the wickedness of humankind was great in the earth, and that every inclination of the thoughts of their hearts was only evil continually." The wicked nature of the human heart was the reason the flood was sent in the first place, but after the waters subside, God's first statement is that humanity is evil to its core. What was the point of sending the flood if the before and after pictures look exactly the same? Was all that death and destruction really necessary? Why did God have to kill every living creature if the outcome did not change anything?

> Does God appear to lack omniscience in the flood story?

This image of the deity is similar to the one that emerges in the garden of Eden, where God goes about creating a suitable mate for Adam by trial and error, appears to be learning as things unfold, and does not always have all the answers. God sends the flood assuming he'll get a do-over and have a clean slate to start afresh with Noah and his family, only to discover that things are exactly as they were prior to the big storm.

The two stories are similar in their portrayals of God because they come from the same J (Jahwist) source that was discussed earlier. One of the hallmarks of that source is an anthropomorphic deity, that is, one who exhibits many human-like traits, in this case an inability to know for certain how things will turn out in the long run. It is worth noting at this point that the source behind the first creation story, called the P (Priestly) source, is also found in the flood story, but with an important difference. While the two sources are found one after another in the creation stories, here they are blended together to create a single narrative. Nonetheless, there are tell-tale signs that the flood story is a cut-and-paste job since there are many repetitions and inconsistencies. For example, the flood is announced twice (6:17; 7:4), Noah is ordered to enter the ark twice (6:18; 7:1–3), and Noah and his family enter the ark twice (7:7, 13). Among the inconsistencies are the length of the flood (40 days or 150 days: 7:4; 8:3), the number of animals brought on board the ark (two of each or seven pairs: 6:19–20; 7:2–3), and the names for God (Yahweh or Elohim). The latter difference can be seen very clearly in an English translation of the Bible like the New Revised Standard Version (NRSV), which renders Yahweh as "LORD" and Elohim as "God." Reading the story with careful attention to where the two names are found in the NRSV allows the reader to easily see how the J and P sources have been woven together to create the story.

> How else might the repetitions and inconsistencies in the flood story be explained?

As in the Garden Story, in which Eve was created only after the animals prove not to be suitable mates for Adam, here too in the flood story God goes to plan B. That adjustment entails God's coming to terms with the evil nature of humanity and accepting it. This is where the rainbow episode comes in. In addition to being an obvious etiology meant to explain the origin of that particular celestial phenomenon, it lays out the parameters of the divine/human relationship going forward. And here, too, a very human-like God is on display.

The rainbow is a sign of the covenant according to Genesis, but it is primarily a sign for God and not for us.

> God said, "This is the sign of the covenant that I make between me and you and every living creature that is with you, for all future generations: I have set my bow in the clouds, and it shall be a sign of the covenant between me and the earth. When I bring clouds over the earth and the bow is seen in the clouds, I will remember my covenant that is between me and you and every living creature of all flesh; and the waters shall never again become a flood to destroy all flesh. When the bow is in the clouds, I will see it and remember the everlasting covenant between God and every living creature of all flesh that is on the earth." God said to Noah, "This is the sign of the covenant that I have established between me and all flesh that is on the earth." (Gen. 9:12–17)

God's anger or frustration with humanity is to the fore in this passage. The human heart inclines toward evil, and God must accept that fact or start looking for another Noah to start over again. Without the rainbow to remind him of the covenant, God might be tempted to let the rain keep falling. The bow in the sky is a sign for God to check the divine anger and come to terms with the imperfect nature of human beings. The more violent subtext of the story is easily lost on modern readers because we often do not understand the symbolism of the rainbow. In the ancient Near East and similar cultures, deities were typically portrayed with objects that represented aspects of their identity. Among these objects were weapons, including the bow and arrow, and that is probably what is being presented in this text.[5] The rainbow symbolizes God's weapon, which is being hung up in the sky rather than being used against wayward humanity.

> What do you think of God's assessment of humanity as evil to the core?

An important aspect of the covenant with Noah is that it encompasses all of creation and is not limited to human beings. After the flood, the relationship that God has with the entire created world is acknowledged and affirmed. In this way, this covenant is meant to establish a sense of order and harmony among all the elements of creation and their creator. Nonetheless, at the core of the covenant that is described in Genesis 9 exists an uneasy relationship

---

5. A discussion of the passage in relation to God's anger can be found in Yair Lorberbaum, "The Rainbow in the Cloud: An Anger-Management Device," *Journal of Religion* 89 (2009): 498–540.

between God and human beings. One of the terms of the alliance is that God must take measures to guarantee that the divine anger does not erupt again. This self-imposed restraint is necessary because of the flawed and imperfect nature of humanity, which is prone to evil and wickedness. With this understanding of the relationship between the two parties of the *berit*, the text is setting the stage for what will be a repeated and consistent theme throughout the remainder of the Old Testament: divine fidelity to the covenant in the face of human weakness and sin.

The Covenant with Abraham

READ: Genesis 15 and 17

The next references to covenant in the Old Testament are found in the Abraham story, specifically in chapters 15 and 17 of Genesis. These two chapters are each identified with one of the two sources of the Pentateuch that have already been discussed. The episode in chapter 15 comes from the J (Jahwist) source, and the one in chapter 17 is a P (Priestly) text. It should be noted that the main character has different, though related, names in the two passages. In chapter 15 he is referred to as Abram, while in chapter 17 he is known as Abraham, variant forms of the same name, meaning "exalted father." Such name changes typically signal a corresponding change of status in a character, and that is clearly the case here.[6] For the sake of simplicity we will refer to him by his better known name of Abraham even when discussing his role in passages prior to Genesis 17.

Although he is considered to be the ancestor of the Israelites, Abraham was not born in the land that eventually became Israel, which was part of an area known as Canaan. He was from a city called Ur of the Chaldeans (11:31–32), in a part of ancient Mesopotamia that is now in the modern country of Iraq.[7] According to Genesis, Abraham was called by God to leave his homeland and journey to Canaan, where he would become the father of a great nation. Upon arriving, he was forced to flee due to a famine and he journeyed to Egypt before returning to Canaan, where he eventually settled. God's promise to make Abraham a great nation was complicated by the fact that he and his wife Sarah (originally named Sarai) were an elderly couple who did not have children (11:30).

---

6. Another example of this can be seen in Gen. 32:22–32, where Jacob's name is changed to Israel.

7. Abraham would not have referred to his city as "Ur of the Chaldeans" since it was not called this until many centuries after the early second millennium BCE, the time period in which these stories appear to be set, according to most scholars. This anachronistic use of the place name is an indication that the text was written long after the purported time of Abraham, a point that will be discussed later in this chapter.

Cutting the Covenant (Genesis 15)

Chapter 15 of Genesis opens with a description of Abraham having a vision in which God promises him that, despite his advanced years, he will have many offspring. God then brings Abraham outside (note the anthropomorphism, an indication of the J source) and tells him that his descendants will be more numerous than the countless stars in the night sky. When God informs Abraham that he has been given the land he is currently residing in, Abraham questions how he is to know that he will possess it (15:1–8).

This leads to a strange scene of a ritual in which Abraham cuts some animals in half. The ritual is described in two parts in verses 9–12 and 17–21. The intervening section (vv. 13–16) reports a brief speech by God that will be discussed below. The text indicates that the ritual is some sort of covenant ceremony meant to express the relationship that has been established between God and Abraham. The term *berit* is found in verse 18.

> Can you think of any rituals in the modern world that are associated with entering into a binding agreement like a covenant?

This is the only passage in the Hebrew Bible that contains a description of such a ceremony, but there is an apparent reference to a similar ritual in Jeremiah 34:18, a verse that helps to clarify the meaning of the Genesis 15 scene: "And those who transgressed my covenant and did not keep the terms of the covenant that they made before me, I will make like the calf when they cut it in two and passed between its parts." According to this passage, the divided animal parts represent what will happen to the partner who violates the terms of the covenant: the guilty party will be cut up just as the animal was. Similar cutting rituals are known throughout the ancient Near East as ways of expressing various types of binding agreements.[8]

The Genesis text describes an ancient practice whereby those entering into a covenant relationship passed between the dissected parts of slaughtered animals. In this instance, God does so in the form of fire (v. 17), similar to how the deity appears elsewhere in the burning bush (Exod. 3:2), a pillar of fire (Exod. 13:21), and the fiery, volcano-like Mount Sinai (Exod. 19:18). This ritual is also the reason why in biblical Hebrew one always "cuts" a covenant. Even though it is often translated here (v. 18) and elsewhere as "make," the Hebrew verb that is typically used in connection with covenants is "cut" (*karat*).

In the midst of the covenant ceremony God relays a future-oriented message to Abraham, who has drifted off into a deep sleep.

Then the Lord said to Abram, "Know this for certain, that your offspring shall be aliens in a land that is not theirs, and shall be slaves

---

8. See Gerhard F. Hasel, "The Meaning of the Animal Rite in Genesis 15," *Journal for the Study of the Old Testament* 19 (1981): 61–78.

there, and they shall be oppressed for four hundred years; but I will bring judgement on the nation that they serve, and afterwards they shall come out with great possessions. As for yourself, you shall go to your ancestors in peace; you shall be buried in a good old age. And they shall come back here in the fourth generation; for the iniquity of the Amorites is not yet complete." (Exod. 15:13–16)

This mini-speech by God makes reference to the time the Israelites will spend in Egypt prior to being set free during the Exodus, a period that the Bible says elsewhere lasted four hundred and thirty years (Exod. 12:40). Given what is taking place in the story, it is a rather strange thing for God to be telling Abraham at the moment. It breaks up the narrative describing the covenant ceremony, and it does not have any connection with the events being described. Why would Abraham care about what will happen to a group of people living four centuries after him? This is an example of *vaticinium ex eventu*, a Latin phrase meaning "prophecy after the fact" that refers to a passage that "predicts" something that had already come to pass at the time the text was written. Such passages are sometimes used in the Bible to legitimate the authority of the one who is speaking, or to address the concerns of later readers. In this case, it is an indication that the text was written long after the events it purports to describe, and it helps to make sense of the period of captivity in Egypt by claiming that it was all part of the divine plan and had already been foreseen by God during Abraham's time.

> What is your reaction to the use of *vaticinium ex eventu* as a literary device?

A couple of aspects of this covenant merit some comment. First of all, it is a unilateral agreement in which God promises something to Abraham but Abraham does not reciprocate by pledging something else in return. The direction is one-way, with God taking the initiative, while the human partner is a passive recipient of divine generosity. In addition, what Abraham receives from God is noteworthy. The wanderer from Ur of the Chaldeans is about to put down roots as he is promised a land he and his descendants will inhabit. The borders mentioned here—from the Nile River to the Euphrates River—encompass the largest area identified with the Promised Land in the entire Old Testament, and the dimensions of Israelite territory never actually extended to those boundaries. It is described as "the land of the Kenites, the Kenizzites, the Kadmonites, the Hittites, the Perizzites, the Rephaim, the Amorites, the Canaanites, the Girgashites, and the Jebusites" (vv. 19–21). Similar lists of the peoples living in Canaan prior to the Israelites are found elsewhere in the Pentateuch, and several of the groups are found only here in Genesis 15. With this reference to

> Does the fact that there were other people living in the Promised Land prior to the arrival of the Israelites raise ethical questions for you?

the land's current occupants the text indirectly raises questions related to their rights as landowners and how they and Abraham's "great nation" will get along, thereby anticipating the future conquest of its inhabitants as related in the books of Joshua and Judges.

Cutting the Covenant Again (Genesis 17)

The first clearly reciprocal covenant in the Hebrew Bible is found in Genesis 17, where both God and Abraham make specific promises to one another. In contrast to chapter 15, where the focus is solely on the land, here God includes Abraham's many offspring as a sign of the covenant. "As for me, this is my covenant with you: You shall be the ancestor of a multitude of nations" (17:4). In addition, God indicates that the covenant with Abraham's descendants will be a perpetual one that will endure for all ages (17:7).

> How is a reciprocal covenant, where both sides make promises to one another, different from a unilateral one, in which only one side has obligations?

God's first words in the chapter reveal the divine name to be El-Shadday, which is often translated as "God Almighty" (17:1). The meaning of this name is uncertain and various proposals have been suggested for its etymology, including "God of the mountains," "God of the beasts," and "God with breasts." In Exodus 6:3 it is stated that this was the name of God known by Abraham, Isaac, and Jacob prior to God's self-disclosure of the name Yahweh to Moses at the burning bush (Exodus 3). The divine epithet El-Shadday is generally held to be found in late biblical texts from the exilic period or later, and it is a characteristic of the P source.[9]

After explaining the obligations on the divine side of the covenant, God then turns to the human side: "God said to Abraham, 'As for you, you shall keep my covenant, you and your offspring after you throughout their generations. This is my covenant, which you shall keep, between me and you and your offspring after you: Every male among you shall be circumcised. You shall circumcise the flesh of your foreskins, and it shall be a sign of the covenant between me and you'" (Gen 17:9–11). God instructs Abraham that all males must be circumcised when they are eight days old, and that practice has continued in Judaism into the present day.

Israel was not the only nation in the ancient Near East to practice circumcision. A passage in the book of Jeremiah identifies other places where circumcision was practiced, including Egypt, Judah, Edom, Ammon, and Moab (9:25–26). Images found on reliefs and other archaeological sources indicate that

---

9. E. A. Knauf, "Shadday," *Dictionary of Deities and Demons in the Bible*, ed. Karel van der Toorn et al. (Leiden: Brill: 1999): 749–53.

as far back as the early third millennium BCE males were being circumcised in Mesopotamia and Egypt. Some iconographic evidence from Egypt indicates that a type of circumcision was present there that kept the foreskin partially attached to the penis, so it is likely that there were different ways of performing the procedure. The origins of circumcision in Israel remain a mystery, and it could be that Genesis 17 is meant to serve as an etiology to explain how it began. It is possible that it originated as a ritual associated with marriage or reaching puberty. This theory is supported by Exodus 4:24–26, which recounts one of the weirdest episodes in the entire Bible. In that story, Moses' wife Zipporah cuts off their infant son's foreskin and then rubs it on Moses' genitals before declaring him a "bridegroom of blood by circumcision."[10]

Even if the origin of Israelite circumcision is unknown, there is no doubt that Genesis 17 gives it theological meaning. In fact, as far as anyone knows, the Israelites were the only people to attach religious significance to the practice. It is the literal mark of the covenant on a man's body, and is a sign of membership in the covenantal community. The drawing of blood that is a part of the ritual is an interesting connection with the animal sacrifices that are described in the covenant ceremony between Abraham and God in Genesis 15. In light of the Hebrew verb typically associated with the term *berit*, one might say that circumcision expresses in a literal way how one "cuts" a covenant. The same type of wordplay is evident in God's final words about circumcision in 17:14, where the possibility of breaking the covenant is mentioned using the same verb that describes making it: "Any uncircumcised male who is not circumcised in the flesh of his foreskin shall be cut off from his people; he has broken my covenant."

Immediately after the command to circumcise, God informs Abraham that his wife Sarah will have a son. Abraham scoffs at this idea due to his and Sarah's advanced years, and suggests that God accept as the child of the covenant Ishmael, Abraham's son with Sarah's servant

> Why would something like circumcision be chosen as the sign of the covenant?

Hagar. But God remains unmoved in the face of Abraham's objection, and states that the yet unborn Isaac will be the son through whom the covenant will be passed (17:19–21).

God had previously promised to establish the covenant with Abraham and his descendants forever, and it is therefore natural for the reader to assume that it will be passed on to both Ishmael and Isaac since they are Abraham's sons. In fact, in ancient Near Eastern cultures the

> How does the choice of Isaac over Ishmael affect your view of God and your idea of covenant?

firstborn son was the primary heir who received the birthright, and so if one

---

10. See Jack M. Sasson, "Circumcision in the Ancient Near East," *Journal of Biblical Literature* 85 (1966): 473–76.

was to be favored it should have been Ishmael. But God goes the other way and chooses Isaac, the younger son.[11] That decision underscores an important aspect of the covenant as it is presented in the Hebrew Bible: God's choice of someone or some group always implies that others have not been chosen. It is Abraham's line that is favored, not someone else's. The Israelites are God's chosen people, not the Kenites, Amorites, Canaanites, or some other group. God goes with Isaac, not Ishmael. The notion of election contains an element of exclusion because it indicates preference and favoritism. In the covenant with Abraham, God takes sides and shows partiality toward one side of the family, thereby rejecting the other.[12]

Ishmael is not completely abandoned by God since he will be blessed, will prosper, and will become a great nation (17:20). The list of his descendants is found in Genesis 25:12–18, along with a reference to where they settled in the desert areas along the Red Sea. But being blessed and having a big family are not the same as receiving a covenantal promise, and so Ishmael suffers the fate of those who must live in the shadow of a more prominent sibling. Ishmael's marginalization is due to the text's role as a foundation document that is meant to establish a shared history and create an identity for a particular group of people. This story tells the Israelites about their origins, who they are, and how their unique relationship with God came about. The traditions about Abraham achieve that purpose by introducing the idea of an eternal covenant with the chosen people through Isaac's line.

The Covenant with Moses

Moses is the main character in what could be considered the most important event described in the Hebrew Bible, the Israelites' escape from bondage in Egypt. This episode, known as the Exodus, is recounted in Exodus 14–15 and is preceded by a set of plagues sent upon Egypt in order to convince the Pharaoh that he should let the Israelites go free (Exod. 7–11). The covenant is not mentioned prior to the Exodus, but once the people leave Egypt and begin their forty-year period of wandering in the wilderness it becomes a common theme.

The Israelite's journey through the desert is described in a lengthy section that runs from Exodus 16 through the end of the Pentateuch at Deuteronomy 34. Early in their trip, the narrative slows down as the people stop traveling and stay in one place for an extended period of time. That layover is located at

---

11. The preference for the younger brother over the older one is a common theme in the Hebrew Bible. In addition to Isaac, other younger brothers who are favored include Jacob, Joseph, David, and Solomon.

12. Regina M. Schwartz argues that such divine partiality is a feature of the monotheistic religions. See her *The Curse of Cain: The Violent Legacy of Monotheism* (Chicago: University of Chicago Press, 1998).

Mount Sinai, where Moses receives the law from God. Many people who are familiar with the Moses-on-the-mountain scene from movies like *The Ten Commandments* assume this is a relatively cut-and-dry episode. The Israelites pull up to Mount Sinai, Moses climbs up the hill, God gives him the tablets containing the law, Moses comes back down, and they're on their way again toward the Promised Land. Actually, it is a much more complicated and lengthy part of the story than most realize, and it takes some sixty chapters to recount: Exodus 19–40, all of Leviticus, and up to chapter 10 in Numbers, as well as a few passages in Deuteronomy.

> What might the law's central location in the Pentateuch suggest about the composition and development of this part of the Hebrew Bible?

Law and Covenant

The giving of the law is the literal center of the Pentateuch, with sixty-seven chapters coming before it and sixty after it. It is the theological center as well, and this is where the covenant comes in. From this point on, the primary way one expresses fidelity to the covenant is through following and observing the law that was revealed on Mount Sinai. The prior covenant to Abraham is rendered less significant because the command to circumcise newborn males on the eighth day after their birth is included in the law given to Moses (Lev. 12:1–3). The law becomes the main theological lens through which the subsequent history of Israel is read and interpreted in the rest of the Old Testament. When things go well, it is because the Israelites are following the law, but when bad things happen, it is due to their inability to obey God's statutes and commands.

Mount Sinai, shown here, is also called Mount Horeb in some parts of the Torah. The presence of multiple names for the same place suggests that the text is a compilation of multiple sources.

Given the amount of text devoted to Mount Sinai, it goes without saying that the law is comprised of more than just the Ten Commandments. Jewish tradition teaches that there are 613 laws in the Torah, but the Ten Commandments, or Decalogue,[13] are the most famous. Less well known is the fact that there are actually two different versions of the Ten Commandments, one at Exodus 20:1–17 and another at Deuteronomy 5:6–21. The most significant difference between the two is in the reason why one should keep the Sabbath day holy. In Exodus, it is because God rested on the seventh day, but in Deuteronomy it is because the Israelites had been slaves in Egypt.

Exodus 24 describes an interesting and unusual scene that is clearly meant to be a covenant-making ceremony.

> Moses came and told the people all the words of the Lord and all the ordinances; and all the people answered with one voice, and said, "All the words that the Lord has spoken we will do." And Moses wrote down all the words of the Lord. He rose early in the morning, and built an altar at the foot of the mountain, and set up twelve pillars, corresponding to the twelve tribes of Israel. He sent young men of the people of Israel, who offered burnt-offerings and sacrificed oxen as offerings of well-being to the Lord. Moses took half of the blood and put it in basins, and half of the blood he dashed against the altar. Then he took the book of the covenant, and read it in the hearing of the people; and they said, "All that the Lord has spoken we will do, and we will be obedient." Moses took the blood and dashed it on the people, and said, "See the blood of the covenant that the Lord has made with you in accordance with all these words." (Exod. 24:3–8)

There are some similarities between this scene and others that have been discussed, especially the one involving Abraham in Genesis 15. Although the verb commonly associated with making covenants is not used here explicitly, the references to sacrificed animals and bloodshed indicate that there is a great deal of "cutting" going on. The altar represents God, just as the fire represents God in the scene with Abraham, and so half the blood being poured on God and the other half on the people recalls the halves of the slaughtered animals that represent the two parties. As with the ritual in Genesis 15, this one is meant to express the binding nature of the relationship and the dire consequences that await the partner who violates it.

The scene stresses the presence and participation of all the Israelites. The people speak in one voice, and the twelve pillars are meant to represent the entire community. This is not a covenant only with Moses. Rather, he plays his usual role as an intermediary between God and the people, who are God's

---

13. The term "Decalogue" comes two Greek words that mean "ten" and "word."

covenant partners. The passage also emphasizes the words of God, which are mentioned directly or indirectly six times. These words are the law that Moses has just received. The people's double pronouncement that they will "do" what the words of the Lord require is their way of affirming that they will abide by and obey the law.

The people did not always follow through on their promise to be faithful to the covenant. In fact, a frequent theme in the narrative describing their wilderness wanderings is their tendency to whine and complain. They lack trust in God and Moses, and prefer to return to their lives of servitude in Egypt rather than journey on to the land that has been promised to them. Things reach their low point in Exodus 32, which describes the episode of the golden calf. While Moses is on the mountain with God, the people become restless and convince Moses' brother Aaron to build them an idol in the shape of a golden calf made of their precious metals. Upon his return, an angry Moses smashes the tablets of the covenant in an act meant to symbolize the rupture of their relationship

This golden calf figurine was found in Canaanite Ashkelon, which later became part of Israel. The calf was often associated with the god Baal in Canaanite religion.

with God. Nonetheless, God continues to be "slow to anger, and abounding in steadfast love and faithfulness, keeping steadfast love for the thousandth generation, forgiving iniquity and transgression and sin" (Exod. 34:6b–7a). Two chapters later, God tells Moses to replace the tablets with new ones so the relationship can be restored. The familiar biblical pattern is established, as God forgives the people for breaking the covenant by violating the law in the shadow of the very mountain on which it has just been given to Moses.

Deuteronomy

Perhaps no other book in the Old Testament focuses more on the covenant than Deuteronomy, which means "second law" in Greek. The book is presented as a final speech from Moses to the Israelites as they are encamped in Moab just prior to their entry into the Promised Land.

> What might be the point of Moses' final speech and lengthy rehearsal of the law in the book of Deuteronomy?

The book ends with Moses' death, and so it functions as a valedictory address in which Moses says farewell to the community he has led through the wilderness for forty years.

The outline of the book indicates that Israel's relationship with God is the central theme of Deuteronomy. Chapters 1–3 give a summary of what has happened since they left Egypt, followed by a section that reminds them to obey the Torah and to not follow other gods in chapters 4 through 11. The main portion of the book is in chapters 12 through 26, which contains an extensive set of laws that treat various aspects of worship and daily life. Chapters 27 to 30 give instructions regarding how the words of the law should be memorialized and when they should be read. This section also includes a list of blessings and curses that explain the consequences of following or not following the law. Chapters 31 to 34 function as an appendix in which Moses writes down the law and prepares to die by reciting a lengthy song and blessing the people a final time. Deuteronomy is not a new covenant, but a renewal of the one God made with Moses on Mount Sinai.

Covenant Elsewhere in the Old Testament

The texts considered so far involving Noah, Abraham, and Moses are the three main examples of divine/human covenants in the Hebrew Bible, but the concept is also found elsewhere in the text. An important passage is 2 Samuel 7, which is sometimes referred to as the "Davidic Covenant" even though the term *berit* is not found in it. The chapter recounts a promise God makes to David whereby the king's descendants are assured of God's protection so that David's line will last in perpetuity (2 Sam. 7:16). This passage validates and legitimates David by giving him the divine seal of approval, and it serves the apologetic nature of the chapter and the Deuteronomistic History

> Why might it be important that the concept of covenant be associated with King David?

(DH) as a whole. In this context, an apology is not a text that admits guilt or asks forgiveness, but one that attempts to explain and justify a person's role or actions. Throughout the DH, David is held up as the perfect king who is the gold standard against whom all subsequent rulers are measured, and this chapter explains why he enjoys such a lofty status.[14]

Even though the word "covenant" is not used in 2 Samuel 7, God's relationship with David is viewed this way in other parts of the Old Testament. David himself understands it in these terms later in 2 Samuel when his last words are reported: "Is not my house like this with God? For he has made with me an everlasting covenant, ordered in all things and secure" (2 Sam. 23:5). A passage

---

14. The apologetic nature of the David story is the focus of Steven L. McKenzie's book *King David: A Biography* (New York: Oxford University Press, 2000).

in the book of Jeremiah expresses a similar sentiment (Jer. 33:20–21). David's relationship with God is also understood in covenantal terms in some of the Psalms (Ps. 89:3, 19–37; 132:11–12), as well as in 2 Chronicles 21:7. All of these texts are generally held to be relatively late, so in all likelihood the idea that 2 Samuel 7 reports a covenant between God and David is a later development in Israelite theology.

Beyond the text noted above, the book of Jeremiah refers to the covenant in several other places. "Do not spurn us, for your name's sake; do not dishonor your glorious throne; remember and do not break your covenant with us" (Jer. 14:21; cf. 11:1–10; 22:9; 31:32). God's covenant with Israel is also mentioned in Ezekiel. "I passed by you again and looked on you; you were at the age for love. I spread the edge of my cloak over you, and covered your nakedness: I pledged myself to you and entered into a covenant with you, says the Lord God, and you became mine" (Ezek. 16:8; cf. 16:59–61). As with the texts that describe David's relationship with God as a covenant, these passages from Jeremiah and Ezekiel are also from a later point in Israel's history. The same can be said of a passage in Hosea (8:1), which is the only other prophetic text to mention the covenant. Related to this are certain texts in the later prophetic literature that envision a future covenant (Isa. 55:3; 59:21; Jer. 31:33; 32:40; 50:5; Ezek. 16:62; 20:37; 34:25; 37:26). The possible implications of the dating of these texts for our understanding of the development of the concept of covenant will be discussed in the next section of this chapter.

This overview of the key passages in the Hebrew Bible that treat the covenant has revealed several important points. First of all, the notion of covenant means something different in each text. The covenant with Noah is with humanity and other living creatures, and its primary purpose is to establish a bond between God and all people. The sign of the covenant is the rainbow, which serves to remind the deity not to destroy humanity due to its evil nature. Although humans are told to refrain from shedding blood, this prohibition is not directly tied to the covenant. The two texts that describe the covenant with Abraham narrow the scope as both of them are limited to the patriarch and his descendants. In Genesis 15, God promises Abraham the land as the two of them participate in a ritual to seal that agreement, but nothing is demanded of Abraham in return. In Genesis 17 the focus is on the offspring God will give to Abraham with the stipulation that all males be circumcised, which is the sign of the covenant. With Moses, the human partner in the covenant is still Abraham's family, which is represented in the twelve tribes named after his great-grandchildren. But now membership in the covenant community is tied to observance of the law that was revealed on Mount Sinai.

Despite these differences, all of these passages share the same basic understanding of the divine/human relationship. To frame that relationship in terms of a covenant is to imply certain things about the parties involved. Like a marriage, for a covenant to work both sides have to want to be in the relationship and must dedicate themselves to doing what it takes to keep it alive. In other words, being part of a covenant is a free choice. God might be the initiator and get things started, but the human partners must be equally involved. Either side can pull out at any time or act in ways that violate the terms of the agreement, but in the Bible it is only the human partner who is at fault in that regard. Sometimes the people backslide and fall short, but God always remains steadfast and faithful. The relationship that is at the core of the Old Testament is best summarized as divine commitment in the face of human betrayal.

> How can we explain the changing nature of covenant throughout the texts involving Noah, Abraham, and Moses?

Second Opinions

Scholars are not completely sure when and how the idea of covenant began in ancient Israel. Most likely, it was initially applied to various social ties like the family and the tribe as a way of uniting different kinship units and helping to bring outsiders into the group. This is probably why common family terms like "father," "brother," and "son" are often used in documents and texts related to covenants. Examples of such covenants between human beings occur in a number of biblical stories that describe arrangements between two parties that help to resolve their differences and make connections between them, and these passages often use the same Hebrew word *berit* that is found elsewhere to describe the divine/human covenant. The Hebrew term is often translated into English as "treaty" in texts that describe political alliances between individuals or groups. These include covenants/treaties between Abraham and Abimelech (Gen. 21:25–34), Isaac and Abimelech (Gen. 26:26–31), Jacob and Laban (Gen. 31:44–50), Joshua and the Gibeonites (Josh. 9:3–21), Nahash the Ammonite and the people of Jabesh-Gilead (1 Sam. 11:1–4), David and Jonathan (1 Sam. 18:3; 20:8; 23:18), Abner and David (2 Sam. 3:12–13), David and the people of Israel (2 Sam. 3:21; 5:3), Solomon and Hiram (1 Kings. 5:12), King Asa and King Ben-hadad (1 Kings 15:19), and Ephraim and Assyria (Hos. 12:1).

The details of how the concept of covenant came to be applied to the divine/human relationship in the Bible are unknown, but it appears that it was a relatively late development that reached full expression sometime around the period of the exile in the sixth century BCE. This seems like a rather odd conclusion to reach since, as already noted, most of the references to the divine/human covenant are found in texts that claim to describe events that took place many centuries before the exile. For example, Abraham's timeframe is usually dated to

> How important is it for you whether or not Abraham existed?

sometime in the eighteenth century BCE, and the Exodus and the giving of the law to Moses are commonly placed at around 1200 BCE. If the covenant figures prominently in those stories, how can it be that it was an idea that took shape in the middle of the first millennium BCE?

Accepting that seemingly illogical conclusion might require a modification in one's understanding of the biblical text, how it came about, and what its purpose is. Many people assume that the Bible is a historical document that provides an accurate and completely reliable account of events that occurred in the past. This is especially the case once the biblical story reaches the time of Abraham, whom many readers take to be the first truly historical figure in the Bible. Scholars are divided, however, on whether or not Abraham was an actual person, with some claiming that Genesis preserves authentic traditions related to him and others arguing that he is a fictitious literary creation.[15]

It is important to acknowledge that the Bible was not written as a historical document, and so it should not be read that way.[16] It is a theological document, and theological writing operates by a completely different set of rules than historical writing. In a theologically-oriented work, "history" is presented in a way that supports a certain belief or illustrates a particular concept related to God. For example, the first creation story in Genesis 1:1–2:4a presents an image of God as an all-powerful being who is in complete control, an image that is informed by the concerns of its Priestly authors and responds to the needs of its original exilic audience. That is how theological history writing works: the theological point being made shapes and determines how the events are presented.[17]

> What are some of the differences between reading a work of history and reading a work of theology?

The same thing can be seen with the covenant theme in the Old Testament. At a somewhat late point in Israel's history it became a useful concept to help express the relationship between God and the people. This was around the

---

15. For a comprehensive study of Abraham and issues related to his historicity, see John Van Seters, *Abraham in History and Tradition* (New Haven: Yale University Press, 1978).

16. Issues related to the reliability and historical accuracy of the biblical material are addressed in most introductions to the Bible that are written from an academic perspective. See, for example, David M. Carr and Colleen M. Conway, *An Introduction to the Bible: Sacred Texts and Imperial Contexts* (Malden, MA: Wiley-Blackwell, 2010); John J. Collins, *Introduction to the Hebrew Bible* (Minneapolis: Fortress, 2014); John Kaltner and Steven L. McKenzie, *The Back Door Introduction to the Bible* (Winona, MN: Anselm Academic, 2012); and Jerry L. Sumney, *The Bible: An Introduction* (Minneapolis: Fortress, 2014). A helpful treatment of how an academic study differs from a faith-based reading of the Bible can be found in Michael Joseph Brown, *What They Don't Tell You: A Survivor's Guide to Biblical Studies* (Louisville: Westminster John Knox, 2000).

17. In the ancient world "history" writing was not meant to be an objective recounting of events, but was always intended to promote a particular perspective. Readers who approach the biblical narratives with the assumption that they are objective history in the modern sense are placing them in a category that did not exist in antiquity.

same time that large portions of the biblical text were reaching their final form through the process of redaction and editing. In order to give the notion of covenant more weight and legitimacy, it was read back into some of the traditions recounting the lives of venerable figures of the past like Noah and Abraham. This served an important rhetorical function in that it helped to create a shared identity within the Israelite community around the idea of covenant by linking those living during the exilic period with their early ancestors. The notion of covenant that was important for people living in the sixth century BCE was traced all the way back to the time of Noah, and this helped to establish a connection among all Israelites who lived in the intervening years.[18]

Covenant in the Pentateuch and the Deuteronomistic History

Most of the references to the covenant in the Pentateuch are from the Priestly source (P) or are in the book of Deuteronomy, both of which can be dated to around the time of the exile. Only three passages that mention the covenant are not from one of these two sources: Genesis 15, Exodus 19–24, and Exodus 34. Because these three texts are generally held to come from an earlier time, they could be interpreted as evidence that the covenant theme is quite a bit older than what is being proposed here. However, all of these passages show signs of having been reworked and given their final shape at a later point, which suggests that the references to the covenant in them are likely later additions.

Genesis 15 and Its Sources

As previously noted, Genesis 15 presents a vivid scene between Abraham and God that demonstrates why, in biblical Hebrew, one "cuts" a covenant. There is evidence from the ancient Near East of similar rituals, but only in later ones are the animals cut in half. The text that is closest to what occurs in Genesis 15 is found in an eighth-century BCE papyrus written in Aramaic, suggesting a fairly late origin for the ritual described in that chapter.[19] It has already been noted that there is a reference to cutting animals in half in a covenant ritual in a passage in Jeremiah (34:18–19), but it appears that the Genesis text is dependent on the Jeremiah text rather than the other way around. This is so because Jeremiah explicitly mentions Abraham and the other patriarchs only one time (33:26), and that is in a very late addition to the book, and so it appears that the author(s)

---

18. Much of the discussion in this section of the chapter draws on Steven L. McKenzie's book *Covenant* (St. Louis: Chalice, 1999). See also Delbert R. Hillers, *Covenant: The History of a Biblical Idea* (Baltimore: Johns Hopkins University Press, 1969).

19. This text is discussed in Joseph A. Fitzmeyer, *The Aramaic Inscriptions of Sefire* (Rome: Biblical Institute Press, 1967).

of Jeremiah is unfamiliar with the contents of Genesis. The Genesis chapter's dependence on Jeremiah is supported by the fact that it also draws upon other prophetic writings for some of its vocabulary. The phrase "the word of the LORD came" (Gen. 15:1, 4) and the designation of the encounter as a "vision" (v. 1) are standard features of prophetic literature. In the same way, nearly 260 of the 280 occurrences of the title "Lord GOD" (literally "Lord Yahweh": vv. 2, 8) are found in the prophets. All of these features are quite common in Ezekiel, where the phrase "Lord GOD" occurs almost 220 times.

Another source Genesis 15 draws upon is the book of Deuteronomy. The promise of descendants as numerous as the stars in the sky (Gen. 15:5; cf. Deut. 1:10; 10:22; 28:62) and the description of the Promised Land (Gen. 15:18–19; cf. Deut. 1:7; 7:1; 9:1) both contain echoes of similar statements made in the last book of the Pentateuch. The books of Jeremiah, Ezekiel, and Deuteronomy were all composed near and after the time of the exile, which means that Genesis 15 reached its final form at a relatively late date; therefore Genesis 15 cannot be understood as the origin of the idea of covenant in the Hebrew Bible. A final point is the reference to Abraham's hometown as "Ur of the Chaldeans." As noted earlier, this place name is an anachronism, since it was not used until late in the sixth century BCE.

Exodus 19–24 and Its Sources

The situation is the same regarding Exodus 19–24, another non-P section, which reports the Israelites' arrival at Mount Sinai and the initial scene describing the giving of the law. It contains three references to the covenant, one at the beginning of the section and the other two at its end. The first is in 19:5 when God tells Moses, "Now therefore, if you obey my voice and keep my covenant, you shall be my treasured possession out of all the peoples." Later on, in the scene that describes the previously mentioned covenant ceremony involving Moses and the people, there is a reference to the "book of the covenant" (24:7) and the "blood of the covenant" (24:8). Here, too, there is clear evidence of dependence on Deuteronomy and the Deuteronomistic History that suggests the section reached its present form at a later time and therefore the idea of covenant is of more recent origin. The first verse (19:5) is found in a passage that contains many words and phrases associated with Deuteronomy. The idea that Israel was carried on eagle's wings (19:4) can be seen in Deuteronomy 32:11. The statement in the same verse that the Israelites have seen what God did to the Egyptians is a common theme in Deuteronomy, where the people are frequently reminded to recall God's great actions in the past (Deut. 29:2; cf. 4:9; 10:21–22; 11:7). Also, the description of Israel as a "treasured possession out of all the peoples" (Exod. 19:5) is an idea that is almost exclusively found in Deuteronomy (7:6; 14:2; 26:18).

Regarding the passage that mentions the book and blood of the covenant (Exod. 24:7–8), it should be noted that the phrase "book of the covenant" is found in the Deuteronomistic History's description of the reign of King Josiah in 2 Kings 22–23. According to the account, in the eighteenth year of Josiah's rule (622 BCE) the "book of the law" was found in the course of renovations on the Temple in Jerusalem. This discovery led Josiah to initiate a major reform of Israelite religion that was in line with what the discovered book contained. The description of that reform in 2 Kings 23 is completely in agreement with Deuteronomic theology, and so it is generally held that some version or form of the book of Deuteronomy was discovered during Josiah's time.[20] In that chapter the book of the law is referred to as the "book of the covenant" (2 Kings 23:2), and in all likelihood this is the origin of the same phrase in Exodus 24. The author has borrowed it, along with other ideas and vocabulary associated with Deuteronomy, to development the theological setting and framework for Moses' covenant ceremony.

Exodus 34 and Its Sources

A similar thing has taken place in Exodus 34, the third passage that has no connection with the Priestly source but mentions the covenant. The first of three occurrences of *berit* in the chapter is in verse 10, which begins with God saying, "I hereby make a covenant." The other two are in verses 27 and 28, after God dictates to Moses what is to be written on the two tablets that replace the ones Moses broke after the golden calf episode.

This chapter's vocabulary and theology show influence from Deuteronomy. God's charge to "observe what I command you today" (Exod. 34:11) is a refrain that is often repeated throughout Deuteronomy (4:40; 6:6; 7:11; 8:1; 10:13; 11:8, 13, 22; 28:1). Listings similar to the one in Genesis 34 of foreign nations who must be driven out of the Promised Land are also a feature of Deuteronomy (7:1; 20:17). In addition, the admonition to avoid the inhabitants of the land lest they become a "snare" (Exod. 34:12) is present in Deuteronomy as well (7:16), as is the order to tear down their cultic sites (Exod. 34:13; cf. Deut. 7:5).

The most fully developed expressions of the covenant in the Hebrew Bible are found in the Priestly source, the book of Deuteronomy, and the Deuteronomistic History (DH), and all that material comes from around the time of the exile or later. The three texts discussed above do not derive from the P source, but the strong presence within them of elements from Deuteronomy and the DH indicates that they have been influenced by Deuteronomic theology and its understanding of the covenant. The

> Why has the book of Deuteronomy been so influential in shaping the biblical idea of covenant?

---

20. It is actually more likely that Josiah's reform was initiated prior to the finding of the book. The accidental "discovery" of a book or scroll that would support a political initiative was a fairly common occurrence in antiquity.

Old Testament's main theology is derived from the DH's presentation of the history of Israel in the books of Joshua through 2 Kings that covers the period from the entry into the land until the Babylonian destruction of Jerusalem in 587 BCE that began the exile. It has already been noted that this is a theological history and therefore interprets events from a particular perspective with a clear agenda in mind. At the heart of that agenda is the idea of the covenant, and so the history is retold and evaluated in light of the relationship between God and the people of Israel. The basic formula operative in the DH is simple and straightforward: when the people remain faithful to the covenant they prosper, and when they violate its terms bad things happen to them.

This pattern is played out over and over again throughout the DH. One of the clearest examples is found in the book of Judges, which describes a series of leaders who rule the Israelites prior to the rise of the kingship. Twelve different judges are mentioned in the book, some in just a few verses and others, like Samson, over several chapters. Six of them are given more extensive treatment, and they are referred to as the major judges. Each of their six cycles is structured in a way that includes all or most of the following eight elements, which is often called the "Deuteronomistic frame":

1. Israel does evil in the Lord's sight.
2. The Lord gives them into the hand of an enemy.
3. Israel serves the enemy for a certain number of years.
4. Israel cries out to the Lord for help.
5. The Lord raises up a judge.
6. The Lord's spirit comes upon the judge.
7. The enemy is defeated.
8. The land rests for a certain number of years.

With the death of each judge, the pattern begins anew. The thing that jump-starts each cycle is the people's inability to abide by the covenant, as can be seen in the beginning of the passage that describes the career of Othniel, the first judge: "The Israelites did what was evil in the sight of the LORD, forgetting the LORD their God, and worshiping the Baals and the Asherahs. Therefore the anger of the LORD was kindled against Israel, and he sold them into the hand of King Cushan-rishathaim of Aram-naharaim; and the Israelites served Cushan-rishathaim eight years" (Judges 3:7–8).

It should be clear in these two verses how the concept of the covenant informs the narrative and shapes the way that the story is told. Worship of other gods is a perennial concern of the DH, and it is the transgression the Israelites are most guilty of in its retelling

> What ideas are being stressed in the repeating pattern that can be discerned in the book of Judges?

of their history. It is therefore probably no coincidence that it is singled out as their offense in the description of the rise of the very first judge. The first four items in the list above focus on the Israelites' sin and the effects such violation of the covenant has on them. But the second half of the list points to an equally important aspect of the covenantal relationship, and the one that keeps it alive: God's faithful response and loving concern for the people.

Ancient Near Eastern Treaties and the Covenant

The DH gets its name from its obvious dependence on the theology contained in the book of Deuteronomy. Deuteronomy itself appears to be dependent upon earlier sources for its organization and structure because the book has much in common with the way ancient Near Eastern treaties were typically arranged. Two different types of treaties were found in the ancient Near East, with the difference between them based on the relationship that existed between the two partners in the agreement. One was the parity treaty, which was made between two parties that were of equal rank and standing. For example, two prominent rulers might enter into an alliance in order to maintain their social status or for their mutual benefit. The other was the suzerain treaty, also sometimes called a vassal treaty, in which one party was more prominent or powerful than the other. In such an arrangement, the lesser partner might be required to pay taxes or offer some other form of tribute in return for its survival or the guarantee of protection. For a long time scholars have argued that, given the nature of the relationship between God and Israel, the biblical idea of covenant is modeled on ancient Near Eastern suzerain treaties.[21]

© posztos / shutterstock.com

The second Jerusalem Temple, depicted here, was built after the Judaean exiles returned from Babylon. The Deuteronomistic History, also the work of the Jewish exiles, explained the destruction of the original Temple as God's punishment for breaking the covenant.

---

21. See Dennis J. McCarthy, SJ, *Treaty and Covenant: A Study in Form in the Ancient Oriental Documents and in the Old Testament* (Rome: Biblical Institute Press, 1978).

Such treaties were typically comprised of six parts: (1) a preamble that mentioned the titles and lineage of the suzerain; (2) a historical preface that gave an overview of the prior relationship between the two parties, particularly any favor the suzerain had directed toward the vassal; (3) the conditions assumed by both parties, especially the stipulations to which the vassal had agreed; (4) a reference to where the treaty document would be stored (often in the temple of the vassal's god) and how often it would be read; (5) a listing of the gods who served as witnesses to the terms of the treaty; and (6) a list of curses and blessings that would be directed toward the vassal based on whether or not the demands of the treaty were met.

> What do the close affinities between the book of Deuteronomy and ancient Near Eastern treaty documents suggest?

Virtually all of these elements are found in the book of Deuteronomy. The preamble is found in Deuteronomy 4:44–49, which states the book contains the decrees and laws that Moses delivered to the Israelites after they defeated King Sihon of the Amorites and King Og of Bashan upon leaving Egypt during the Exodus. Chapters 5 through 11 are the historical preface that gives an overview of the relationship between God and the Israelites, recalling all that God has done for them. The set of laws that are outlined in Deuteronomy 12:1–26:15 function as the conditions that are placed upon the Israelites as the vassals in the relationship. Provisions to deposit the treaty document and periodically read it are found in a few places. The two tablets on which the law is written serve this purpose (10:1–5), and they are placed in the Ark of the Covenant that will travel with the people wherever they go (31:24–26). In Deuteronomy 31:9–13 it is stated that the law should be read aloud to the people every seventh year. Not surprisingly, no other gods are called upon as witnesses, so that part of ancient Near Eastern treaties is not found in Deuteronomy, but in several places heaven and earth play this role (4:26; 30:19; 31:28). Finally, a lengthy list of blessings and curses is found in Deuteronomy 28:1–68.

> Why do you think Deuteronomy contains such a long list of curses if the covenant is violated?

Among the ancient Near Eastern treaties that have been found, the closest connections with Deuteronomy are seen in those from Assyria in the eighth and seventh centuries BCE. For example, the biblical book contains some striking similarities to the vassal treaties of King Esarhaddon, who ruled until 669 BCE. In particular, both contain unusually long lists of curses that parallel each other closely not just in terms of the various punishments that will be experienced, like blindness, skin disease, and having one's corpse eaten by birds, but the orderings of the curses in both also match up very well. It is quite likely that the treaty relationship outlined in documents like Esarhaddon's formed the basis for the biblical idea of covenant.[22] A key difference is that Deuteronomy is presented as a series of speeches by Moses rather than a treaty statement, but nonetheless the contours of a treaty document are clearly discernible in the biblical book.

Most scholars believe that the Priestly source was written after the DH and that it was meant to serve as an introduction to it. It affirms and incorporates Deuteronomy's view of the covenant and its role in history as presented by the DH, but it also includes the history of the covenants prior to the giving of the law at Mount Sinai. Virtually all of the law given to Moses is P material, and the main organizing structure throughout P is the series of covenants with Noah, Abraham, and Moses. The most significant covenant for P is the one with Moses, and consequently it is much longer than the others, taking up about one-third of the entire Pentateuch.

The covenant serves as a bridging theme that unites the first two major sections of the Hebrew Bible, the Pentateuch and the Deuteronomistic History. Those two parts were joined together toward the end of the period of the composition of the text when the final form of the Pentateuch, with its emphasis on covenant from the Priestly tradition, became the introduction to the DH. Prior to the Pentateuch's expansion by the Priestly writers it does not appear that the covenant was included in the traditions about Israel's earliest ancestors. Consequently, those behind the P and Deuteronomistic material were the ones responsible for developing and introducing into the Old Testament the concept that has become the primary way of understanding the relationship between God and the people.

> How significant is the idea that the covenant is likely a relatively late addition to the biblical text?

Covenant in the Prophets

A careful examination of the prophetic writings of the Hebrew Bible supports the idea that the covenant theme was a late development. As in the Pentateuch and DH, the term *berit* in the prophets can sometimes describe treaties or agreements between two human parties, and so the word does not always refer to the divine/human relationship. Those relatively few passages where *berit* is used in reference to the relationship between God and Israel are found in texts from a later period. The three major prophets (Isaiah, Jeremiah, and Ezekiel) all contain the term, and its use in Isaiah is especially interesting because of the history of the composition of that book.

---

22. A thorough exploration of the connections between Deuteronomy and Assyrian treaty documents can be found in Moshe Weinfeld, *Deuteronomy and the Deuteronomic School* (Oxford: Clarendon, 1972).

Isaiah and Covenant

Scholars are in agreement that Isaiah is a composite work. Its contents span a period of some two centuries, with a key dividing point being chapter 40. Virtually everything prior to that chapter comes from the time of the prophet Isaiah of Jerusalem, who lived in the eighth century BCE, and chapters 1–39 of the book are commonly referred to as "First Isaiah." But the material from chapter 40 on (known as "Second Isaiah")[23] comes from a much later period; it was written for an audience that was living in exile, and so it is typically dated to the sixth century BCE. A textual clue that supports this division of the material is the way the enemy is identified in each part. While Assyria (eighth century) is referred to several times as the adversary in the first part, Babylon (seventh and sixth centuries) is the foe in the second part, while Assyria is never mentioned.[24]

The word *berit* is found four times in First Isaiah. Two of those occurrences (28:15, 18) use the term metaphorically, to refer to a covenant with death, so they are not relevant for our purposes. The other two places mention the violation of a *berit*, but the nature of that *berit* is not specified. The first is in 24:5, which is part of a lengthy section in chapters 24–27 that describes the future destruction of Israel's enemies. The verse recounts in general terms some of the offenses humanity is guilty of committing: "The earth lies polluted under its inhabitants; for they have transgressed laws, violated the statutes, broken the everlasting covenant." While it might be tempting to see this as a reference to the covenant between God and Israel, the verse's wider literary context urges caution against this. The chapter contains a broad condemnation of humanity in general and does not identify any group by name, and so the laws, statutes, and covenant referred to in the verse are most likely meant to serve as examples of the types of obligations and agreements people violate without having particular ones in mind.

The other passage in First Isaiah that mentions a *berit* is 33:8, and a similar thing can be seen here. The relationship is not described in any detail, but the context suggests that the term is being used in reference to a political agreement or arrangement that has been violated. The NRSV translation of the verse supports this interpretation and probably seeks to avoid confusion with the covenant between God and Israel by rendering the word "treaty." The NRSV is not completely faithful to the Hebrew because it adds a definite article ("the treaty") where there is none in the original text. This indicates that the author did not have a particular treaty or covenant in mind and is another reason why the word *berit* in this verse should not be equated with the divine/human covenant.

---

23. It has been argued that there is also a "Third Isaiah" in chapters 56 through 66 of the book. Since all the material from chapter 40 on is dated to the exile or later, this further subdivision of the material is not an important issue for our purposes.

24. The text of Second Isaiah and its relationship to First Isaiah is discussed in great detail in Joseph Blenkinsopp, *Isaiah 40–55* (New Haven: Yale University Press, 2002).

In Second Isaiah, on the other hand, there are a number of references to God's covenant with Israel: "And as for me, this is my covenant with them, says the LORD: my spirit that is upon you, and my words that I have put in your mouth, shall not depart out of your mouth, or out of the mouths of your children, or out of the mouths of your children's children, says the LORD, from now on and forever" (Isa. 59:21; cf. 54:10; 55:3; 56:4, 6; 61:8). The presence in Second Isaiah of several uses of *berit* that refer to God's relationship with Israel, coupled with the absence of any such clear usage in First Isaiah, supports the contention that this meaning came along relatively late in Israelite history. This assertion is further strengthened by the frequent occurrence of *berit* with this meaning in Jeremiah and Ezekiel, both of which are works from the time of the exile or later (Jer. 11:2–3, 6, 8, 10; 14:21; 22:9; 31:31–33; 32:40; 33:20–21; 34:13, 15, 18; 50:5; Ezek. 16:59–62; 20:37; 34:25; 37:26; 44:7).

Jeremiah and Covenant

A passage in Jeremiah is especially noteworthy because in it a different understanding of covenant is put forward that is meant to speak to the audience's unique context.

> The days are surely coming, says the LORD, when I will make a new covenant with the house of Israel and the house of Judah. It will not be like the covenant that I made with their ancestors when I took them by the hand to bring them out of the land of Egypt—a covenant that they broke, though I was their husband, says the LORD. But this is the covenant that I will make with the house of Israel after those days, says the LORD: I will put my law within them, and I will write it on their hearts; and I will be their God, and they shall be my people. (Jer. 31:31–33)

Jeremiah's notion of a new covenant is likely a response to the circumstances he and his community faced in the early sixth century as Babylon became more powerful and threatened the survival of Judah. The Babylonians eventually invaded Jerusalem in 587 BCE in an event that led to the destruction of the Temple and the loss of the Ark of the Covenant containing the tablets of the law. As he anticipated that outcome, Jeremiah needed to reassure the people that the law was more than merely words on stone. Therefore he interiorized the concept so that the law became something that each person could preserve in his or her heart. The destruction of the Temple and loss of the Ark of the Covenant would not mean the covenant would be null and void, because the law would continue to live on in the heart of each person. Jeremiah also makes use of the

How does Jeremiah's idea of a covenant written on the heart develop the meaning of covenant in the Old Testament?

marriage analogy in this passage in order to present an image of the covenant that would be easily recognizable to his audience.

The Minor Prophets and Covenant

The minor prophets contain very few references to the divine/human covenant in their writings, and they all support the conclusion that it is a late idea in Israelite theology. The book of Zechariah has a single reference at 9:11: "As for you also, because of the blood of my covenant with you, I will set your prisoners free from the waterless pit." The only other passage that contains both the words "covenant" and "blood" in it is in Exodus 24, discussed above, where Moses throws blood on the people before reading from the book of the covenant.[25] This verse is found in the second part of Zechariah, and that section of the book is usually dated very late. Some would put it as late as the second half of the fourth century BCE because of the reference to the Greeks two verses after this one.

Two other possible references to the covenant between God and Israel are found in Malachi, which immediately follows Zechariah in the canonical order. There is a likely allusion to the covenant at Mount Sinai in 2:10: "Have we not all one father? Has not one God created us? Why then are we faithless to one another, profaning the covenant of our ancestors?" Later, in 3:1, a verse that is the basis for the book's name (Malachi means "my messenger"), another ambiguous reference is made to what could be the divine/human covenant: "See, I am sending my messenger to prepare the way before me, and the LORD whom you seek will suddenly come to his temple. The messenger of the covenant in whom you delight—indeed, he is coming, says the LORD of hosts." The book of Malachi presumes the presence of the rebuilt Temple in Jerusalem after the exile, so it is generally dated to the late sixth or early fifth centuries BCE.

The only other references to *berit* in the minor prophets are in the book of Hosea, who was an eighth-century BCE contemporary of Isaiah of Jerusalem. The term *berit* is mentioned five times in the book, but three of them clearly do not refer to the covenant between God and the Israelites (Hos. 2:18; 10:4; 12:1). The fourth occurrence, at Hosea 6:7, is in a verse whose meaning is not completely certain. The NRSV reads, "But at Adam they transgressed the covenant; there they dealt faithlessly with me." The original text actually reads "like Adam" instead of "at Adam," and so the verse appears to be referring to some violation of the covenant that Adam made in the Garden of Eden. But a covenant between Adam and God is never mentioned in Genesis or

---

25. The connection between these two passages is considered in Carol L. Meyers and Eric M. Meyers, *Zechariah 9–14* (New Haven: Yale University Press, 1998), 138–40.

anywhere else in the Old Testament. For this reason, many translations render the phrase "at Adam" because the Hebrew letters that mean "like" and "at" are almost identical and there are other examples of confusion between them in the biblical text. A further reason why the NRSV translation is preferable is because of the presence of the word "there" later in the verse in reference to Adam. This indicates that Adam is a place, and a Transjordanian town by that name is mentioned in the description of the Israelites crossing the Jordan River upon entering the Promised Land in Joshua 3:16. It is therefore likely that the passage refers to some transgression at Adam in the past that cannot now be identified, but it is not impossible that it could be an allusion to the covenant between God and Israel.

> Bible scholars sometimes propose alternative readings of passages because of a presumed mistake, like the confusion between "like" and "at" in Hosea 6:7. How comfortable are you with such emendations to the text?

The final mention of *berit* in Hosea (8:1) is clearly a reference to the covenant with God: "Set the trumpet to your lips! One like a vulture is over the house of the LORD, because they have broken my covenant, and transgressed my law." In all likelihood, then, this is the earliest mention of the covenant between God and Israel in the Hebrew Bible. The fact that it is referred to only once or twice in the book indicates that the covenant was not a very important concept for Hosea, probably because the concept was in its infancy and had not yet taken full shape. Consequently, the biblical literature does not show any evidence of the idea of covenant before the eighth century BCE, and it was not fully developed until much later, as seen in texts from around the time of the exile, like the Priestly source and the Deuteronomic tradition.

Covenant is a theme that would have suited well the theology and purposes of the prophets. The biblical book attributed to Amos, another northern prophet of the eighth century BCE, is a case in point. Amos was deeply concerned about the way the behavior and actions of the Israelites were having a negative effect on their relationship with God. He was especially critical of the many social injustices he observed in the ways the wealthy exploited and oppressed the poor. He, like other prophets, believed that one's relationships with other people intimately influenced one's relationship with God, and he thought that the Israelites could not be right with God until all people were treated fairly. The idea of God's covenant with the people and the need for them to follow the law in all matters, including their relationships with others, would have fit perfectly into Amos's theology—and that of many other prophets. And yet it is not mentioned a single time in his book and, as we have

> Can you think of any other reasons that might explain why the prophets don't mention the covenant until a late period in Israel's history?

seen, it is rarely mentioned in the prophetic literature prior to the time of the exile. The most logical explanation for its absence is that covenant was not yet an important component of Israelite religion at the time in which Amos and his contemporaries were writing.

When it finally did emerge on the scene, covenantal theology played a critical role in helping the community come to terms with and make sense of themselves and their experiences. The DH demonstrates this clearly with its retelling of Israelite history based on how well the people kept the covenant and followed the law. All setbacks and tragedies, including the invasion of the land by foreign forces and the exile, were punishments from God due to the Israelites' inability to remain faithful to the terms of the covenant. In a number of texts, the Assyrians and Babylonians are nothing but God's instruments who help to bring about the divine will by invading the land and punishing the Israelites (Isa. 10:5–11; 45:1–7). This theologizing of historical events served a vital purpose because it helped to explain disasters and crises, and did so in a way that allowed God to still be in charge and more powerful than ever because the great political powers of the time were simply pawns in God's hands. It is the idea of covenant that made this reinterpretation of events possible, and the biblical understanding of God's relationship with the people would be completely different without it.

A MODERN TAKE ON COVENANT

An interesting attempt to apply the idea of covenant to an important issue in today's world can be seen in the Catholic Climate Covenant. This initiative, which began in 2006, is an effort to address environmental concerns through an appeal to Catholic social teaching on the ecology. Familiarize yourself with the group and its mission by reading through the material on its website (*http://www.catholicclimatecovenant.org/*) and viewing some of the videos it has produced (*https://www.youtube.com/channel/UC9BbDlrf07gipbLGs4MfSjQ*).

1. How has the idea of covenant informed and shaped the group's identity and activities?

2. Can you identify specific connections between the Catholic Climate Covenant and the biblical notion of covenant? Are there significant differences between them?

3. Can you think of other ways that the idea of covenant might be used in our day to address social issues?

Implications and Applications

1. How has your understanding of the Bible changed after reading this chapter?
2. How has your understanding of the idea of covenant changed after reading this chapter?
3. How is God presented in texts that mention the covenant? Identify the main qualities and features of the deity in these sections and explain how they contribute to the portrait of God that emerges from the Hebrew Bible.
4. How is humanity presented in texts that mention the covenant? Identify the main qualities and features of human beings in these sections and explain what they suggest about the human condition.
5. Do you think the relationship between God and humanity as it is presented in the Old Testament is primarily healthy and positive?
6. What issues does the relatively late introduction of the notion of covenant into the Bible raise for you?
7. Do you think covenant is a concept that speaks to modern people? Are there other ways of talking about the divine/human relationship that might be more relevant in our day and age?
8. Is one (or more) of the covenants discussed in this chapter a more appropriate way than the others of understanding God's relationship with humanity in the modern world?
9. Do the texts discussed in this chapter play a role in shaping your views about humanity and God? If so, how? If not, why not?

Perspectives on Liberation

Of all the people who populate the pages of the Hebrew Bible, only King David's name is mentioned more frequently than that of Moses. Moses is cited about eight hundred times in the text, but that number does not begin to get at the reasons why he is such a prominent and popular biblical figure. It would be hard to come up with another Old Testament character who led a more fascinating and exciting life than Moses. He starts out as a newborn with a price on his head. His mother has to abandon him to guarantee his survival, which leads to his becoming part of a powerful royal family. He then has an encounter with God at a burning bush that puts him at odds with his adopted people. After escaping the clutches of a mighty ruler by taking a miraculous path through a body of water, he eventually leads a large group of nomads on a forty-year trek in the desert that includes other private audiences with God on a mountain. Moses is the quintessential action figure of the Bible. His life is the stuff of movies, so it is not surprising that everyone from Charlton Heston to Ben Kingsley to Christian Bale has wanted to portray him on the screen.

As profitable as the story of Moses has been for famous actors like Heston, Kingsley, and Bale, his real value can be seen in the impact it has had on the not-so-famous. Countless people throughout history have been inspired by what Moses does and says in the Bible, and their lives have been radically transformed by the lessons contained in the passages about him. In particular, the theme of liberation that is at the heart of the Exodus story has resonated down the ages as a beacon of hope and a call to action for those who have been the victims of oppression, marginalization, and various forms of servitude. Moses' name is synonymous with liberty, and his journey from slavery to freedom has inspired many people to pursue a similar course. It is a sad fact that in our world persecution, domination, and tyranny are ever present, while Moses-like figures are in short supply. That is why reading and reflecting on this part of the Bible is an essential task for anyone who claims to be committed to justice and equality. The story of Moses offers a challenge and a reminder that lives can be transformed, no matter how hopeless the situation might appear to be.

First Impressions

Unless you read the text very carefully, you can easily miss the fact that God plays no role in Moses' life until he is a married adult with a child. Moses is born at the beginning of the second chapter of the book of Exodus, which contains the famous story of his mother placing him in a basket that she floats on the Nile River in order to save him from Pharaoh's command to kill all the boys born to the Hebrew people (2:1–10). Many readers see this as a story of divine protection, with God intervening to insure the survival of the child, but God is not mentioned a single time in this narrative. Pharaoh's unnamed daughter rescues Moses from a watery demise and sets him on his path to becoming the liberator of his people. God is missing in action, although it is not uncommon for Bible readers to assume the deity is busily working behind the scenes to bring about a happy ending that gets Moses back on *terra firma*.[1]

The same thing happens in the stories that follow in Exodus 2. The Bible provides no information on Moses' early childhood; the next time we encounter him he is a grownup who kills an Egyptian after he witnesses the man beating a Hebrew. When Pharaoh gets word of what Moses has done, he calls for his death. Throughout this episode as well, God is nowhere to be found (Exod. 2:11–15a). Upon hearing that

> Why do you think God is not mentioned in the chapters that describe Moses' early life?

there is a warrant for his arrest, Moses flees from Egypt and goes to an area called Midian, in southern Transjordan, where he meets a priest who gives his daughter to Moses in marriage. That union produces a son named Gershom, who is Moses' firstborn child. In this section, too, there is no explicit mention of God.[2]

Only at the end of chapter 2 is the deity mentioned, in a passage that connects the Moses story with the traditions about venerable figures from the past who play prominent roles in the book of Genesis (Exod. 2:23–25). The reference in that passage to the Israelites' status as slaves whose cries are heard by God subtly introduces the liberation theme and raises the possibility that they will be freed from their oppression. The stage is now set for Moses' initial encounter with God, which will be their first step on the road to freedom.

---

1. The Qur'an, the sacred text of Islam, also contains an account of Moses' birth, but in that version of the story God plays an active role in the events of the narrative (28:3–13).

2. There is, though, an indirect and ironic reference to God in the description of Moses' father-in-law as a priest (2:16; 3:1). While the religion his father-in-law practiced is left unidentified in the text, he expresses belief in the God of Israel in 18:1–12.

A Revealing Chat

READ: Exodus 3:1–4:20

This is arguably the longest conversation God has with a human being in the entire Bible. Some might object that the exchange between Job and God in chapters 38 through 42 in the book of Job is actually the lengthiest exchange between the deity and a person in biblical literature, but God does practically all the talking in that instance. Exodus 3–4, on the other hand, is a true back-and-forth, give-and-take dialogue that goes on for thirty-six verses in which each party has the opportunity to speak at least six times.

The scene is often referred to as God's self-revelation to Moses, but there is a lot more going on than that one-way description might suggest. Moses does in fact learn much about God, but in the course of their tête-à-tête the deity (and the reader) discovers a great deal about Moses as well. In other words, it is a good example of what often happens when two parties sit down for a heart-to-heart: each side comes away with a better understanding of what makes the other tick.

As their talk unfolds, it becomes clear that God's agenda is different from Moses'. It is a classic case of two conversation partners speaking at cross pur-

Moses encounters God at the burning bush in this Byzantine-era mosaic from Saint Catherine's Monastery on Mount Sinai. The monastery is located near the traditional site of the burning bush.

poses, with neither of them willing to give an inch or concede to the other. Things get off on the wrong foot when God first speaks to Moses from out of the burning bush by using language similar to what is found at the end of chapter 2 of Exodus by self-identifying as the God of important figures in the book of Genesis: "I am the God of your father, the God of Abraham, the God of Isaac, and the God of Jacob" (3:6). And what is Moses' response? He hides his face. The text explains that this reaction is rooted in Moses' fear and hesitancy to look at God, but in light of the way the conversa-

tion develops it is also a sign of things to come.

God's commission to Moses is spelled out in no uncertain terms when, in their next exchange, the deity sends Moses to Pharaoh in order to free the Israelites from the oppression they have been experiencing under the Egyptians (3:7–10). Moses is told that liberation is something near and dear to God's heart and that he, Moses, has been tapped to help bring it about for the Israelites. In the verse that follows, Moses responds in a self-deprecating way that lets God know he is not the man for the job: "Who am I that I should go to Pharaoh, and bring the Israelites out of Egypt?" This reluctance is met with an assurance that God will go with Moses, so there is nothing to fear. In addition, God tells Moses that he will be given a sign to further reassure him; he and the Israelites will worship God on the very mountain at which they are now speaking, which is identified as Mt. Horeb at the beginning of the chapter (3:11–12).[3] At this point, Moses shifts gears and goes from asking, "Who am I?" to, "Who are *you*?" Moses tries to clarify the identity of his conversation partner by asking, "If I come to the Israelites and say to them, 'The God of your ancestors has sent me to you,' and they ask me, 'What is his name?' what shall I say to them?" (3:13)

After revealing the divine name, the deity goes on to predict how the conversation between Moses and Pharaoh will go and explains that the Israelites will be brought to their own land after a series of miraculous works God will perform (3:14–22). Once again, the deity keeps the liberation theme front and center in the conversation. At nine verses, it is the longest speech in the encounter between Moses and God, but the most interesting part of it comes at the outset when God's identity is disclosed. Rather than give a simple answer to Moses, God's response is in multiple parts.

Why does Moses try to get out of doing what God wants him to do? Does the text offer any clues?

> God said to Moses, "I Am Who I Am." He said further, "Thus you shall say to the Israelites, 'I Am has sent me to you.'" God also said to Moses, "Thus you shall say to the Israelites, 'The Lord, the God of your ancestors, the God of Abraham, the God of Isaac, and the God of Jacob, has sent me to you': This is my name forever, and this my title for all generations." (Exod. 3:14–15)

The details of this passage will be discussed later in this chapter, but for now the key point to keep in mind is that in these verses God has answered Moses' question "Who are *you*?" in a comprehensive way that identifies the deity by both name and deed.

It is a lengthy response that is meant to end the conversation, but Moses doesn't take the hint. He instead proposes yet another hypothetical scenario designed to give him some wiggle room and avoid doing what God is asking. Moses answers, "But suppose they do not believe me or listen to me, but say, 'The Lord did not appear to you'" (4:1). At this point, God resorts to the

---

3. In other passages Mt. Horeb is referred to as Mt. Sinai, reflecting the presence of different sources behind the story.

equivalent of magic tricks to convince Moses that he is up to the task at hand. God first transforms Moses' staff into a snake and returns it to its original form. Then he does the same thing with Moses' hand, which is turned leprous and then healed (4:2–7). These are symbolic actions that are meant to convince the people of Moses' legitimacy as God's envoy, and if they should fail to persuade them God has one final ace up the divine sleeve: "If they will not believe you or heed the first sign, they may believe the second sign. If they will not believe even these two signs or heed you, you shall take some water from the Nile and pour it on the dry ground; and the water that you shall take from the Nile will become blood on the dry ground" (4:8–9).

Even this display of divine power is not enough to sway Moses, who points his finger back at himself once again to remind God of his unworthiness. "O my LORD, I have never been eloquent, neither in the past nor even now that you have spoken to your servant; but I am slow of speech and slow of tongue" (4:10). This

> What might be behind Moses' claim that he has difficulty speaking?

claim that he is physically incapable of doing what God wants has led some to suggest that Moses had a speech impediment or some other condition that made it difficult for him to speak properly. Whether that is the case or not, God has a quick remedy for Moses' claim that he would be a lousy spokesperson. "Who gives speech to mortals? Who makes them mute or deaf, seeing or blind? Is it not I, the LORD? Now go, and I will be with your mouth and teach you what you are to speak" (4:11).

God has responded to each objection and hypothetical situation, and Moses is at the end of his rope. He is finally forced to come clean, and utter the words he probably wanted to say when he first heard the voice speak to him from the bush but did not dare to do so: "O my LORD, please send some-one else" (4:13). He has run out of excuses and can now only politely command God to start searching for another spokesperson. God does just that, but the search process does not end in the way that Moses had hoped it would. God identifies another candidate in Moses' brother Aaron, but in an ironic twist to the story Moses is not set free (at least not yet) and it will now be a team effort (4:14–15).

God gets the last word, and Moses' slowness of tongue finally catches up with him. The next time we see him he is back in Midian with his father-in-law, seeking his permission to make the trip to Egypt he so desperately tried to avoid.

Reading between the Lines

The conversation between God and Moses is a fascinating exchange with a seven-part structure in which divine self-disclosure alternates with Moses' reluctant responses.

God	Moses
I am the God of Abraham, Isaac, and Jacob.	Hides his face, afraid to look.
I hear the cry of the people and I send you to tell them; I will deliver them.	Who am I to go to Pharaoh and deliver the Israelites?
I will be with you and you will worship me on this mountain.	Who are you? What if the Israelites ask me your name?
I am who I am, and I will bring them out and strike Egypt.	What if they do not believe me?
Turns Moses' staff into a serpent and turns Moses' hand leprous.	I am slow of speech and slow of tongue.
I will be with your mouth and teach you what to say. Go to them!	O Lord, send someone else!
Your brother Aaron will go with you, and he will be your mouth.	Goes to Egypt.

As the dialogue deepens, each side learns much about the other. God learns that Moses is an unwilling partner who is averse to the mission that is being thrust upon him. Moses eventually relents and makes his way to Egypt, but by the end of the encounter the reader (and God?) can't help but wonder if Moses will be up to the task.

God comes across as equally relentless. Each objection by Moses is met by a response that not only addresses Moses' concern but draws him deeper into the relationship until he is literally speechless and must concede to God's will. God will not let Moses off the hook and deftly counters every one of his doubts and concerns. It is not completely clear why Moses responds as he does. It could be due to fear, self-centeredness, a lack of interest in the fate of the Israelites, or any number of other factors. But his attempts to avoid what God is asking him to do put him in a negative light and raise questions about his character. This is not the case with his conversation partner. God is motivated by concern and compassion for the Israelites, who are being oppressed and mistreated by the Egyptians. His people's liberation is foremost in the divine mind, and the deity deftly responds to each of Moses' parries with a thrust of his own in order to bring about the Israelites' freedom. Their words suggest that Moses cares about himself, while God cares about others.

The scene describes a theophany, a term coming from two Greek words that can be loosely translated as "divine appearance." In several other places in the Hebrew Bible, fire is associated with God's presence (Gen. 15:17; Exod.

13:21; 19:18; Ezek. 1:27), and that is clearly the case here as well. The command to Moses to remove his sandals because he is on "holy ground" (3:5) serves to reinforce the idea that he is standing before God.

> Why do you think God is sometimes associated with fire in the Bible?

Several things about how the deity is designated are important to keep in mind. In the first place, one might be tempted to wonder if the passage is describing a divine identity crisis because in 3:14–15 God refers to himself in three different ways: first "I Am Who I Am," then "I Am," and finally "the Lord." These three phrases are etymologically related because they all come from the same Hebrew root that means "to be." They will be discussed in more detail below, but for now the key thing to keep in mind is that the divine name(s) connotes the idea of being or existence.

As already noted, in several places God is referred to as "the God of Abraham, the God of Isaac, and the God of Jacob" (3:6, 15, 16; 4:5). In each case this title is found in direct speech by God, and it is a way of establishing a link between the God who will bring Israel out of Egypt and the God of the ancestors. The covenant in Genesis is tied to the promise of the land, and the references here to God leading the Israelites to a new land highlight the covenantal connection (3:8, 17).

An important fact is highlighted both times the new land is mentioned: it is already occupied. The description of it as "the land of the Canaanites, the Hittites, the Amorites, the Perizzites, the Hivites, and the Jebusites" indicates that several other groups are living there, so when the Israelites arrive they will not be its original tenants. This creates the potential for conflict between the current residents and the newcomers and causes the reader to wonder where all this might be headed. In particular, it raises important questions about freedom, oppression, and the relationship between the two. In

> What are some of the issues involved with the Israelites being promised a land that already has other people living in it? How can those issues be addressed?

several places, God refers to the mistreatment the Israelites have received at the hands of the Egyptians and promises to improve their situation by leading them to a new place (3:7, 9, 17). But what will happen to the people already living in that land? Will all parties live side-by-side in peace, or will the freedom of the Israelites come at a cost to others?[4]

---

4. The question of the land and its prior occupants is at the heart of the modern Israeli-Palestinian conflict. When the state of Israel was created in 1948 there were already people living there, some of whom were displaced while others remained and continue an uneasy coexistence with their Israeli neighbors into the present day.

Take That!

READ: Exodus 7-11

In the section of Exodus that follows, the deity goes on to unleash a series of punishments against Pharaoh and Egypt that demonstrate God's power and authority and do as much to establish his identity as the "I am" speech to Moses did earlier. Chapters 7 through 12 of Exodus describe an impressive display of divine feats and pyrotechnics that culminate in the Old Testament's most dramatic moment: the parting of the waters that allows the Israelites to pass through on dry land and begin their journey to the land God promised them. As with the burning bush episode, God's desire for his people's freedom drives the story forward and is the ultimate endgame.

These chapters are commonly referred to as the "plagues narrative," but that designation probably is not the most apt. The term "plague" can conjure up certain images and ideas that do not accurately reflect what is going on in the story. Many people think of a plague as some kind of a disease or other physical ailment that threatens the health and wellbeing of an individual. There is often an element of contagion associated with the word as well, since plague is commonly thought of as something that can be passed from an animal or a person to others without their being aware of it until it is too late and they become infected. The Black Death outbreak of the fourteenth century, which wiped out nearly half the population of Europe, as well as the HIV-AIDS epidemic of more recent times, are often referred to as examples of plagues, but chapters 7–11 of Exodus do not describe a situation like either of those. Another reason why its usual name does not quite fit is that the word "plague" is not mentioned at all in this section of the Bible. The most common verbs used in these chapters to describe what happens to the Egyptians come from Hebrew roots that mean "to touch or strike," so perhaps something like "punch," "hit," or "wallop" would better convey the sense of the original language.[5]

When nouns are used to describe the plagues the two words that are consistently found are "signs" and "wonders." Both these terms are significant because they highlight God's role as the one who is behind the events. A sign is something that points beyond itself to some other reality, and in this case each plague is meant to remind the Egyptians (and the Israelites) of God's supreme authority over creation. Similarly, a wonder also points to the power of the one who is responsible for it. By using this vocabulary, the text identifies God as the supreme wonderworker and sign maker, and the plagues are the vehicles through which God's power and sovereignty are expressed in order to realize the goal of his people's liberation. The first time the terms "signs" and "wonders" are found they are

---

5. In fact, our word "plague" comes from a Greek word that means "to strike or hit," which explains why this section came to be called "the plagues of Egypt," but "plague" has since taken on different connotations for most English speakers.

spoken by God, and their primary purpose is to demonstrate his complete authority over Pharaoh and the Egyptian people (7:3–5; cf. 7:9; 8:23; 10:1–2; 11:9–10).

Plotting the Plagues

Although they have been traditionally termed the "ten plagues," they are not numbered in the text and nowhere does it say that there are ten of them. The last one
describes the deaths of the firstborn children throughout Egypt, and because it is
of a different nature from the others and is described in more detail than they are
we will treat it separately from them. The last plague is what allows the Israelites to
finally be freed from their enslavement to Pharaoh, and so it will be discussed with
their escape from Egypt in the next section. The other nine share a similar outline that includes the following elements: (1) a description of the plague by God;
(2) Moses, or Moses and Aaron, serving as God's agent(s); (3) a reference to Moses'
or Aaron's staff; (4) the Israelites being protected from the plague; (5) a reference
to Pharaoh's heart being hardened; and (6) Pharaoh's initial acquiescence, followed
by his refusal to let the people go. Not each of these elements is found with every
plague, but the pattern is clearly discernible as can be seen in the following chart.

Plague	Agent(s)	Staff	Israelites protected	Pharaoh's heart	Pharaoh acquiesces
Water to Blood (7:14–24)	Moses and Aaron	Yes	No	Yes	No
Frogs (7:25–8:15)	Moses and Aaron	Yes	No	Yes	Yes
Gnats (8:16–19)	Moses and Aaron	Yes	No	Yes	No
Flies (8:20–32)	Moses	No	Yes	Yes	Yes
Livestock (9:1–7)	Moses	No	Yes	Yes	No
Boils (9:8–12)	Moses	No	No	Yes	No
Hail storm (9:13–26)	Moses	Yes	Yes	Yes	Yes
Locusts (10:1–20)	Moses	Yes	No	Yes	Yes
Darkness (10:21–29)	Moses	No	Yes	Yes	Yes

A careful examination of the chart allows some observations to be made. Each plague is connected to an element of nature, and in each case God takes something from the created world and has it comply with the divine will. In some cases, these are living creatures like frogs and flies, and elsewhere they are inanimate objects like water and the sun. This is meant to show God's control over all of creation. After the first three plagues, in which Moses and Aaron both play important roles, the attention shifts to Moses as God's primary agent. Aaron is mentioned in a few other places for the other plagues, but his role is clearly secondary after the third one. In more than half the plagues the staff of Moses or Aaron plays a key role in the story, and it functions in a quasi-magical way that enables its wielder to perform feats of wonder. If we include the tenth one, in one-half of the plagues the Israelites are protected by God from the punishments and consequences that the Egyptians experience. This relates to the theme of election and God's preference for Israel as the Chosen People who are set apart.

How might we explain the fact that Aaron's role becomes secondary after the third plague?

Although they are not listed in the chart, Pharaoh's magicians play an interesting role in the narrative. At first they have no difficulty keeping up with Moses' and Aaron's deeds as they duplicate the first and second plagues (7:22; 8:7). We see a similar thing in 7:8–12, where Aaron turns his staff into a snake and the Egyptian magicians do the same, only to have theirs devoured by Aaron's staff/serpent. But when they try to copy the third plague and produce gnats, the Egyptian sorcerers are unable to do so (8:18). They even acknowledge the power of Moses' and Aaron's God after their failure by proclaiming, "This is the finger of God!" The last time we hear of them is at the end of the description of the sixth plague when they suffer from the boils that also afflict their fellow Egyptians (9:11).

What purpose do the Egyptian magicians serve in the story?

Over the course of the story, the Egyptian magicians become more and more impotent until they cannot even come before Moses because they are so debilitated. An interesting question related to their role concerns why Pharaoh would want them to replicate the plagues and why they would agree to do so, since doing so merely inflicts more pain and punishment on the Egyptian people. Perhaps it is an example of the Hebrew Bible's penchant for poking fun at foreigners, or is meant to be a critique of them as being so blinded by their desire to prove their superiority over the agents of Israel's God that they are prepared to harm themselves in the process.

A Heart Attack

Pharaoh is the most interesting character in the narrative for a number of reasons. The hardening of his heart is mentioned with every plague, and it is an important aspect of the story that is theologically significant but easy to misunderstand. The hardened heart motif is relatively rare in the Old Testament, and outside this section is found in only a handful of other texts (Josh. 11:20; 1 Sam. 6:6; Ps. 95:8; Isa. 63:17).[6] In chapters 4 through 14 of the book of Exodus, Pharaoh's hardened heart is mentioned twenty times, so it is obviously a central theme in the story. In some of those verses it says that God hardened Pharaoh's heart (4:21; 7:3; 9:12; 10:1, 20, 27; 11:10), and elsewhere the passive voice is used to state that Pharaoh's heart was hardened (7:13, 14, 22; 8:19; 9:7, 35). In three places, it is said that Pharaoh hardened his own heart (8:15, 32; 9:34).

> What do you think is happening to Pharaoh when it says that God hardens his heart?

Those passages in which there is no subject for the verb are most probably examples of what is sometimes termed the "divine passive," where God is understood to be the actor even if it is not explicitly stated. This interpretation is supported in several ways. The first time that Pharaoh's hardened heart is mentioned God takes credit for it in words that suggest that the deity is the one behind the hardening each time it happens. "When you go back to Egypt, see that you perform before Pharaoh all the wonders that I have put in your power; but I will harden his heart, so that he will not let the people go" (4:21). Another reason why God should be understood as the one responsible is because almost every time the passive voice is used to describe Pharaoh's heart being hardened it is accompanied by the phrase "as the Lord had said." There is therefore an interesting juxtaposition in the story in that as God's goal of freeing the Israelites from their oppression comes closer, Pharaoh himself becomes less free as he increasingly comes under God's authority.

But what exactly is God doing when Pharaoh's heart is hardened? This is where some confusion and misunderstanding are possible because modern views of the heart were not shared by ancient people. For us, the heart is associated with our feelings and emotions, especially love. This would have seemed odd to people in biblical times, because the heart was not the seat of the emotions for them. Rather, it was where thinking took place. We associate thinking with the brain, but people of long ago did not see things that way. The difference can be noted in ancient Egyptian burial practices in which

> What do you think of ancient views regarding the heart and other organs of the body?

---

6. See Andreas K. Schuele, "Harden the Heart," in *The New Interpreter's Dictionary of the Bible*, ed. Katharine Doob Sakenfeld (Nashville: Abingdon, 2007), 2:735–36.

the stomach, lungs, intestines, and liver were all placed in vessels called canopic jars that were meant to preserve the organs that would be needed in the afterlife. And the brain? The Egyptians removed it either by cracking open the skull or by using tools that allowed it to drain through the nose, and then they discarded it. They also typically left the heart in the body because ancient Egyptians believed it was where the soul of a person resided. In ancient sources, including the Bible, the kidneys often were associated with feelings and emotions in a way similar to how the heart is perceived today.

The connection between the heart and thinking is clearly stated in some biblical passages: "But to this day the Lord has not given you a mind [literally "heart"] to understand, or eyes to see, or ears to hear" (Deut. 29:4).[7] This has important implications for how we interpret what is happening between God and Pharaoh in the plagues narrative. By hardening Pharaoh's heart, God isn't influencing how the Egyptian ruler feels about the Israelites so that he cannot love them or have compassion for them. Rather, God is affecting Pharaoh's rational powers and his ability to think straight. His judgment is impaired and his thinking has become cloudy, and so he is incapable of making the right decisions.

The hardening-of-the-heart motif lends a tragic quality to Pharaoh's character because in a number of places it appears that he wants to do the right thing but he cannot because he is mentally incapacitated and incapable of acting as he wishes. Several times he even expresses a belief in the power of Israel's God or asks Moses to pray for him, and then accedes to the request to let the people go (8:8; 9:27–28; 10:16–17). But each time God hardens Pharaoh's heart yet again, causing him to rethink his decision to free the Israelites and to crack down even harder on them.

In these scenes, Pharaoh comes across as a puppet that is being manipulated by God. He wants to act one way, but then the divine puppet master intervenes and pulls him in another direction. This is meant to stress God's power and authority, but in places it seems that the deity takes things a step further and is intent on embarrassing and humiliating Pharaoh and the Egyptian people: "Go to Pharaoh; for I have hardened his heart and the heart of his officials, in order that I may show these signs of mine among them, and that you may tell your children and grandchildren how I have made fools of the Egyptians and what signs I have done among them—so that you may know that I am the Lord" (10:1–2; cf. 9:14, 16).

This is an image of God that some might find disturbing and troubling. To cut right to the chase, is God being cruel in the plagues story? Even when Pharaoh is ready to do the deity's bidding and free the Israelites, God tugs on the strings again and causes him to renege on his promise. Why not just allow Pharaoh to do what he wants to do and be done with it? On the other hand,

---

7. The NRSV doesn't render the Hebrew literally in order to reflect the modern understanding of how the body works.

the text presents Pharaoh as a harsh taskmaster under whom the Israelites have suffered greatly, so maybe the tyrant is getting what he deserves. But what about the Egyptians, many of whom were also tormented and victimized by their auto-cratic ruler? What does God have against them? Nothing more than collateral damage in the battle between Pharaoh and God, the Egyptians are implicated in things that were not their doing. These are profound theological questions hav-ing a significant bearing on how one interprets God's role in the story.[8]

> What do you think of the idea that God is being cruel to Pharaoh and the Egyptians during the plagues story?

Despite their dramatic nature and their close connection to the central event of the Exodus, the plagues do not play a prominent role in the rest of the Old Testament. In the book of Deuteronomy there are a few references to the "signs and wonders" God performed in Egypt (Deut. 7:17–19; 11:2–3; 29:2–3; cf. Ps. 135:8–9). In addition, one passage in the book of Joshua uses the same verb that refers to the plagues in Exodus to explain how God "hit" Egypt and freed the Israelites (Josh. 24:5). Specific plagues are mentioned in the book of Psalms, which contains two lists of the punishments that God visited on Egypt (78:44–51; 105:27–36). The lists have some items in common, but they are not identical and neither one matches the account in the book of Exodus in terms of the number, order, or nature of the plagues. All three agree that the death of the firstborn of Egypt was the final plague.

The Great Escape

READ: Exodus 12–15

The tenth and final plague leads directly to the Exodus and the Israelites' flight from bondage, so it is best to treat it separately from the previous plagues as the precursor to the Exodus. This is obviously the main event to which the entire story has been building, and here more than anywhere the theme of liberation is to the fore because the people actually take the first steps of their journey from captivity that will continue for the next forty years. At the burning bush, God made himself known to Moses, but it is here, when he leads them to freedom, that God is most fully revealed to the Israelite people.

A Plague unlike Any Other

While it shares much in common with the other plagues, certain things about the tenth one set it apart. In the first place, the description of it is

---

8. For an overview of the hardening-of-the-heart motif, see David M. Gunn, "The Hardening of Pharaoh's Heart: Plot, Character, and Theology in Exodus 1–14," in *Art and Meaning: Rhetoric in Biblical Literature*, ed. David J. A. Clines, David M. Gunn, and Alan J. Hauser (Sheffield: JSOT Press, 1982), 72–96.

considerably longer than those of the other nine. The main reason for this is that the plague is presented in two parts that create a bookend or sandwich effect. Chapter 11 of Exodus gives the background to the plague and tells how Moses warns Pharaoh about what is to come, and then the actual plague is described in 12:29–36. Between these two sections is a middle part—the meat of the sandwich—that explains the origins of the two feasts of Passover and unleavened bread (12:1–28). According to the text, these two festivals trace their roots back to the tenth plague and the Exodus. The somewhat detailed explanation of the feasts lengthens the account of the final plague, making it much longer than its predecessors.

Another important difference between this plague and the others is its nature and the devastating effect it has on Egypt. While the previous ones each focused on some aspect of creation (such as water, frogs, and the sun) that was somehow temporarily manipulated by God in an attempt to convince Pharaoh to let the Israelites go free, this one is a much more impressive and permanent display of divine power as the firstborn of all Egyptians, both humans and animals, are put to death more or less instantaneously (12:29–30).

The magnitude of their loss and the degree of pain that is inflicted upon the Egyptians in this case are much greater than what they had experienced with the previous nine plagues, and the theological questions that ensue are also amplified. Why does the death toll have to be so high and all-inclusive? The body count ranges from "the firstborn of Pharaoh who sits on the throne to the firstborn of the female slave who is behind the hand-mill, and all the firstborn of the livestock" (11:5). That description is fraught with dramatic irony as one set of slaves is set free while the burden of another only increases. It appears that the Egyptians' greatest offense is the unfortunate (and uncontrollable) fact that they are not Israelites. Once again the question must be asked, is God being cruel?

> Is there a way of interpreting the tenth plague that does not put God in a negative light?

Despite those differences, the tenth plague shares much in common with the other nine as all of the elements in the chart discussed earlier are found here. Moses continues to be God's main agent in the confrontation with Pharaoh. While his staff is not mentioned explicitly in the description of the plague, it figures prominently in the ensuing account of the parting of the sea and the Exodus (14:16). As with some of the other plagues, the Israelites are singled out and treated in a special manner by God (11:7). There is a reference to Pharaoh's heart being hardened in 11:10 after Moses warns Pharaoh about the plague, and this is followed by the final three instances of the hardened heart motif during the Exodus itself (14:4, 8, 17). In all four of these verses the passive voice is not used; God is clearly identified as the one who is hardening the Egyptian ruler's heart. Finally, like some of the earlier plagues, the account of this plague and its aftermath has Pharaoh initially agree to Moses' request only to reverse himself and pursue the Israelites (14:5–6). All of these similarities suggest that the account of the final plague follows closely the overall pattern that can be discerned in the other plague accounts.

Out of Egypt

The Exodus is arguably the central event of the entire Old Testament, and it has profoundly shaped the biblical understanding of God because it is directly tied to important theological concepts. One of these is the idea of covenant. In the book of Genesis, God enters into a special relationship with Abraham and his offspring by pledging to be with them forever. Related to this is the theme of election, which marks the Israelites as the Chosen People who will be protected and cared for by God. In the Exodus, the covenant is fully experienced and Israel's special status is realized in a dramatic and powerful way. The Exodus results in their freedom from that bondage, and serves as a reminder that the covenantal relationship endures because the Chosen People still enjoy their special status.

But the Exodus is not only an occasion for the Israelites to look back to the time of their ancestors and remember the covenant that long ago forged their unique relationship with God. It is also an opportunity for them to look ahead and to anticipate the realization of the other part of the covenantal pledge: the promise of a land of their own. The word *exodus* comes from two Greek words that mean "out" and "way, path," but this story is as much about going *to* someplace as it is about going *out from* someplace; the destination is as important as the departure point. The land is a key theological concept in the Hebrew Bible because it is intimately tied to the covenantal promise and Israel's role as the Chosen People. Thus it is important to remember that the Exodus is just the beginning of a very long journey that will culminate in the Israelites' entry into the land God promised them. According to the text, that trek will take forty years, and many of those who left Egypt, including Moses himself, will die on the way.

The first steps of most lengthy journeys are often long forgotten before the destination is reached, but that is not the case here. After a dramatic buildup that recounts the mass deaths of the firstborn of Egypt, the Exodus gets underway with what might be the most miraculous event described in the entire Hebrew Bible. As the forces of Pharaoh close in on the fleeing Israelites and pin them down with their backs to the water, God creates a pathway of dry land through the sea that allows them to escape to safety. The Egyptians rush headlong in pursuit, but at God's command the waters return to normal and Pharaoh's forces and horses are drowned (13:17–14:31).

A chink in the Israelite armor is revealed just before the miracle at the sea when Pharaoh is closing in on them and the people second-guess the entire escape plan: "Was it because there were no graves in Egypt that you have taken us away to die in the wilderness? What have you done to us, bringing us out of

Egypt? Is this not the very thing we told you in Egypt, 'Let us alone and let us serve the Egyptians'? For it would have been better for us to serve the Egyptians than to die in the wilderness" (14:11–12). The Israelites are speaking to Moses here, but the real target of their complaint is God, because Moses is simply following orders from his higher-up. Their lack of confidence and faith is surprising given the front row seats they had for the plagues, but this is only a taste of what's in store. Throughout the next forty years they will regularly murmur in the wilderness as they question Moses' leadership and express their desire to return to the relative security of Egypt.

In several places there are references to God being with the people in the form of a pillar of cloud and a pillar of fire (13:21–22; 14:19–20, 24). This is the first of a number of references to this same phenomenon in the Old Testament, and sometimes Moses converses with God in the cloud (Exod. 14:19–20, 24; 33:9–11; Num. 10:33–36; Deut. 31:14–15). This type of encounter is similar to what occurs in the burning bush episode, and as in that case it should be seen as an example of a theophany or divine appearance.

> Why do you think the theme of the Israelites' lack of faith is so prevalent in the Bible?

As already noted, the account of the tenth plague is divided in two and there is an explanation of the origins of two feasts in the middle of it. This intervening material (12:1–28) disrupts the narrative, which would flow smoother if the two outer sections followed one after the other. Chapter 11 of Exodus ends with Moses angrily leaving Pharaoh after explaining to him what the tenth plague will entail, followed by a brief summary that reiterates how the Egyptian leader would not let the Israelites go because God had hardened his heart (vv.8–11). The section on the two feasts comes next, and then in 12:29 the action resumes with the report of God striking down the firstborn throughout Egypt. The material on the feasts is likely a later insertion that breaks up the account of the tenth plague and creates the sandwich effect mentioned above.

The two holidays discussed in the chapter are Passover and the festival of unleavened bread, springtime feasts that have been celebrated together in the post-biblical period.[9] Their location here connects them to the tenth plague and Israel's flight from Egypt, and so the text is an etiology to explain how the feasts came about. The slaughtered lamb's blood is to be smeared on the doorposts of the Israelites as a way of marking their residences so that God will not inflict harm on them. In reality, the feasts' origins were more complex than what is described in the Bible, but their association with the Exodus has a strong rhetorical function that serves to legitimate them and their ongoing observance. In several places, it is stated that these feasts should be celebrated forever (12:14, 17, 24–27).

---

9. For the history of Passover, see Baruch M. Bokser, *The Origins of the Seder* (New York: JTS Publications, 2002).

From the ancient synagogue of Dura-Europos in Syria (mid-third century CE), comes this fresco of Moses parting the Red Sea. The Israelites, on the left, cross unharmed, while the Egyptians, on the right, are swept away.

The plagues account describes scenes that appear to violate the laws of nature. There have been attempts to explain some of these events naturally, but others defy explanation. In particular, the circumstances surrounding the Israelites' departure from Egypt fly in the face of science and common sense. How is it possible that all firstborn humans and animals in Egypt could die on the same night at more or less the same time? How could a body of water form walls on the right and left that would allow people to pass through them (14:22)? How likely is it that a group of six hundred thousand men, not counting women and children, would be able to escape from a well-trained army and then survive in the wilderness for forty years?

Most of chapter 15 is a poem that is a lyrical version of the events described in the previous chapter. This composition, sometimes referred to as "The Song of Moses," is considered by many scholars to be one of the oldest portions of the Old Testament.[10] While the prose in chapter 14 is a narrative report of the episode, the poetry is a response to it that offers praise and thanksgiving to God for rescuing Israel from its enemy. A few verses after the conclusion of the song, Moses' sister Miriam repeats its opening lines and exclaims, "Sing to the LORD, for he has triumphed gloriously; horse and rider he has thrown into the sea" (15:21). The passage describes her and other women dancing with tambourines as they sing, a scene that is similar to one recounted later in the Old Testament after David slays Goliath (1 Sam. 18:6–7).

Second Opinions

The book of Exodus contains some of the best-known stories in the Hebrew Bible, like the burning bush episode, the plagues, and the escape from Egypt.

---

10. A similar arrangement of a prose account followed by a much older poetic version of it can also be seen in the story of Deborah in Judges 4–5.

However, these are not likely to be historical events. In some cases, evidence from extra-biblical sources is lacking or fails to corroborate the text, while in other places it appears that the story is dependent upon traditions from outside the Bible.[11] And then there is the matter of plausibility. The preponderance of events in the narrative that appear to violate the laws of nature gives it a strongly legendary—as opposed to historical—feel.

Questioning the Exodus

In addition, there are a number of anomalies in these chapters that raise issues about the text's historicity, composition, and development. Several oddities in the text have generated discussion among scholars and raise questions about its formation. In 13:17 a reference is made to a geographical location that is chronologically out of place: "When Pharaoh let the people go, God did not lead them by way of the land of the Philistines, although that was nearer; for God thought, 'If the people face war, they may change their minds and return to Egypt.'" The Philistines were a people from the western Mediterranean Sea who settled in southwestern Canaan in the early twelfth century BCE. By the time of the rise of the Israelite monarchy under Saul and David around the year 1000 BCE, they were well established in the land, and they are presented in the biblical text as enemies of the Israelites. But to refer to this area as the "land of the Philistines" during the time of the Exodus is anachronistic because the Philistines were just beginning to settle in the region at this point and so it would not yet have been known by that name. Using that name here is equivalent to describing the landing of the Mayflower at Plymouth in 1620 as its arrival in the United States of America.

Another problem is that two of the main characters in this section of Exodus are actually both "not all there." After playing a visible role in the first three plagues, Aaron pretty much drops out of the picture after that. He makes cameo appearances for many of the other plagues, but Moses is the one who takes the lead and does all the speaking and most of the acting. In some cases, it says that Aaron is standing with Moses before Pharaoh, but then the text refers only to Moses' departure (8:30; 10:6, 18). Aaron is not even mentioned in the description of the ninth plague, and after briefly returning for the tenth plague (12:31, 43, 50) he drops out of the story again until 16:2. During the parting of the sea and the departure from Egypt the entire focus is on Moses as his brother Aaron becomes a bystander.

Pharaoh, of course, is no onlooker, but there is still something missing in the portrayal of his character: his name. From the time Moses comes on the scene as an infant until he departs as an adult—notice how water plays a key

---

11. These will be discussed shortly.

role both when Moses enters Pharaoh's life and when he leaves it—the Egyptian ruler is mentioned more than ninety times in the text, but never by name. This continues a trend that begins in the book of Genesis, which also never identifies the Pharaohs it mentions (Gen. 12:10–20; 39–50). In fact, in the rest of the Hebrew Bible only four kings of Egypt are named: Hophra, Neco, Shishak, and So. Speaking of names, depending on what Bible you are reading the location of the great escape might appear to be a misprint with an additional vowel. While most people know it as the Red Sea (13:18), the Hebrew name (*yam suph*) better translates as "Reed Sea."[12] The more common "Red Sea" is based on the Greek translation of the Old Testament known as the Septuagint, but it is not supported by the Hebrew.

> Why might it be that Pharaoh is never referred to by name?

For these reasons the historical accuracy of Exodus has been called into question at times, leading some scholars to conclude that Moses was not an actual person but rather a fictional invention by the author(s). At the other end of the spectrum are those who dismiss these concerns and believe the book of Exodus provides a reliable account of events as they happened. Still others adopt a middle position and say that at least some of the traditions recorded in the book can be traced back to someone called Moses, whose lifetime is usually located somewhere between the fifteenth and thirteenth centuries BCE. Despite this range of scholarly views regarding historical accuracy, there is more or less universal agreement that the theological agenda of the author(s) has had a significant impact on the final shape of the text; to ignore that fact would be a mistake. With that in mind, the key question to be asked is not, "Did it happen?" but, "What does it mean?" In other words, even if some readers have serious reservations about what is "true" in the text, they can still grapple with the truth claims it makes.[13]

> What is your reaction to the idea that Moses might not have been a real person?

Meeting Moses

When we first meet Moses, he is an infant floating to safety on the Nile River inside a basket made by his mother (Exod. 2:1–10). Ironically, he is heading right toward Pharaoh, the very person who has called for his death but will soon

---

12. It is also possible that the Hebrew could mean "Sea of the Endpoint," but this alternative has not been as widely accepted as "Sea of Reeds." For an argument in favor of this translation see Bernard F. Batto, "The Reed Sea: *requiescat in pace,*" *Journal of Biblical Literature* 102 (1983): 27–35.

13. An overview of the main views regarding whether or not Moses existed is provided in Dennis T. Olson, "Moses," in *The New Interpreter's Dictionary of the Bible*, ed. Sakenfeld, 4:142–44.

welcome him as the newest member of his household. That is the first encounter modern readers have with Moses, but if you were someone living in the ancient Near East that story would likely have a familiar ring to it.

A similar story was told about a legendary ruler named Sargon, who was in power more than a thousand years before the time in which many scholars date the Exodus. According to the text that has come down to us, which is told in Sargon's own voice, his mother was a priestess and he did not know his father. She had her child in secret, probably because priestesses were supposed to remain childless, and then put him in a reed basket that was sealed with pitch and placed on the river. He was eventually rescued by a gardener named Aqqi, who adopted Sargon and raised him as his own son.[14] The similarities between the birth stories of Sargon and Moses are quite apparent, and the simplest explanation for them is that the former was used as a model for the Exodus text.

> What do you make of the similarities between the birth stories of Sargon and Moses?

It was noted earlier that God is not mentioned explicitly in the story of Moses' birth, and that absence indirectly supports the idea that the Bible has recycled the Mesopotamian tradition. The Sargon story does not refer to a deity either, and perhaps the biblical author/editor preferred not to introduce that element into the tradition. Its placement in Exodus 2 is in keeping with a well-known pattern sometimes found in ancient literature whereby the birth or early life of a hero is full of dangers or complications. According to the accounts of their lives, many newborns who go on to achieve greatness as adults were endangered early on, including Oedipus, Paris, Gilgamesh, Cyrus, Hercules, and Jesus. With that formula in mind, the Bible reader is predisposed to assume that the child Moses is destined to do great things.[15]

The birth story of Moses concludes with a reference to his name and its presumed meaning: "When the child grew up, she brought him to Pharaoh's daughter, and she took him as her son. She named him Moses, 'because,' she said, 'I drew him out of the water'" (2:10). Pharaoh's daughter gives Moses a name that she connects to a Hebrew verb that means "to draw out," but this does not make sense within the context of the story. Why would an Egyptian woman adopt a child and then give it a Hebrew name? It is unlikely she would have even known the language. This detail is clearly meant for the Hebrew-reading

---

14. The text of Sargon's birth story can be found in William W. Hallo, ed., *The Context of Scripture: Canonical Compositions from the Biblical World* (Leiden: Brill, 2003), 1:461.

15. The biblical writer is not the only one who has reused the Sargon birth story to burnish the reputation of a later figure. Saddam Hussein, the former despot of Iraq, tried to model himself after his long-ago predecessor at his fifty-third birthday party by having a baby doll in his likeness placed in a basket and floated down a stream. See Paul Kriwaczek, *Babylon: Mesopotamia and the Birth of Civilization* (New York: St. Martin's Press, 2010), 112–13. Eyewitnesses did not comment on whether or not the doll had a mustache.

audience of the text and might be anticipating the later scene when Moses plays a key role in "drawing out" the Israelite people from the water in the Exodus event. The name Moses probably derives from an Egyptian word that means "to beget" or "son of." It is seen in the names of certain Pharaohs, like Thutmose and Ahmose, which describe the individual as the offspring of a particular god.[16]

What in God's Name?

Moses' name is not the only one that has been discussed by Bible scholars. As previously noted, at the burning bush Moses poses a hypothetical scenario and asks how he should respond if the Israelites ask him about God's identity. The deity's answer comes in multiple parts as God gives Moses three options to choose from.

> God said to Moses, "I Am Who I Am." He said further, "Thus you shall say to the Israelites, 'I Am has sent me to you.'" God also said to Moses, "'Thus you shall say to the Israelites, 'The Lord, the God of your ancestors, the God of Abraham, the God of Isaac, and the God of Jacob, has sent me to you: this is my name forever, and this my title for all generations.'" (3:14–15)

In Hebrew, God's self-designation as "I Am Who I Am," "I Am," and "the Lord" would be similar to a man who identifies himself in English as "Joe," "Joey," and "Joseph." The three are obviously related and sound similar to one another, but they are not identical. The phrase translated here as "I Am Who I Am" is *'ehyeh 'asher 'ehyeh* in Hebrew, and it can also be translated in other ways, like, "I am that I am," "I will be who I will be," or "I will be what I will be." God's second response to Moses ("I am") in Hebrew, the "Joe" one, is simply the first word of his first one: *'ehyeh*. The third one ("the Lord") appears to be unconnected to the other two, but it is actually etymologically related to them because it comes from the same Hebrew root. "Lord" is the way that many English translations choose to render the Hebrew word *yahweh*, which is a verbal form that probably means something like "he causes to be." All three forms of the divine name in this passage come from the same Hebrew root that means "to be," and this passage has played a foundational role in the theological understanding of God as self-existent, eternal, and uncreated.

In the earliest form of the Hebrew text, this name was written with only its four consonants, and so it is found sometimes in English as YHWH. In this form it is known as the "tetragrammaton," a term based on two Greek words that mean "four letters." Many devout Jews do not pronounce the tetragrammaton,

---

16. See the discussion of Moses' name in Dennis T. Olson, "Literary and Rhetorical Criticism," in *Methods for Exodus*, ed. Thomas B. Dozeman (New York: Cambridge University Press, 2010), 40.

and when reading the biblical text aloud they substitute '*adonay* or another word for it.[17] The divine name "Jehovah," which is mostly used by some Christians, is actually a hybrid form that combines the consonants of the tetragrammaton with the vowels of '*adonay*. Appearing almost seven thousand times in the Old Testament, Yahweh is the most common name for God in the text. Ironically, though, its precise meaning and origin remain shrouded in mystery.

> What does the divine name's basis in the verb "to be" suggest about God's nature?

A Prophet like Moses

As discussed earlier, the encounter at the burning bush has a back-and-forth, cat-and-mouse quality to it that pits God's persistence against Moses' reluctance. The deity has a specific mission for Moses to undertake that will bring him into the Egyptian halls of power, but the soon-to-be liberator of his people responds with a barrage of excuses and what-ifs meant to keep him safely at home.

That conversation between Moses and God at the bush contains elements that are sometimes found in the biblical books associated with the prophets. The three major prophetic books in the Hebrew Bible are Isaiah, Jeremiah, and Eze-kiel, which are among the longest works in the Old Testament. They have quite a bit in common: soaring poetry, stern warnings about the punishment to come if people do not change their ways, and call narratives.

Somewhere near the beginning of all three books are scenes in which each prophet is called by God. These sections vary in length and details, but they have a similar outline, comprised of five main parts: (1) a meeting between God and the person, (2) a commission from God for the person to do a particular task, (3) an objection from the person, (4) a reassurance by God that the person can do the task, and (5) a sign from God validating the person's call to be a prophet. Every element is not found for each prophet and they are not always in the same order, but the overall pattern is similar enough that it is generally held that the prophetic call narrative is a discernible genre in the Old Testament. Examples of it can be seen in Isaiah 6, Jeremiah 1, and Ezekiel 1–3.

It should be obvious that the prophetic call pattern maps nicely onto the burning bush story since all five elements of it are found in Exodus 3:1–4:17. What is interesting is how two of the elements are repeated multiple times as Moses continues to object to his call and God has to reassure him again and again that

> What do its similarities with the prophetic call narratives suggest about the composition of the burning bush story?

17. One of the most common replacement words for "Yahweh" among Jews is *ha-shem*, which is Hebrew for "the name."

he is up to the challenge. The repetition of those parts is what extends the narrative and increases its dramatic tension as the conversation shifts back and forth between God demanding that Moses go to Pharaoh and say, "Let my people go!" and Moses pleading, "Let go of me!"

Moses may not be a prophet in quite the way that Isaiah, Jeremiah, and Ezekiel are, but he is described as a prophet elsewhere (Deut. 34:10) and he even considers himself to be one (Deut. 18:15). But that is only one aspect of his multi-faceted identity in the Bible, where he also plays the roles of God's agent, political leader, mediator, and intercessor, among others. It is interesting, though, that his first encounter with God is presented in a way that puts him squarely in the prophetic camp and yet sets him apart from the other prophets by making him even more reluctant to do God's will than they are.

Oddly, there are no unambiguous references to the burning bush story in the rest of the Old Testament. There is a possible mention of it in a passage in the book of Deuteronomy (33:16), but it is unclear whether the verse is referring to God as "the one who dwells in the bush" or "the one who dwells on Sinai," because the words for "bush" and "Sinai" are almost the same in biblical Hebrew. References to this episode are actually more common in the New Testament, where it appears four times (Mark 12:26; Luke 20:37; Acts 7:30, 35). Its virtual absence from the rest of the Hebrew Bible is an argument in favor of seeing the burning bush tradition as a somewhat late addition to the text. But despite its likely status as a relative latecomer, Moses' encounter with God at the bush has remained a popular image throughout history, and has been represented in countless works of art.

Parsing the Plagues

The plagues narrative in Exodus 7–11 describes a series of punishments against the Egyptians that are sent by God through the agency of Moses and Aaron. This devastating succession of blows is meant to cripple the entire land and incapacitate all its inhabitants except the Israelites.[18] These "signs and wonders" are presented as events that are not of human origin, and this appears to be the Egyptian magicians' understanding of their cause; when they are unable to replicate the swarm of gnats they exclaim, "This is the finger of God!" (8:19). Despite the text's insistence on their divine source, though, attempts have been made to argue for a more worldly explanation of the problems that plagued Pharaoh and his people.

---

18. The universal nature of the plagues can be seen in the fact that the Hebrew word for "all" (*kol*) appears more than fifty times in these chapters. This point is made by Terence E. Fretheim in his essay "Issues of Agency in Exodus," in *The Book of Exodus: Composition, Reception, and Interpretation*, ed. Thomas B. Dozeman, Craig A. Evans, and Joel N. Lohr (Leiden: Brill, 2014), 14.

Explaining the Inexplicable

Some have suggested that virtually all of the plagues can be explained by natural phenomena, many of which have been known to occur one after another in a cause-and-effect sequence.[19] Flowing for more than four-thousand miles, the Nile is the longest river in the world and the major water source for Egypt and much of northeast Africa. Until 1970, when the High Dam was completed in the southern Egyptian city of Aswan, the banks of the Nile would swell each year and flood the land on both sides of the river. As the floodwaters subsided they would leave behind large deposits of silt, which resulted in the rich and fertile soil that allowed Egyptian civilization to develop and thrive despite the area's desert conditions. It has been proposed by some scholars that the first plague's reference to the river turning to blood is actually a description of the silt-filled Nile that occasionally would take on a reddish shade.

The second plague can be accounted for by the frogs that would be brought onto the land by the floodwaters, and then after the water had subsided the decaying bodies of the frogs left behind would attract the gnats and flies mentioned in the third and fourth plagues.[20] Those insects would then come in contact with livestock and humans, who would become infected by the germs they bore from the frog carcasses, resulting in the diseases described in plagues five and six. In this way, more than one-half of the plagues can be explained as stemming from a chain of events that were due to the annual flooding of the Nile.

As far as the other plagues are concerned, most of them can also be connected to observable phenomena. While not very common, hail does sometimes fall in Egypt and so the scene described in the seventh plague is not impossible. The eighth plague is similar, since locust infestations are well documented in Egypt, like the one that occurred in 2013 that included more than thirty million of the creatures flapping their wings over the land of the pyramids. It coincidentally happened less than a month before Passover, and many media reports made the obvious association with the biblical story.[21]

Are attempts to explain the plagues by natural means persuasive?

---

19. See, for example, James K. Hoffmeier, *Israel in Egypt: The Evidence for the Authenticity of the Exodus Tradition* (New York: Oxford University Press, 1999); and Colin J. Humphries, *The Miracles of Exodus: A Scientist's Discovery of the Extraordinary Natural Causes of the Bible Stories* (San Francisco: HarperOne, 2003). In a similar vein, scientific explanations for the miracle at the sea have been proposed by Doron Nof and Nathan Paldor, "Are There Oceanographic Explanations for the Israelites' Crossing of the Red Sea?" *Bulletin of the American Meteorological Society* 73 (1992): 305–14; and Doron Nof and Nathan Paldor, "Statistics of Wind over the Red Sea with Application to the Exodus Question," *Journal of Applied Meteorology* 33, no. 8 (1994): 1017–25

20. The Exodus story has left its mark on zoology since the scientific name of a species of frog that is commonly found near the Nile River is *Rana Mosaica*, the "Moses frog."

21. See "Swarms of Millions of Locusts Plague Cairo, Egypt ahead of Passover," *https://www. youtube.com/watch?v=Olh4pBbUFYg.*

The loss of sunlight that is the subject of the ninth plague has been explained in different ways. One theory posits that the locusts of the previous plague were so numerous that they blocked out the sun's rays from reaching the earth, thus causing darkness to fall. The video cited above suggests this is a rather unlikely scenario, since the number of locusts involved in such a lights-out event would have to be astronomical. More plausible is the idea that a solar eclipse or a sandstorm, again not uncommon phenomena, was responsible. The one plague that is *sui generis* and inexplicable is, of course, the final one. The deaths of large numbers of people in a short time span have been recorded during times of epidemic and similar public health emergencies, but what makes this different is that only the first-born male child of each Egyptian family is affected. Throw in the same thing happening to the animals, and you have a situation that cannot be explained away or chalked up to coincidence.

Such efforts to assign a cause for each plague are ultimately misguided for several reasons. First, an explanation like the one above that ties many of the events to the annual flooding of the Nile River is not supported by the text itself. According to the book of Exodus, the effects were actually broader than such a hypothesis claims. For example, the first plague affects not just the Nile but all the water sources in Egypt, including standing pools of water that are not physically connected to the river (7:19). Similarly, the punishments are not felt just by the Egyptians who live near the river but have an impact on all of them. In virtually each case, the point is made that the entire land of Egypt, not just the area near the river, experienced these hardships (7:21; 8:2, 6, 16, 21, 24; 9:9, 22, 25; 10:5, 14, 22).

A more important reason why natural explanations of the plagues should be rejected is that they go against the very reason why the events have been recounted in the first place, and to ignore that reason is to misunderstand the genre and whole point of the narrative. The central message of the text is a theological one, not a historical one. Whether or not the plagues can be rationally explained is inconsequential because, in a sense, it does not really matter if they actually happened or not. The primary purpose of the account is to acknowledge and celebrate the power of the God of Israel, who came to the aid of his people when they needed assistance. To claim that all these things just happened and were not due to God's intervention would strip them of that meaning and render them theologically irrelevant. God is the central actor of the story, and, as elsewhere in the Bible, we need to keep in mind that often events that are presented as "history" in the text are actually theological interpretations of things that may or may not have happened.

An Anonymous Pharaoh and Missing Records

There are certain indications, both within the text and outside it, that suggest we should not read the plagues narrative as straight history. One is the fact mentioned earlier that the Pharaoh is never identified by name despite being referred to ninety-plus times in the first thirteen chapters of Exodus. Such anonymity, especially of a central character, is often the hallmark of a fictional work that is more interested in exploring ethical and existential themes than in reporting actual events. Think of all those fables and tales that feature figures described as "a scarecrow," "a tin man," or "a lion" without ever naming them. In the present case, the unnamed Pharaoh is power personified, and he symbolizes all those bullies at the top of the heap who always get what they want and don't have to answer to anyone. The story pits that unbridled authority against a motley crew of nobodies and their reluctant leader, and it delivers a message of hope to underdogs everywhere. That message comes through loud and clear partly because the Pharaoh's identity remains a mystery. If he has a name it becomes a story about a particular person at a specific moment in time, but keeping it vague makes it something we can all relate to more easily.

His namelessness has not discouraged attempts to identify who the Pharaoh of the Exodus was and therefore provide a chronological context for the events described in the text. Due to the lack of explicit evidence, any proposal is nothing more than a conjecture, but one verse in particular has been the subject of some scrutiny. The first chapter of Exodus describes the Israelites building two supply cities for Pharaoh, named Pithom and Rameses (1:11), and Egyptian sources indicate that the construction of the latter city was completed during the reign of Ramesses II (1279–1213 BCE). The final form of the text has to come from a time after he ruled Egypt, but it is possible that it was composed in a much later period and the reference to the city of Rameses is anachronistic— like the reference to the land of the Philistines, previously noted. Even though the evidence is inconclusive, Ramesses II is the Pharaoh who is most commonly associated with the plagues and the Exodus.

© David Henderson / iStockphoto.com

Ramesses II, represented in this statue from Luxor, is one of several Pharaohs that have been proposed as the Pharaoh of the Exodus. The biblical account, however, gives no name.

Another reason why some healthy skepticism is not a bad thing when considering the historicity of the story has to do with another absence, only this time on the Egyptian side: there is not a single reference to the plagues in the extra-biblical sources. The Egyptians were meticulous record-keepers and their scribes were highly regarded members of society, but within the countless documents that have come down to us the plagues are not mentioned at all. That includes the final blow of the death of the firstborn, an event bound to make headlines if ever there was one. The same is

> How big a problem is it that the Egyptian sources do not mention any of the plagues?

true of the Bible's account of the parting of the waters and the Israelites' miraculous escape on dry land, which does not merit even a footnote in the Egyptian historical record. That scribal silence is deafening. Granted, these events would be embarrassing to the Egyptian people and their ruler, and so there would likely be a tendency to downplay them. But such momentous happenings would certainly have been cited somewhere in the mountain of ancient Egyptian data if they had taken place as recorded in the Old Testament.

The Role of Religion and Theology

A general understanding of ancient Egyptian religious beliefs and practices helps to highlight the theological dimension of the plagues narrative.[22] It was a polytheistic system comprised of dozens of gods and goddesses, many of whom were associated with various aspects of the created world. This means that when God exercises control over parts of the natural world through the plagues, God is also demonstrating power over the gods who were identified with those natural elements. The first plague shows God's superiority over Hapi, the god of the Nile River, just as the sending of the frogs during the second one expresses God's authority over Heqet, the goddess of childbirth and fertility, who was commonly depicted in the form of a frog. The diseases visited upon the livestock were attacks on the god Apis and the goddess Hathor, who were identified with the bull

> If the plagues story is not historical, what effect does that have on how we should interpret this section of the Bible?

and the cow. And, of course, the plague of darkness is a direct attack on the sun god Ra, who was one of the major deities of the Egyptian pantheon. Add to this the fact that Pharaoh himself was considered to be divine, and the theological purpose of the plagues becomes clear: this is a battle *royale* in which the God of Israel wins all ten rounds by taking on and defeating the gods of Egypt, including its overmatched ruler with a hardened heart.

Prior to the plagues, Pharaoh claims he does not know who Israel's God is (Exod. 5:2), but that changes throughout the course of the narrative, as even

---

22. See Byron E. Shafer, *Religion in Ancient Egypt: Gods, Myths, and Personal Practice* (Ithaca, NY: Cornell University Press, 1991).

before the first plague is sent God announces his intention to fill in the missing information for Pharaoh and his people (7:5). From that point on, that theme is reiterated: the plagues have been sent so that the Egyptians might know who God is (7:17; 8:10, 22; 9:14, 29; 10:2; 11:7). In this way, the punishment of Pharaoh and his people is simultaneously an education that is meant to instruct them about the nature and power of Israel's God.

Hovering over this section of Exodus, not unlike the cloud that leads the Israelites from Egypt to their Promised Land, is the question of how God's character should be evaluated. In particular, what does it mean that God continually hardens Pharaoh's heart so that he is prevented from doing the very thing God commands him to do? God wants Pharaoh to know that he is God but, ironically, the repeated hardening of his heart prevents Pharaoh from achieving that knowledge. One way to address this issue is to focus on genre and remember that theological—not historical—concerns drive the way the story is told. With that in mind, the take-away message is clear: God's power is supreme and transcends the authority of Pharaoh and the gods of Egypt.

Still, the questions linger. One way of addressing them is to recognize that the theological perspective reflected in the narrative is one of *monolatry* rather than monotheism.[23] The idea that the God of Israel is the only God that exists will be a later development in the biblical tradition. These texts acknowledge the existence of the Egyptian gods, but they argue for Yahweh's supremacy over them, and it is not surprising that he comes out victorious. Yahweh is the God of the Hebrews, and not of the Egyptians, and he therefore saves the one and destroys the other. In a truly monotheistic perspective—if there is only one God—Yahweh would be the God of both the Hebrews and the Egyptians, and in that case the sort of behavior attributed to God in the Exodus account would be inappropriate. But it took Israel some time to develop a more universal understanding of God and to adopt a fully monotheistic view. When these texts were reaching their final form, the Israelites had not yet made the jump to monotheism and its accompanying belief that God is the God of all people. The image of God in the Exodus narrative therefore doesn't fully agree with the understanding of the deity that many Jews and Christians hold today, and so they have a hard time accepting certain aspects of God's character in the story.

> Does a focus on its theology successfully address questions regarding God's character in the plagues story?

---

23. In simplest terms, *monotheism* is the belief that only one God exists, whereas *monolatry* is the exclusive worship of one god; in the latter, worshippers do not deny the existence of other gods, but refuse to worship them.

A One-Way Ticket to Nowhere?

The Exodus is referred to approximately 120 times in the Old Testament, more than any other past event. It is mentioned in sources as varied as the historical books, the prophetic writings, and the book of Psalms, and is cited in relation to many different themes and teachings. Among other topics, these texts discuss the Exodus as a demonstration of God's power (Josh. 24:5–7), as a reason why the people should obey the law (Deut. 7:7–11), as a cause for judgment against them when they do not follow God's will (Jer. 7:21–26), and as a source of hope for the future (Ps. 77:15–20).

The Historical Problems

While the Exodus theme is well documented within the Hebrew Bible, scholars continue to debate how old it is and how far back it can be traced. Many believe that most of the texts related to it in the Pentateuch should be dated to the time of the exile (sixth century BCE) or later.[24] It is likely that the earliest references to the Exodus in the Bible come from eighth-century prophets like Amos, Hosea, and Micah: "For I brought you up from the land of Egypt, and redeemed you from the house of slavery; and I sent before you Moses, Aaron, and Miriam" (Mic. 6:4; cf. Hos. 2:15; 8:13; 11:1, 5; 12:9, 13; 13:4–5; Amos 2:10; 3:1; 9:7; Mic. 7:15). Like this passage, almost all of the references to the Exodus within the early prophetic books speak in general terms about the Israelites being brought out of Egypt by God without any details regarding how it happened or descriptions of the events as presented in the book of Exodus. An exception is in Amos 4:10, which appears to make an allusion to the plagues and uses a Hebrew term for pestilence (*dever*) also found in Exodus 9:15. The lack of specificity about the Exodus in the earliest texts suggest that a general form of the tradition was known among Israelites certainly by the eighth century BCE, but the specific description of it as presented in the book of Exodus comes from a later time.

> What are the implications of the idea that the Exodus theme comes from a relatively late time in Israel's history?

This conclusion is supported by extra-biblical evidence because some of the details mentioned in the text do not match up well with what we know about Egypt during the New Kingdom period (sixteenth–eleventh centuries BCE) in which the story is set. There are references in the Egyptian sources to people from Asia who worked in Egypt during that time, but there were no subjected ethnic groups similar to the way the Israelites are presented in the biblical text. These workers tended to assimilate into Egyptian society, unlike the Hebrews in Exodus, and they did not typically make bricks or engage in activities similar to

---

24. The oldest pictorial representation of the Exodus is the third-century CE painting in the Dura-Europos synagogue in Syria, reproduced in this chapter.

those of the Israelites in this story (Exod. 5:1–14). In addition, there are problems associated with some of the place names. The Hebrew form of "Rameses" (Exod. 12:37) is written in a way that comes from the eighth century BCE at the earliest. It is found earlier in the Hebrew Bible in the phrase "the land of Rameses" (Gen. 47:11), but such a place is never mentioned anywhere in the Egyptian sources. On top of this is the fact that a number of Egyptian towns and locations that were very prominent during the time in which the story is set are not mentioned at all in the biblical narrative. These and other factors better reflect conditions in Egypt during the seventh through the fifth centuries BCE, and point to a later date of composition.[25]

And so we find ourselves in a double bind, since very little in the biblical account agrees with what we know about Egypt from reliable sources, and there is not a single reference to the incredible events described in Exodus in the entire Egyptian written record. The verifiable Egyptian data in the biblical account are meager at best and consist of the personal names Moses, Shiphrah, and Puah (Exod. 1:15), and the place names Pithom and Rameses, which were known sites in the eastern delta region of Egypt. Such an almost complete lack of information specific to a time and place is unusual in a contemporaneous account, and argues in favor of the position taken above that the Exodus story comes from a later time. For most scholars, the absence of references to the Exodus events in the Egyptian written sources clinches the argument: "From the Egyptian viewpoint, the Old Testament narrative records a series of earthshaking episodes that never happened."[26]

Such a statement dismisses the book of Exodus as a work of fiction that is of no help in efforts to reconstruct what happened in the past. This is in line with the idea stated earlier that it is a theological document whose purpose is not to recount events as they actually happened. Rather, it relates traditions that are considered foundational for a particular community and it presents them in a way that aligns with and supports the theological perspective of the author(s).

Who Were the Israelites, and Where Did They Come From?

Despite its limited historical value, in the minds of many scholars the Exodus story still plays an important role in attempts to imagine and explain how the Israelites came to exist as a people. As already noted, there are no explicit references in Egyptian sources to biblical stories like the burning bush episode, the plagues narrative, or the escape through water. But if we turn to the other end of what the Bible describes as the Israelites' forty-year journey through the

---

25. A discussion of the issues treated in this paragraph can be found in Lester L. Grabbe, "Exodus and History," in *The Book of Exodus: Composition, Reception, and Interpretation*, ed. Thomas B. Dozeman, Craig A. Evans, and Joel N. Lohr (Leiden: Brill, 2014), 61–87.

26. William A. Ward, "Summary and Conclusions," in *Exodus: The Egyptian Evidence*, ed. Ernest S. Frerichs and Leonard H. Lesko (Winona Lake, MN: Eisenbrauns, 1997), 105.

wilderness and we consider their arrival at the land God promised them, the situation is a little different. The only mention of Israel in an Egyptian text is found on a stela, or stone slab, that commemorates a military campaign of Pharaoh Merneptah, who ruled from 1213 to 1203 BCE. This stela, from around 1208 BCE, contains the earliest reference to Israel outside the Bible. Its inscription lists the different enemies Merneptah defeated in a campaign to Canaan, including one called "Israel." That name is identified as a group of people and not, like the others on the list, a place. This means that by 1208 BCE there was an entity in Canaan known as Israel. It does not tell us how or when they arrived, so it has no bearing on the historicity of the Exodus story, but it is the earliest extra-biblical starting point we have for the history of Israel.

It is conceivable that the people who eventually came to be called "Israel" actually began as smaller subgroups that banded together over time to form one larger entity. The traditions and stories of each group were shared with the others, and some of those traditions were eventually accepted as the foundation stories of the entire community. According to this theory, within that assembly was a (small?) group of people who had

> Is the theory that Israel began as a set of smaller groups that eventually joined together plausible?

traditions about their ancestors escaping from Egypt with help from their God, who had set them free and had provided for them on their journey to Canaan. As this and other traditions were accepted by the group, they were expanded upon and developed until they reached the form that they now take in the Bible. If this is what happened, then the story of the Exodus as we have it, including its theological perspective and emphases, is not identical to its original form but reflects the concerns and interests of a later, likely exilic, context.

While it is impossible to determine the historical reliability of the traditions that were eventually incorporated into the Exodus account, one aspect of them suggests that they could have some basis in actual events. That is, it stretches the imagination to assume that any population group would simply make up such an unflattering account of their origin. Why invent a story in which one's people had such a dishonorable beginning—as escaped slaves—unless there were some truth to it? Bible scholars often refer to this as the "criterion of embarrassment" in their efforts to determine which sections of the biblical literature are more likely to be based in history. According to its logic, the presence in a text of something that could be a source of shame or disgrace for the community that produced it increases the likelihood of its being authentic.[27]

---

27. In 2013 a symposium was held on the Exodus at the University of California, San Diego, that brought together natural scientists and humanities scholars. The topic was addressed from many different perspectives, and the conference papers are available in Thomas E. Levy, Thomas Schneider, and William H. C. Propp, eds., *Israel's Exodus in Transdisciplinary Perspective* (New York: Springer, 2015).

There is no way to precisely identify the group of people who made their way from Egypt to Canaan, but one term related to them stands out because of its frequent use in the biblical text. The word "Hebrew(s)" is found thirty-four times in the entire Hebrew Bible, with fifteen of those occurrences in the first ten chapters of the book of Exodus. In six places the deity is referred to as the "God of the Hebrews," and these are the only places that title is used in the Old Testament (3:18; 5:3; 7:16; 9:1, 13; 10:3). Sometimes the term is used as a marker of ethnicity, but it could be that there is also some connection between it and the word *habiru* (sometimes spelled *hapiru*), that is often found in ancient Near Eastern texts to describe a particular segment of society. The Habiru are typically presented as outsiders, and often outlaws, who were a marginal group throughout the area in the period 1850–1150 BCE. The etymology of the word is uncertain, but some have argued that the terms *Habiru* and *Hebrew* are related. Whether or not they are, the reputation and description of the Habiru have much in common with the way the Hebrews are presented in the opening chapters of the book of Exodus (1:8–2:15). Were the ancient Israelites the equivalents of modern-day gypsies whom the Egyptians looked upon as foreign rabble-rousers who were often up to no good? The text does not come right out and say that, but the similarities are tantalizing and raise provocative questions about the origin of at least some of the Chosen People.[28]

> If some of the Hebrews were in fact Habiru, would that change your view of them?

However much they may disagree over how historically reliable this part of the Bible is, people can all agree on one undeniable fact: the Exodus is a story about human freedom and liberation. It graphically captures the competing desires of the powerful and the powerless, and it illustrates how the latter group can sometimes emerge victorious and shake off the chains of oppression and enslavement. This is why it has been a go-to story and an inspiration for those who have experienced persecution and marginalization throughout history.[29]

Exodus in Modern Times

In recent times, the Israelites' journey from slavery to freedom has been embraced as a paradigm and blueprint for many individuals and groups. During the 1950s and 1960s a movement emerged in South America that came to be known as Liberation Theology. It gained international attention at a 1968 gathering of Latin American Roman Catholic bishops who met in the city of Medellín, Colombia, to address the unjust social conditions that were imposed

---

28. A brief discussion of the Habiru and their possible connection to the Hebrews can be found in Norman K. Gottwald, "Habiru, Hapiru" in *The New Interpreter's Dictionary of the Bible*, ed. Sakenfeld, 2:709–10.

29. For an in-depth treatment of the role the book of Exodus has played in this regard, see Scott M. Langston, *Exodus through the Centuries* (Malden, MA: Blackwell, 2006).

upon many of the people they served. The gap between the relatively few rich and the countless poor was growing wider and wider, and the vast majority of people were living in abject poverty. As the bishops and Latin American theologians began to study this situation and seek a solution to it, they saw in the Exodus story a biblical tradition that mirrored their experience, and that became the lens through which they attempted to

> If God has a preferential option for the poor, what does that mean for wealthy people?

address the problem. In the memorable words of that Medellin gathering, the Exodus story and other biblical texts make it clear that God has a "preferential option for the poor" and that all people have the right to free themselves from the forces that enslave them. Liberation Theology continues to be a powerful force for social change throughout Latin America, and its Exodus-based call for freedom from oppression has been embraced by many.[30]

At around the same time, the civil rights movement was reaching a crucial juncture throughout the United States. Many of the leaders of that struggle were clergy and other people of faith who framed their efforts in terms that drew upon the Exodus story and the Israelites' passage from slavery to freedom, a transition that was being reenacted by many within the African-American community. On the night before he was assassinated on April 4, 1968, in Memphis, the Rev. Dr. Martin Luther King Jr. gave a final address in Mason Temple that has come to be known as the "I've Been to the Mountaintop Speech." In it he made a direct allusion to the Exodus story by identifying himself with Moses, who was unable to enter the land that God had promised to the Israelites (Deut. 34:1–4): "Like anybody, I would like to live a long life; longevity has its place. But I'm not concerned about that now. I just

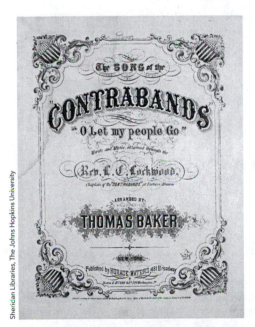

Sheridan Libraries, The Johns Hopkins University

The Exodus has long been a symbol of hope for the African-American community. This edition of the spiritual "Let My People Go" was published in 1862, in the middle of the Civil War.

---

30. The most influential work within the movement is Gustavo Gutierrez, *A Theology of Liberation: History, Politics, and Salvation* (Maryknoll, NY: Orbis, 1973); the original Spanish edition appeared two years earlier.

want to do God's will. And He's allowed me to go up to the mountain. And I've looked over. And I've seen the Promised Land. I may not get there with you. But I want you to know tonight, that we, as a people, will get to the Promised Land."[31]

In recent times, forms of liberation theology have emerged among a variety of marginalized and excluded groups that have turned to the Exodus tradition in their efforts to overcome the obstacles that have prevented them from experiencing the freedom they seek. Among those groups are African-Americans, Native Americans, Palestinians, South Africans, and members of the LGBTQ communities.[32] Probably no other part of the Old Testament has had a more profound effect on people's lives than the story of Moses and the Exodus. Even if it did not actually happen the way the text presents it, the impact of its message of freedom is undeniable and enduring.

A MODERN TAKE ON LIBERATION

Artists have often drawn upon the biblical story of the Exodus to express their views on freedom and liberation. An example can be seen in the song "Freedom (Song for Egypt)," which was written by the musician Wyclef Jean in response to the Egyptian revolution that took place during the height of the Arab Spring in early 2011. Read through the lyrics of the song (http://www.azlyrics.com/lyrics/wyclefjean/freedomsongforegypt.html), and view the video of Wyclef Jean performing it (https://www.youtube.com/watch?v=NgOgCsZ45CQ).

1. How does the song make use of biblical themes and imagery?
2. How is the Exodus motif reimagined to fit the modern Egyptian context?
3. Can you think of other examples of contemporary art that address themes related to liberation?

---

31. For a discussion of the role that the Exodus tradition has played within the African-American community, see the chapter titled "'Let My People Go': Exodus in the African American Experience," in David W. Kling, *The Bible in History: How the Texts Have Shaped the Times* (New York: Oxford University Press, 2006), 193–230.

32. A collection of essays that treats such groups within the United States can be found in Stacey M. Floyd-Thomas and Anthony B. Pinn, eds., *Liberation Theologies in the United States: An Introduction* (New York: New York University Press, 2010). An important work in Palestinian liberation theology is Naim Stifan Ateek, *Justice and Only Justice: A Palestinian Theology of Liberation* (Maryknoll, NY: Orbis, 1989). South African varieties of liberation theology are explored in Gerald O. West, *Biblical Hermeneutics of Liberation: Modes of Reading the Bible in the South African Context*. For an interpretation of the Exodus story from an LGBTQ perspective, see Mona West, "Outsiders, Aliens, and Boundary Crossers: A Queer Reading of the Hebrew Exodus," in *Take Back the Word: A Queer Reading of the Bible*, ed. Robert E. Goss and Mona West (Cleveland: Pilgrim, 2000), 71–81.

Implications and Applications

1. How has your understanding of the Bible changed after reading this chapter?

2. How has your understanding of the Moses story changed after reading this chapter?

3. How is God presented in the texts that treat Moses and the Exodus? Identify the main qualities and features of the deity in these sections and explain how they contribute to the portrait of God that emerges from the Hebrew Bible.

4. How are the human characters presented in the texts that treat Moses and the Exodus? Identify the main qualities and features of human beings in these sections and explain what they suggest about the human condition.

5. Does the miraculous nature of many of the events described in the plagues narrative and Exodus story make them less relevant for modern readers?

6. What issues does the relatively late introduction of the theme of the Exodus into the Bible raise for you?

7. How would the story of the plagues and the Exodus be different if it were retold from the Egyptian perspective?

8. Where is liberation most needed in the world today? Do you think the story of the Exodus has anything to say to that situation?

9. Do the texts discussed in this chapter play a role in shaping your views about human freedom and liberation? If so, how? If not, why not?

4

CHAPTER

Perspectives on the Human Condition

Did you know that every year the American Bible Society issues what it calls its "State of the Bible" report? (Did you know that there is an organization known as the American Bible Society?) It is based on the results of a telephone and on-line survey the group conducts, in which approximately two thousand Americans are asked questions about their perceptions and use of the Bible. Each spring they release a lengthy document with lots of fancy pie charts and detailed analysis that offers a fascinating overview of the survey's findings. Here is a fun fact that you might not have known: the average number of Bibles in each American household is 4.4. That includes households that self-identify as having no faith. No other tome comes close to matching that type of presence on our bookshelves and coffee tables, and that number explains why business is booming for Bible publishers. The annual American Bible Society report is a must-read for those who like to keep a finger on the pulse of the nation's complex relationship with the Good Book.[1]

The latest report has some interesting things to say about what people think regarding the Bible's relevance for their daily lives. Just about one-half (49 percent) of all Americans believe that the Bible contains all one needs to know to live a meaningful life. Among those who had read the Bible at least once during the previous week, a whopping 93 percent gave some thought or a lot of thought to how the Bible applies to their lives. Among those who had heard the Bible read in the previous week, the percentage did not reach that level but was still quite high (78 percent). Those numbers have remained more or less consistent in similar surveys the American Bible Society has conducted in recent years.

The takeaway from those results is that a lot of people are of the opinion that the Bible can serve as a guide or manual for how to live what Aristotle and his philosophical heirs have referred to as "the good life." What many folks probably have in mind when they think of the Bible in this way are the countless

---

1. The most recent "State of the Bible" reports can be found at *http://www.americanbible.org* under the link titled "Bible Resources."

commands and prohibitions that are found within it—the dos and don'ts, the thou shalts and thou shalt nots that pepper the pages of certain books like Exodus, Leviticus, and parts of the New Testament. All one needs to do, so the logic goes, is to act as the Bible teaches and all will work out in the end.

As important as the question "What is the good life?" might be, a prior and more fundamental query is, "What is life?" The answer to that question, as hard as it might be to discover, can help determine the quantity and quality of goodness (and badness) that a particular life contains. In other words, once the purpose and nature of life have been identified, we are in a better position to ascertain whether one's life is good or not so good. This question is the topic of this chapter, as we try to get a handle on the biblical view of the exhilarating and frustrating experience of being alive that we all share. To wit, what is the Old Testament's view of human nature?

Two of the most insightful and sustained attempts in the Bible to wrestle head-on with that question are found in the books of Job and Qohelet.[2] Each work features a protagonist who is trying to come to terms with circumstances that make no sense to him and that do not mesh with his conception of how things work. As each reflects upon his situation, he reaches certain conclusions about the way of the world and humanity's place within it. In both cases the problem is resolved, but here's the kicker: Job and Qohelet are the Bible's equivalent of actress Scarlett Johansson and her twin brother Hunter. They start out in more or less the same place, but end up worlds apart. Qohelet's view of the mystery of life is one that Job would have a hard time signing off on, and vice versa. In short, this is one of those topics—and there are more of them than many people realize—about which the biblical literature sends mixed messages, and that should caution us against making blanket claims about what the Bible "says" or teaches.[3]

First Impressions

Job and Qohelet are two of the three books of the Old Testament that are commonly identified as "wisdom writings," the other being the book of Proverbs.[4] These works are given that designation because of certain features they share with examples of a literary genre found throughout the ancient Near East that is known as wisdom literature. Wisdom works take a variety of forms, but they all attempt to explore and understand aspects of common human experience whose

2. In most English translations, Qohelet is titled Ecclesiastes; this will be discussed later in the chapter.

3. For more on this issue, see the chapter titled "'In this Corner . . .': Competing Perspectives," in John Kaltner and Steven L. McKenzie, *The Back Door Introduction to the Bible* (Winona, MN: Anselm Academic, 2012), 141–54.

4. The Roman Catholic and Greek Orthodox canons would include two more: Wisdom and Sirach. These books are not found in the Hebrew Bible, and Bibles intended for use by Protestants typically do not include them.

meaning and purpose are elusive or mysterious, like pain, suffering, and death. A question that frequently underlies wisdom literature is, "Why are things the way they are?"[5]

Posing such questions might seem a waste of time because there are often no satisfactory answers to them, but that has never stopped people from asking. Such questions often cross our minds as we struggle to make sense of some problem or tragedy (real or imagined) that we have had to confront. This is a universal reaction because it is in our nature to reflect on our circumstances and grapple with what it means to be a human being, especially when things are messy or confusing. Whenever we do so, we are engaging in a time-honored intellectual activity that can be traced back to the earliest stages of recorded history.

Among the ancient thinkers who sought answers to life's enigmatic questions are the authors of Job and Qohelet, who took on two of the thorniest and most irresolvable issues that people have ever pondered. For Job, the question was the existence of innocent suffering. Why do some people experience untold pain and misfortune through no fault of their own? For Qohelet, the question was existence itself. What is this mortal coil we all inhabit called life, and why is it so arbitrary and unfair?

Job Gets Jobbed

At forty-two chapters, Job is the longest of the three wisdom books in the Old Testament. It has a bookend or "sandwich" arrangement in which a prose prologue (1:1–2:13) and epilogue (42:7–17) surround a much longer central part that is written in poetry (3:1–42:6). The prose sections relate a classic example of a reversal story that describes the loss of Job's personal possessions and family in the prologue and their restoration to him in the epilogue. The poetry section presents a conversation between Job and three of his friends (a fourth person joins them toward the end), during which they debate the reasons for Job's losses. The poetic material has its own arrangement with three cycles of speeches in which Job speaks, his first friend (Eliphaz) responds, Job speaks again, his second friend (Bildad) responds, Job speaks once again, and his third friend (Zophar) responds. The third cycle is incomplete since Bildad's speech is quite brief and Zophar doesn't speak at all.[6]

---

5. A good overview of the biblical wisdom material can be found in James L. Crenshaw, *Old Testament Wisdom: An Introduction* (Louisville: Westminster John Knox, 2010), and David Penchansky, *Understanding Wisdom Literature: Conflict and Dissonance in the Hebrew Text* (Grand Rapids: Eerdmans, 2012).

6. There are many studies and commentaries on the book of Job, including Robert Gordis, *The Book of Job: Commentary, New Translation, Special Studies* (New York: The Jewish Theological Seminary of America, 2011); Gustavo Gutiérrez, *On Job: God Talk and the Suffering of the Innocent* (Maryknoll, NY: Orbis, 1987); Kathleen M. O'Connor, *Job* (Collegeville, MN: Liturgical Press, 2012); and C. L. Seow, *Job: Interpretation and Commentary* (Grand Rapids: Eerdmans, 2013).

The Prose

READ: Job 1:1–2:13; 42:7–17

The prologue begins with an introduction that provides background on Job's character (1:1–5). Its opening sentence sounds like the beginning of a fairy tale: "There was once a man in the land of Uz whose name was Job." We are then told what kind of person he is: "That man was blameless and upright, one who feared God and turned away from evil." Some details follow about his family and possessions, and the list of his property makes it clear that he is a prominent and important individual in society. Just so no doubt is left in the reader's mind about his standing, Job is described as "the greatest of all the people of the east" (1:3).

Job's sterling reputation extends to his role as a family patriarch. All ten of his children regularly socialize together, and Job presents offerings on their behalf just in case they might have sinned or done something wrong. His children's welfare is always foremost in his mind because, "this is what Job always did" (1:5). This is about as close as the Bible comes to describing a family that could star in a sappy 1950s television sitcom like *Ozzie and Harriet* or *Leave it to Beaver*, but the story quickly takes a *Simpsons*-like turn as things get ugly and head south.

> What purpose might the opening section of the book of Job serve?

The bulk of the rest of the prologue is composed of two scenes that describe how Job loses his possessions, his family, and his health, in that order (1:6–22; 2:1–10). They are mirror images of one another, and the scenes' parallel structure is tipped off by the identical words that begin each one: "One day the heavenly beings came to present themselves before the Lord, and [the] Satan also came among them" (1:6; 2:1).[7] In both cases this statement is followed by a scene that contains the following elements: (1) God and the Satan converse about what the latter has been doing; (2) God singles out Job as an outstanding servant and believer; (3) the Satan issues a dare that would allow him to harm Job; (4) God agrees to the dare after setting the terms of the contest; (5) the Satan leaves; (6) the scene shifts to earth, where Job experiences tragedy; (7) Job maintains his faith in God.

The main differences between the two scenes are in the third and fourth elements. The first time around, the Satan tells God that the only reason Job is such a good servant is because nothing bad has happened to him, but he will turn on a dime as soon as he experiences hardship (1:11). God takes up the Satan's challenge and gives him control over all that Job has, with the stipulation that Job not be physically harmed in any way. The Satan agrees to this

---

7. The NRSV translation does not include the word "the" before "Satan," although it is present in the Hebrew text. It is included here for reasons that will become obvious later in this chapter.

condition, and in a series of rapid-fire disasters Job loses his animals, servants, and children. This does not shake Job's faith or resolve, so the Satan has to go to plan B. In the second scene, he suggests that if God ups the ante Job will show his true colors (2:5). The deity allows Job to be physically harmed provided that he not be killed, and the Satan returns to earth to afflict Job with painful sores all over his body. Once again Job remains faithful, and refuses to follow his wife's recommendation that he "curse God, and die" (2:9). As the prologue draws to a close, Job is now bereft of his possessions, his family, and his health, and his three friends arrive to commiserate with him and try to cheer him up.

Over on the other side of the poetry, the epilogue is a relatively brief account of the reversal of Job's misfortune. It opens with God chastising the three friends because they did not speak well of God as Job had, and they then obey God's command to sacrifice animals to atone for their offense (42:7–9). This is followed by a description of how Job's final days were more blessed than the earlier ones, as he receives twice as many animals as he owned before and he fathers ten more children. According to the book's final verses, Job died at the age of one hundred and forty years, and he lived to see four generations of descendants. In a nice touch, the book ends with the same fairy-tale feel with which it began: "And Job died, old and full of days" (42:17).

By this point, you might be wondering why the definite article "the" has been used with the word "Satan." Simply put, its inclusion more accurately conveys what the Hebrew text says. In the original language, each time this figure is identified as *ha-satan*, with the Hebrew particle *ha* being the equivalent of English "the." Many English translations render the term as simply "Satan," but to do so runs the risk of confusing readers and introducing an element into the story that does not belong there. In the English language, the word "Satan" is generally considered to be a proper name, an alias for the devil, the personification of evil.[8] The modern understanding of Satan is a much later development that would not have made sense to ancient readers, and to interpret the story in light of it is to engage in *eisegesis*, or reading something into a text that isn't there.

> How serious a mistake do you think it would be to equate the Satan figure in Job with the devil?

The Hebrew word *satan* means "accuser" or "adversary," and it is used in Job to describe a figure who is charged with monitoring what is happening on earth. The references at the beginning of each scene to the heavenly beings, including the Satan, gathering before the Lord likely reflects the common belief throughout the ancient Near East in the existence of a divine court composed of angels and others who assisted God (1:6; 2:1). The details of the

---

8. This identification can be seen in the venerable Oxford English Dictionary, where the first meaning for "Satan" is "the proper name of the supreme evil spirit, the Devil."

text suggest that it was the Satan's role to keep an eye on what people were doing on earth and to report back to God. In effect, "Satan" is a job description and not a name. At a later point in the biblical period, as seen in the New Testament, the Satan figure becomes more closely associated with the devil, but that is not yet the case here.[9]

What Do You Know?

The reader naturally feels a great deal of sympathy for Job. We are told in the opening verses that he is a good man who believes in God and takes care of his family. It is possible that his financial and social success can be directly attributed to those personal qualities. Nonetheless, unspeakable tragedies befall the man as all he holds near and dear is stripped from him and he is reduced to sitting on an ash heap trying to scrape the scabs and sores off his body with a piece of broken pottery (2:7–8). His reputation appears to be squeaky-clean, and so this is not an example of "what goes around, comes around"; Job is not simply getting what he deserves.

There is an additional reason why we feel for Job: we know something he does not know. The manipulation of knowledge is a powerful tool in an author's bag of tricks, and figuring out who knows what helps to determine the kind of story you are reading. If the character knows more than the reader we have the makings of a mystery, and the reader is drawn into the story in a quest to fill in the missing knowledge to discover whodunit. The flip side is when the reader knows more than the character, which creates suspense as the reader wants to warn the character not to open that closet door, where her would-be killer is waiting. A third type of reading position is one in which the character and the reader acquire knowledge at more or less the same time, which helps to establish a connection and bond between the two in the reader's mind.

The way that knowledge is parceled out and withheld is a fascinating dimension of storytelling, and the next time you read a story or watch a movie, pay attention to what you know and when you know it in relation to the characters. It will open up new ways of thinking about what you read on the page or see on the screen. Most narratives move back and forth between the three different reading positions mentioned above, and the story of Job is no different. Sometimes it is a character-elevating situation, as Job knows more than we do. For example, we have no idea how he is going to react to the tragedies that come his way. In other places, the situation is even-handed, as we and Job gain knowledge at the same time. This is what happens when the messengers come to tell

---

9. Sometimes in the Bible the word *satan* refers to a normal person and not a supernatural being. An example of this is in 1 Kings 11:14, where Solomon's enemy is clearly a human being: "Then the Lord raised up an adversary (*satan*) against Solomon, Hadad the Edomite; he was of the royal house in Edom."

him that he has lost all his possessions and his family, heartbreaking news that he and we receive together. Elsewhere the reading position is reader-elevating, as we the readers are privy to information that Job lacks. The clearest examples of this in the prologue are the two scenes in the heavenly court, where God and the Satan come up with their plan to test Job. The reader is on top of things every step of the way, but poor Job doesn't have clue one about what has been agreed upon behind his back. An intriguing dimension of the story is that Job remains in the dark permanently, since there is no indication that he ever learns about the conversations between the Satan and God.

Questioning God

The conversations between God and the Satan, as the author tells the story, are disturbing, especially in how they portray the divine character. They have the feel of a backroom bargain being struck, with each party wheeling and dealing to get what he wants. The Satan wishes to expose Job as a fraud whose wholesome and faithful demeanor is just a façade that will crumble at the first whiff of adversity. God, on the other hand, is intent on putting the lie to the Satan's claim by having Job demonstrate that even in the midst of hardship he truly is who he appears to be.

Why would God enter into such an arrangement with the Satan? God already knows that Job is a good person, something the reader learns in the book's very first verse, so why not just leave well enough alone? The text does not tell us what motivates God to enter into the pact with the Satan, and so we are left to speculate about its cause. Is God not completely convinced of Job's sincerity? Does he perhaps wonder along with the Satan about what kind of person Job really is? If so, that seems to point to a lack of omniscience on the deity's part. Has God been tricked or manipulated by the Satan to do something he normally would not do? This would also place limitations on God, who seemingly would not have complete control and authority over the created world. Maybe God is well aware of Job's true character and is completely confident that Job will remain faithful no matter what comes his way, and so he enters into the contest as a way of demonstrating this to the Satan and putting him in his place. If that is the case, it raises important questions about the treatment of Job. Why would God permit pain to be inflicted on a blameless and upright person who is forced to twist in the wind just so the Satan can be proved wrong? Another possibility is that God is testing Job by sending all these punishments his way in order to make him stronger or instruct him about life. If so, it seems like a harsh and cruel ordeal to put someone through just to prove a point or teach a lesson.

> Does Job's lack of knowledge about the deal between God and the Satan raise any theological issues for you?

Some unanswered questions remain as this happily-ever-after ending draws the book to a close. What would Job's first set of children think about the way things turn out? Was Job still the same person after these experiences? How would Job react if he were to find out about the deals that God made with the Satan? Does the epilogue satisfactorily resolve the story of Job?

> Can you think of any other reasons why God would allow Job to suffer?

The Poetry

READ: Job 3–11; 38:1–42:6

As already noted, the bulk of the poetic portion of the book is comprised of an extended conversation between Job and his three friends, consisting of three cycles, the third of which is incomplete. That discussion is abruptly ended in chapters 32 through 37, when a young man named Elihu weighs in with his views. This leads directly into a lengthy speech by God in chapters 38 through 41 that is briefly interrupted by Job in 40:3–5 and concluded by Job's second response in 42:1–6. The primary topic of all this material is the reason for Job's suffering, as each character (God included) offers a perspective on its cause. In this way, the poetry is in the form of a disputation in which various opinions are expressed and debated in the hope of reaching a deeper understanding, if not agreement, about the matter at hand.

A Tale of Two Jobs

There is a striking difference in the way Job's character is presented in the prose and the poetry portions of the book. The accepting, even docile, Job of the prose is replaced by someone who is much more combative and aggressive in the poetry. This can be seen in the initial words he utters in reaction to the situation in which he finds himself. Upon being informed of the loss of his animals and his children in the prologue, he replies, "Naked I came from my mother's womb, and naked shall I return there; the LORD gave, and the LORD has taken away; blessed be the name of the LORD" (1:21). He strikes a similar note in the next chapter after he is tormented with sores all over his body and his wife tells him to curse God (2:10): "You speak as any foolish woman would speak. Shall we receive the good at the hand of God, and not receive the bad?" How different his tone is in the poetry when his very first words also make reference to his mother's womb, but in order to rail against his circumstances.

> How can we explain the differences between the Job of the prose and the Job of the poetry?

After this Job opened his mouth and cursed the day of his birth. Job said:
"Let the day perish in which I was born,
and the night that said, 'A man-child is conceived.'
Let that day be darkness!
May God above not seek it, or light shine on it.
Let gloom and deep darkness claim it.
Let clouds settle upon it; let the blackness of the day terrify it.
That night—let thick darkness seize it!
Let it not rejoice among the days of the year;
let it not come into the number of the months.
Yes, let that night be barren;
let no joyful cry be heard in it.
Let those curse it who curse the Sea,
those who are skilled to rouse up Leviathan.
Let the stars of its dawn be dark;
let it hope for light, but have none;
may it not see the eyelids of the morning—
because it did not shut the doors of my mother's womb,
and hide trouble from my eyes." (3:1–10)

It is hard to imagine the Job of the prologue speaking those words, but this is the manner he adopts throughout much of the poetry. Rather than passively accept his new situation, as he does in the prose, here Job tells his friends that God has entrapped him and has treated him unjustly (3:23; 19:5–7). He repeatedly protests that he is innocent and has done nothing to deserve the torment he is experiencing (9:11–24; 12:4–6; 23:10–12). Job is particularly troubled by the double standard he sees in the world around him; the evildoers in society prosper and are not held accountable for their actions, while good people like him suffer for no apparent reason (21:7–26).

Chapter 31 is the most impressive self-defense Job mounts in the entire book. He begins by pointing out the absurdity of his situation, since he is being treated in a way that his actions do not warrant and God is well aware of this (31:2–4). In the remainder of the chapter he proposes fifteen different hypothetical scenarios that would find him guilty of some social or religious infraction, and each one is posed in a way that suggests he would never do such a thing: "If I have raised my hand against the orphan, because I saw I had supporters at the gate; then let my shoulder blade fall from my shoulder, and let my arm be broken from its socket. For I was in terror of calamity from God, and I could not have faced his majesty" (31:21–23).

Job's friends aren't buying any of it, because they are sure that Job must have done something to deserve what he is getting. The first speaker, Eliphaz, gets the ball rolling in that direction with his questions and observations: "Think now, who that was innocent ever perished? Or where were the upright cut off?

In William Blake's *The Book of Job* (1825), Job's three friends accuse him of having sinned against God, for God would not allow a righteous person to suffer. But the reader knows that Job has done nothing wrong.

As I have seen, those who plow iniquity and sow trouble reap the same. By the breath of God they perish, and by the blast of his anger they are consumed" (4:7–9). In other words, "Come on, Job, own up to what you've done! Do you take us for fools?" They go on to offer some examples of the sort of offenses he might be guilty of (22:4–11), and they advise him to come clean and throw himself on God's mercy (8:1–6) because everyone knows it would be foolish for a guilty person like Job to think he can get away with it (20:1–11). The latecomer, Elihu, also joins in the fray and asks Job to exercise his good judgment (34:10–12).

Job will have none of it, though, and continues to maintain his innocence. In several places, he frames things in legal terms and states that he wants his day in court.

> Today also my complaint is bitter;
> his hand is heavy despite my groaning.
> Oh, that I knew where I might find him,
> that I might come even to his dwelling!
> I would lay my case before him,
> and fill my mouth with arguments.
> I would learn what he would answer me,
> and understand what he would say to me.
> Would he contend with me in the greatness of his power?
> No; but he would give heed to me.
> There an upright person could reason with him,
> and I should be acquitted forever by my judge. (23:2–7; cf. 13:3; 31:35)

A Questioning God

A hearing before God is what Job wants, and a hearing is what he gets. Things do not go according to plan, though, because Job is the one who does most of the listening. In chapters 38 through 41, God finally responds to Job's concerns by delivering the deity's longest speech in the entire Old Testament. It is a real stemwinder, interrupted only by Job's brief comment in 40:3–5. It also gives Job a taste of his own medicine. He initiated the conversation with a series of questions he wanted answered, but God turns the tables by firing off question after question back at Job. There are about sixty of them throughout the four chapters, and they are all of the rhetorical variety. In other words, their purpose is to make a point rather than to request information, and after the first few questions that point is painfully obvious: "Where were you when I laid the foundation of the earth? Tell me, if you have understanding. Who determined its measurements—surely you know! Or who stretched the line upon it?" (38:4–5).

> What do you think of God's strategy of answering Job's questions with more questions?

The words drip with sarcasm, and as the questions pile up it becomes apparent why Job has so little to say in this section of the book. The barrage of queries concerns matters related to creation and the natural world, about which Job has no knowledge or experience, and if he were to attempt to reply he would be reduced to sputtering the same non-responses over and over again: "No, of course I can't." "You got me again there." "Only you can do that, Lord." As the interrogation mercifully comes to an end, Job raises the white flag and concedes that he has met his match: "I know that you can do all things, and that no purpose of yours can be thwarted. . . . Therefore I have uttered what I did not understand, things too wonderful for me, which I did not know. . . . I had heard of you by the hearing of the ear, but now my eye sees you; therefore I despise myself, and repent in dust and ashes" (42:2–6).

In the next verse, God says to Job's three friends, "You have not spoken of me what is right, as my servant Job has" (42:7). How did Job speak rightly of God? What does he know now that he did not know earlier? How has he changed? The answers to these questions are tied to Job's new understanding of life and the way the world works. Prior to this, he had a view of things that was quite predictable and based on the principle of cause and effect. He (and his friends) believed that if he lived a good life and did the right things, he would be rewarded. Conversely, according to this way of thinking, those who do the wrong things will suffer the consequences. There is a logical dimension to human existence: you get out of it what you put into it. This can be thought of as a litmus-test view of life. If certain qualities and elements are present in the way you live, a positive outcome is more or less guaranteed. If they are not there, you are out of luck. By that reasoning, Job's life should have been one big success story, but things didn't work out that way. His experiences, especially his encounter with God, taught him that litmus-test logic is not the way the world works, and he became the wiser for it.

A Full-Time Job

Read: Qohelet 1–12

If Job has a doppelgänger in the biblical literature, it can be found just a few books away in Qohelet, whose author struggles with many of the same issues regarding everyday existence and the purpose of life. Their shared interest in existential questions and the similar ways they probe them are among the reasons why both books are categorized as wisdom literature. In each work, common human experiences become the springboard to explore gnawing mysteries that continue to haunt people and that have caused sleepless nights for millennia, but Qohelet's musings led him to some pretty dark places that Job probably never dreamed of going near. He is the alpha Job whose troubled ruminations ratchet things up several notches in the anxiety department, but they do not result in the quasi-happy ending that comes Job's way. As far as we know, Qohelet never had his day in court with God like Job did, and so he remained consigned to a life of unending speculation that lacked a resolution.[10]

An Elusive Author

Who is the person behind this book that is generally held to be the most pessimistic read in the entire Bible? We are not completely sure. Early on, the reader is left with the impression that the author is a member of royalty, but that idea soon falls by the wayside. The very first verse of the book identifies him as "the son of David, king in Jerusalem," and his blue-blood status is reinforced in several other places (1:12; 2:4–10, 12), but after the second chapter it is not mentioned again. The reference to him as the son of David and the description of his tremendous wealth suggest that he is none other than the great king Solomon, whose reign is recounted in the first eleven chapters of 1 Kings. The allusions to his wisdom (1:13, 16–18; 2:3, 9, 12–15, 19, 21) also point in the same direction, since this is a trait that is commonly associated with Solomon, as seen in 1 Kings 3 and elsewhere. But Solomon is never mentioned by name anywhere in the book, and in all likelihood this is an example of a practice that was fairly common among ancient Near Eastern authors of associating a text with an important figure from the past in order to give it more status and significance.

The first verse is a superscription or title that provides us with further information about the author: "The words of the Teacher, the son of David, king in Jerusalem." The word translated as "teacher" is the Hebrew term *qohelet*, from which the name of the book is derived. Within the Bible it is found only in

---

10. Among the commentaries and studies on the book of Qohelet are Eric S. Christianson, *Ecclesiastes through the Centuries* (Malden: Blackwell, 2007); James L. Crenshaw, *Ecclesiastes: A Commentary* (Louisville: Westminster John Knox, 1987); Michael V. Fox, *The JPS Bible Commentary: Ecclesiastes* (Philadelphia: Jewish Publication Society, 2004); and James Limburg, *Encountering Ecclesiastes: A Book for Our Time* (Grand Rapids: Eerdmans, 2006).

this book, where it appears seven times (1:1, 2, 12; 7:27; 12:8, 9, 10). The English translation "teacher" is a bit misleading, since the Hebrew root the word comes from has the basic meaning of "to gather," especially to describe people being gathered together. A more accurate translation of the title would be "the gatherer," perhaps in reference to the role someone plays in bringing others into some type of assembly.[11] It is also possible that the term is being used in connection with the great amount of wealth or wisdom the author has accumulated in his lifetime.

The book is also commonly known as Ecclesiastes. This word comes from the Septuagint, the ancient Greek translation of the Bible, and it is based on how the Hebrew *qohelet* is rendered in Greek (*ekklēsiastēs*). That term also describes someone who is in charge of a congregation or assembly, and so it is semantically close to the Hebrew original. The book is rarely referred to as "Ecclesiastes" within Judaism, but it is a common way of identifying it in Christianity because of the important role the Septuagint has played within the Christian community throughout history.

An Unambiguous Message

The overall structure of Qohelet somewhat mirrors that of Job with its three-part arrangement of a prologue, a central portion, and an epilogue. The key difference is that while the opening and closing sections of Qohelet are fairly well defined, there is very little agreement on how the middle portion is organized and should be divided up. The book's first eleven verses comprise its opening section. The one-verse superscription mentioned above, which identifies the author, is followed by a brief statement of the same length that introduces a central theme of the book: "Vanity of vanities, says the Teacher, vanity of vanities! All is vanity" (1:2). This verse will be treated in detail below, but for now its obvious use of repetition should be noted. The word "vanity," whose meaning will be discussed shortly, is repeated again and again throughout the rest of the book.

The remainder of the opening section is a poem that functions in a way similar to a musical prelude that introduces melodies and rhythmic motifs that will recur throughout the rest of the composition. In these nine verses, Qohelet offers observations about life and the world that he will circle back to time and again in the remainder of the book.

> What do people gain from all the toil at which they toil under the sun?
> A generation goes, and a generation comes, but the earth remains forever.
> The sun rises and the sun goes down, and hurries to the place where
>   it rises.
> The wind blows to the south, and goes around to the north;

---

11. Strictly speaking, "gatherer," rather than "the gatherer," would be closer to the way the term is used in the book, since it is found with the Hebrew definite article ("the") only one time (12:8).

round and round goes the wind, and on its circuits the wind returns.
All streams run to the sea, but the sea is not full;
to the place where the streams flow, there they continue to flow.
All things are wearisome; more than one can express;
the eye is not satisfied with seeing, or the ear filled with hearing.
What has been is what will be, and what has been done is what will
    be done;
there is nothing new under the sun.
Is there a thing of which it is said, "See, this is new?"
It has already been, in the ages before us.
The people of long ago are not remembered,
nor will there be any remembrance
of people yet to come by those who come after them. (1:3–11)

This dreary assessment of the world we inhabit paints a pretty un-rosy picture of the way things are: pointless, cyclical, static, predictable, boring, and unchanging. That's life in a nutshell, at least according to Qohelet. His view of humanity in the last couple of lines is particularly harsh, since he sees us as nothing but a bunch of insignificant and anonymous nobodies who are forgotten soon after we bite the dust.

> Can you find anything positive in Qohelet's poem in 1:3-11?

At first that bleak appraisal might sound like a gross exaggeration, but let's stop for a moment and think about those last two lines within the context of our own lives. How many of your grandparents did you get to know? If you are like most people, probably at least two or three of them lived long enough to see you get your driver's license or go on your first date. How about your great-grandparents? Here the numbers drop off dramatically. Even if one of them was still around when you joined the family, how well did you really know one another? We do not even need to push things back further to your great-great-grandparents, so that is two generations (counting your parents), three tops, with which you have had personal contact. Extend things out in the other direction, and odds are you will live to see your own grandkids and, if you are lucky, a great-grandchild or two. But beyond that, the chances are slim to none. Modern technology allows us to record images and messages that presumably will be available in the future, but will that be the same as being remembered? Let's face the facts. Within a few short decades after our deaths, the vast majority of us will be forgotten. Maybe Qohelet had a point.

The closing section of the book begins with a reminder to enjoy what life has to offer before it's too late (11:7–12:7). In several places this message is directed specifically to young people, and it is presented in a way that suggests that the author is looking back on his own life and drawing upon his experiences as he shares his wisdom with the next generation (12:1). This is followed by a one-verse statement that is almost identical to the one in the opening section in 1:2: "Vanity of vanities, says the Teacher; all is vanity" (12:8). While the key terms "vanity/vanities" are found three times instead of five times, as in the first chapter, the use of repetition and the verse's connection to the earlier one are obvious. In this way, the two verses serve as a frame that opens and closes the book and unites it by highlighting the central theme that runs through the text. The ending of Qohelet is a two-part epilogue (12:9–11, 12–14) whose most important feature is a theological perspective that is at odds with the message found in the rest of the book. The point of these final words and what they suggest about the history of the text will be discussed below.

Vanity Unfair

Have you ever wondered what bestselling song has the oldest lyrics? If so, you came to the right place to answer that question when you opened your Bible to the book of Qohelet. The first eight verses of chapter 3 should be at least vaguely familiar to even the most tone-deaf among us, since it was the inspiration for one of the biggest hits in rock and roll history and it continues to get a lot of airtime on the radio. "Turn! Turn! Turn! (To Everything There Is a Season)" was written in the 1950s by the legendary folksinger and activist Pete Seeger as a peace anthem. In the next decade, it was recorded by the rock group The Byrds, whose version soared to the top of the charts, thus earning it the distinction of being the number one song with the oldest lyrics. It was a "golden oldie" the day it was released.

> For everything there is a reason, and a time for every matter under heaven:
> a time to be born, and a time to die;
> a time to plant, and a time to pluck up what is planted;
> a time to kill, and a time to heal;
> a time to break down, and a time to build up;
> a time to weep, and a time to laugh;
> a time to mourn, and a time to dance;
> a time to throw away stones, and a time to gather stones together;
> a time to embrace, and a time to refrain from embracing;
> a time to seek, and a time to lose;
> a time to keep, and a time to throw away;
> a time to tear, and a time to sew;
> a time to keep silence, and a time to speak;
> a time to love, and a time to hate;
> a time for war, and a time for peace. (3:1–8)

When you read those verses, especially out loud, you cannot help but feel there is a song somewhere in there waiting to break out, so it is not surprising that Pete Seeger chose this particular passage to put to music.[12] The steady rhythm and repetition ("A time for this, a time for that . . .") create a sense of predictability and inevitability that is at the heart of his book's message. The impression is that human beings are in the hands of a fate that is greater than

> What feelings or thoughts does the poem in 3:1-8 leave you with?

they are, and all they can do is respond in the appropriate way based on what "time" it is.

Like The Byrds and Pete Seeger before him, Qohelet was not a one-hit wonder, since several other things he penned have stood the test of time and have continued to resonate into the modern day like a tune that is stuck in your head. One note that reverberates throughout his entire book is the term "vanity/vanities" mentioned earlier, which is repeated in the opening and closing sections (1:2; 12:8). The word appears seventy-six times in the Old Testament, with exactly one-half of those occurrences (38) found here in Qohelet. That is a very high concentration, and its frequent usage suggests that it is a key to understanding what the book is all about.

There is a problem, though, in that it is easy to misunderstand what the term means. In modern parlance, vanity is most often a quality associated with a "vain" person, someone who is conceited, narcissistic, egotistic, and self-centered. This is the way the term typically used today, but many people do not realize that it has another meaning. That other sense is best seen in the phrase "in vain," as in, "The Red Sox tried in vain to move ahead of the Yankees during the last week of the season, but New York's lead was too big for them to overcome." In this case vanity has to do with something that is futile or pointless, and that is the way it is used in Qohelet.

The Hebrew word that is translated "vanity" is *hebel*, which can also describe a breath or a vapor. Just as each breath we take is passing and fleeting, so too does *hebel* refer to something that is temporary, transitory, and ephemeral. So when Qohelet says something is "vanity," he is making a comment about its short-lived, momentary, and ultimately

> What is your reaction to Qohelet's idea that everything is hebel, or vanity?

worthless nature.[13] The "frame" verses at the beginning and the end of the book make it clear that Qohelet evaluates everything in this way—"All is vanity" (1:2; 12:8)—but throughout the text he identifies specific elements of human life that

---

12. It's interesting to compare the biblical text with the lyrics that Seeger wrote. The differences are not very significant, but they clearly show his editorial process at work and they are likely due to the fact that he was crafting an anti-war song. The lyrics are available at this link: *http://www.lyricsfreak.com/b/byrds/turn ι turn ι turn_20026419.html.*

13. *Hebel* is also the Hebrew name of Adam and Eve's son Abel, which is a not-so-subtle way the author lets the reader know that this character will not be around for long.

he labels as *hebel*. Among these are all deeds done under the sun (1:14; 2:11, 17); enjoyment (2:1); the fact that his descendants will get what he has worked for (2:19, 21; 6:2); the pain and vexation of life (2:23); human envy and jealousy (4:4); human toil and work (4:8); the fact that people are forgotten when they die (4:16); human desire (6:9); the laughter of fools (7:6); the way the good are punished while the wicked prosper (8:10, 14); the fact that good people and wicked people both die (9:1–3); and youth itself (11:10). Qohelet has a decidedly pessimistic view of life, and in *hebel* he found the perfect word to help him express its pointlessness and emptiness.[14]

If that's all there is, what's a person to do? Qohelet's advice is a surefire hit with college students and working stiffs everywhere: kick back, enjoy the ride, and don't sweat the small (or big) stuff. He suggests that we might as well turn our attention to other pursuits that can help us pass the time enjoyably as we make our way along this long strange trip called life. And for Qohelet that entails all the ingredients that would have gone into the ancient Near Eastern equivalent of a barbecue: food, drink, and friends. Interspersed throughout the book is a refrain that is a slacker's call to inaction as Qohelet counsels us to think of life as one long Fourth of July weekend: "So I commend enjoyment, for there is nothing better for people under the sun than to eat, and drink, and enjoy themselves, for this will go with them in their toil through the days of life that God gives them under the sun" (8:15; cf. 2:24; 3:12–13, 22; 5:18; 9:7–10; 11:7–10).

> Is Qohelet's advice to "eat, drink, and be merry" a good philosophy of life?

An Awesome Absence

The reference to God in that verse raises the important question of the image of the deity that is put forward in the book. Qohelet believes that the proper attitude a person should adopt toward God is one that is often translated as "fear" in English (5:7; 7:18; 8:12; 12:12–14). Here, too, it is important to avoid giving this word a meaning that would read something into the text that is not there. In these passages, fear of God is not meant to convey a sense of terror or fright, nor is it a phobia that creates a feeling of dread and anxiety within a person. It is rather a state of mind that is filled with awe or reverence before the power and majesty of God. Fear of God is a common motif throughout wisdom literature in the ancient Near East, as can be seen in the first verse of the book of Job: "There once was a man in the land of Uz whose name was Job. That man was blameless and upright, one who feared God and turned away from evil" (Job 1:1; cf. 1:8; 2:3; 28:28).

---

14. For a book-length treatment of the term *hebel*, see Douglas B. Miller, *Symbol and Rhetoric in Ecclesiastes: The Place of Hebel in Qohelet's Work* (Atlanta: Society of Biblical Literature, 2003).

Qohelet believes that the only appropriate attitude toward God is fear and awe because, for him, the deity is incomprehensible and inscrutable. It is impossible to determine God's purpose or motive in anything, and that is a big reason why life remains a bewildering enigma: "I have seen the business that God has given to everyone to be busy with. He has made everything suitable for its time; moreover he has put a sense of past and future into their minds, yet they cannot find out what God has done from the beginning to the end" (3:10–11).

> What is your reaction to Qohelet's view of God?

The deity is mentioned quite a few times throughout the book, but there are virtually no references to the covenant or the nuts and bolts of Israelite worship. God is responsible for all that humans have and do, but the book never suggests that there is a special relationship between the two. We may be as dependent upon God as a child is on its parents, but the deity's ways are so far beyond ours that an unpassable chasm separates us: "Just as you do not know how the breath comes to the bones in the mother's womb, so you do not know the work of God, who makes everything" (11:5; cf. 1:13; 2:24–26; 3:12–19; 5:18–20; 7:13–14, 29; 9:7).[15]

Given this understanding of God as distant and aloof, it is not surprising that Qohelet is not keen on the idea of divine/human interaction (5:2). He is quick to take his own advice; he never addresses God directly or tries to initiate a conversation with the deity. And the favor is returned, since God does not speak in the book. This is in contrast to what happens in Job, where the main character keeps badgering the deity for a conversation until God finally takes the bait. The two have a lengthy talk that eventually resolves the differences between them, and each one comes away having learned something about the other. It is hard to imagine such an exchange taking place between Qohelet and God. What would they talk about? Qohelet believes that he and God have nothing in common, and that it would be a complete waste of time to try to interact with one another, since the two of them do not even speak the same language. And so, unlike Job, he never gets an answer to the perplexing questions that continue to confound him.

Life as Lottery

If you have ever consulted a Magic 8 Ball, spun a roulette wheel, flipped a coin, or played bingo, you have a fairly good sense of Qohelet's view of life. There is not much skill or strategy involved, and it pretty much all boils down to fate and dumb luck. As far as he is concerned, the random nature of human existence gives it a hit-or-miss quality that is no more predictable than a game

---

15. For more on Qohelet's view of God, see Stephan de Jong, "God in the Book of Qohelet: A Reappraisal of Qohelet's Place in Old Testament Theology," *Vetus Testamentum* 47, no. 2 (1997): 154–67.

of chance. Call it the "life-as-lottery" model of the way things work: we plunk down our money, pocket our tickets, and then wait to see if we hit it big. Everything is out of our hands, and it is all up to Lady Luck or whoever/whatever controls our destiny by smiling or, more likely, frowning on us.

One of Qohelet's big complaints is that life is not fair, an idea that is expressed in a number of different ways. Something that really bugs him is that there is no difference between what happens to good people and bad people after they die: "Everything that confronts them is vanity, since the same fate comes to all, to the righteous and the wicked, to the good and the evil, to the clean and the unclean, to those who sacrifice and those who do not sacrifice. As are the good, so are the sinners; those who swear are like those who shun an oath. This is an evil in all that happens under the sun, that the same fate comes to everyone" (9:1b–3a; cf. 2:14–17). To make matters even worse, Qohelet detects an unjust principle operative in the world whereby sometimes good people are punished while evil ones are rewarded. This same complaint is raised in the book of Job, and it is a common theme throughout wisdom literature (7:15; 8:14; 10:5–7). As with Job, this strikes Qohelet as unfair because it flies in the face of the cause-and-effect view of life that is common in the Bible and says that persons will be judged based on how they lived their lives.

> What are the pros and cons of Qohelet's view of life?

When all is said and done, Qohelet concludes that human beings are no different from animals in that we have no control over our lives and things just happen to us without rhyme or reason. Any sense of order or logic that we discern in the world is nothing but an illusion, since our fates are determined by a cosmic roll of the dice that takes place without our even knowing it: "Again I saw that under the sun the race is not to the swift, nor the battle to the strong, nor bread to the wise, nor riches to the intelligent, nor favor to the skillful; but time and chance happen to them all. For no one can anticipate the time of disaster. Like fish taken in a cruel net, and like birds caught in a snare, so mortals are snared at a time of calamity, when it suddenly falls upon them" (9:11–12; cf. 3:18–21).

Second Opinions

He's a Real Nowhere Man, Sitting in His Nowhere Land

Very few biblical characters have the cachet and recognizability that Job enjoys. All you have to do is drop his name, and even people who have never peeked inside a Bible know exactly who you're talking about. "Oh yeah, he's that guy who loses everything he has, but gets it all back in the end." Job is such a well-known figure because he is so closely identified with one particular quality that he has a complete monopoly on it. Ask a hundred people to fill in the blank in the sentence "So-and-so has the patience of _____," and ninety-nine of them will scribble in "Job." (The other one would probably go with "a saint.") A search on Google for the expression "patience of Job" turns up over ninety-four million hits—that's what you call

> Can you think of another biblical character who is identified with a particular trait the way Job is?

establishing a brand. To put that number in perspective, consider that the phrase "LeBron James best basketball player in the world" results in a paltry thirteen million hits. Is any other biblical character so exclusively tied to a single quality or trait?

It is therefore more than a little ironic that one of the most famous characters in the best-selling book of all time is such a mystery man. In fact, many scholars maintain that pretty much everything about Job and the text that is named after him is up for grabs. As with virtually all of the biblical literature, we have no idea who wrote the book and we are not completely sure about when it was composed. It is likely that more than one author wrote it because of the significant differences between the prose and poetic sections, but exactly how many writers had a hand in it is impossible to say. The best educated guess is that it is a product of somewhere around the sixth or fifth century BCE, during the time of the Babylonian exile when the Israelites were living far from their land.

The text itself is of no help because there are no clear historical references within it that help to anchor it to a particular place or moment in time. Certain linguistic features of the Hebrew text point to a quite early date of composition around the tenth century BCE, but this is far from conclusive evidence by which to date the work. It could be that these are examples of intentional archaizing to give the book the appearance of being much older, as when you come across words like "thee" and "thou" in something that was written last week.

The names that are mentioned in the story do not contribute much either. Job's name means something like "Where is the father (i.e., God)?" and so it is a fitting designation for a main character who is on a quest to encounter the deity. The names of his three friends—Eliphaz, Bildad, and Zophar—are not well attested within or outside the Bible, and there is no agreement on their meanings or even what language(s) they come from. However, four other people in the Old Testament have the name of Job's fourth interlocutor, Elihu, which is a Hebrew term that means "He is my God." Job's homeland is identified as Uz, and there is a general consensus among scholars that it should be located in Edom, which was an area bordering ancient Israel at the southern end of the Dead Sea. This identification is supported by the book of Lamentations, which mentions Uz in relation to Edom (4:21), and in a genealogical list in Genesis (36:28) that has Uz as a descendant of the inhabitants of Edom. In addition, the birthplaces of all three of Job's friends—Teman (Eliphaz), Shuah (Bildad), and

Naamah (Zophar)—are in the same general area and have been identified with sites in northwest, northeast, and central Arabia, respectively. But beyond those general parameters, we do not know where Job hails from.

The great amount of uncertainty regarding whether Job even existed, who the Bible says he was, where and when he lived, who wrote the book, and when it was written creates a sense of timelessness about the story and reinforces the idea that it is a legendary tale whose message is enduring and meant to speak to all people everywhere. In this way, the lack of specificity functions in a way similar to the words in the opening crawl of the *Star Wars* movie: "A long time ago in a galaxy far, far away. . . ."

> How important is it whether or not Job was an actual person?

Another factor that contributes to the fictional quality of the book of Job is the fact that there were almost as many variations of it floating around the ancient Near East as there are installments in the *Star Wars* series. The tale of a man down on his luck who starts to question it all and turns to the gods in his misery was a tried and true formula among the scribes of antiquity, especially those living in Mesopotamia. Many of these texts predate the Bible by centuries, with some of them going back to the early part of the second millennium BCE.

Among the Mesopotamian writings that share features in common with the biblical book of Job, the one that is closest to it is a text that is often referred to as the *Babylonian Theodicy*, which was written sometime around 1000 BCE. It takes the form of a dialogue between a man who is suffering and his friend, both of whom are unnamed. The sufferer complains about how unfair his life has been because he was orphaned at a young age and has experienced nothing but hardship and persecution. His friend responds that inexplicable pain is something all people have to go through, but those who endure patiently will benefit in the end. At times, the sufferer's comments echo some of Job's sentiments regarding life's injustices and the pointlessness of being a believer.

> Those who seek not after a god can go the road of favor,
> those who pray to a goddess have grown poor and destitute.
> Indeed, in my youth I tried to find out the will of my god,
> with prayer and supplication I besought my goddess.
> I bore a yoke of profitless servitude:
> My god decreed for me poverty instead of wealth.
> A cripple rises above me, a fool is ahead of me;
> rogues are in the ascendant, I am demoted.[16]

---

16. The text of the *Babylonian Theodicy* can be found in William W. Hallo, ed., *The Context of Scripture: Canonical Compositions from the Biblical World* (Leiden: Brill, 2003), 1:492–95; his translation is quoted here. An overview of the ancient Near Eastern texts that are similar to Job is available in Samuel E. Balentine, "Job, Book of," in *The New Interpreter's Dictionary of the Bible*, ed. Katharine Doob Sakenfeld (Nashville: Abingdon, 2008), 3:319–23.

This person and Job are definitely kindred spirits, but there are important differences between texts like this one and the biblical book. The *Babylonian Theodicy* mentions only one friend rather than Job's three, and the sufferer never hears from his god like Job does. It is unlikely that the biblical author borrowed or copied from this or other ancient sources, but their striking similarities point to a shared set of concerns that this type of literature is trying to address. In their efforts to unravel the mysteries of human existence, the question of suffering was one that many ancient Near Eastern wisdom writers tried to address.

Interrogating Job (the Book, Not the Person)

The prose prologue and epilogue are the oldest sections of the book of Job. They were likely originally one literary unit that was an ancient folktale about a man who continues to serve God even when everything is taken away from him. He proves his faithfulness after he is tested twice, and so, despite the Satan's best efforts to cause him to waver, he is blessed by God and all is returned to him. At a certain point this folktale was broken in two and became the framework within which the poetic material was placed. In the process, a relatively brief story about why an individual (in this case, Job) should serve God became the narrative background for a much longer work that addresses the question of why human beings suffer.

Poetry That Bears Repeating

The lengthy middle section containing speeches by the various characters exhibits features commonly found in poetry, including meter, imagery, and figurative language. Another element that is often, but not always, associated with poetry is rhyme. This is not a quality of biblical Hebrew poetry, so when two adjacent lines end with the same or a similar sound in Hebrew it is a rare occurrence that is probably an accident rather than the intention of the author. The dominant feature of biblical poetry, many would say its defining characteristic, is something called "parallelism." On its most basic level, parallelism is a type of repetition whereby a similar thing is stated in two consecutive lines of a composition. This repetition is on the level of the text's meaning rather than its sound, and it does more than simply restate something that has already been said.

The primary unit of a poem in biblical Hebrew is a bicolon that is composed of two adjacent lines. Colons with three or more lines are sometimes found in Old Testament poetry, but the bicolon is the main building block. Parallelism can take several different forms, but the most common type is when there is a semantic development from the first line of a bicolon to its second line. In other words, what is being communicated in the first line is somehow advanced or expanded upon in the subsequent line. This can be illustrated by considering the very first lines of poetry in the book of Job (3:3), which were discussed earlier:

> Let the day perish in which I was born,
> and the night that said, "A man-child is conceived."

There is a clear parallelism in the vocabulary, as the two word pairs "day"/"night" and "born"/"conceived" match up. The same thing is true on the level of meaning. The two lines are saying almost the same thing, but they are not identical. In fact, upon closer examination it becomes clear that Job is expressing two related but separate thoughts. In line A he curses the day he was born, but in line B the target of his anger is the event nine months earlier that made his birth possible.

In the second line Job ratchets things up a notch and gives us a glimpse into just how dark his thoughts have become. In the space of two brief lines, the very first words he speaks to his friends, the reader becomes vividly aware of how despondent and miserable Job is through the author's use of a literary feature that allows the character to say the same thing twice, only with a certain nuance the second time.

> What are some of the other benefits of employing a literary device like parallelism?

That is how parallelism typically works. Something is stated, and then it is followed up by a "not just that, but also . . ." partner statement that develops the thought further. It is the motor that makes biblical Hebrew poetry dynamic, keeping it moving and creating added meaning.[17]

Poets are notorious for regularly using language and turns of phrase in ways that the rest of us normally do not encounter as we go about our non-poet lives. Sometimes we can be familiar with all the words found in a poem, but because of the company they are keeping we are not exactly sure what they mean. Take the first few lines of Sylvia Plath's poem "Daddy," for example:

> You do not do, you do not do
> Any more, black shoe
> In which I have lived like a foot
> For thirty years, poor and white,
> Barely daring to breathe or Achoo.

There is not a word there that would trip you up if you had to define it. But when you put them all together, that is when the fun starts and people begin to debate the poem's meaning and significance. A good poet can work magic by taking terms that are commonplace and turning them on their heads by putting them in unusual surroundings.

---

17. The features of biblical Hebrew poetry, with special attention to parallelism, are treated in Robert Alter, *The Art of Biblical Poetry* (New York: Basic Books, 1985), and Adele Berlin, *The Dynamics of Biblical Parallelism* (Grand Rapids: Eerdmans, 2008).

Words, On Their Own and In Groupings

While this same thing sometimes happens in biblical Hebrew poetry,[18] another issue that interpreters often have to wrestle with is the presence of *hapax legomena*. These two Greek words, which mean "spoken once," refer to a word that appears only one time in the Bible. Frequently such words do not appear in any other literature either. The problem here is not a familiar word in an unfamiliar setting, but an unfamiliar word that is not attested in any other setting. Sometimes the precise meaning of such a term can be hard to pin down, but that is not always the case. It could be that the literary context makes it pretty obvious what the word means, or can at least help you make an educated guess that will put you in the ballpark. In other cases, there is a cognate word whose meaning is well known in a language similar to Hebrew—like Akkadian or Arabic—that can be used to make sense of an unknown Hebrew word. On occasion, though, there are no clues available to help solve the riddle of a *hapax* and the exact meaning of a passage cannot be deciphered.

Approximately fifteen hundred words are found only one time in the Old Testament, but most of them are related to Hebrew roots whose meanings are well established. About four hundred of them can be categorized as strict *hapax legomena* in that they appear only one time in the text and they do not come from a known Hebrew root. Of that four hundred or so, sixty are found in the book of Job. That ties it with Isaiah for the most *hapax legomena* in a single biblical book. For the sake of comparison, the book of Psalms has the next highest number with thirty-seven. Both Isaiah and Psalms are much longer than Job, so that means it has the highest concentration of *hapax legomena* in the Bible.[19] This may be partially due to the relatively late date of the composition of the book of Job, which has been suggested based on some of its linguistic features.

It has already been noted that the Job of the prose is somewhat different from the Job of the poetry. The same might be said about the deity, at least as far as the divine titles are concerned. In the prologue and epilogue, the word "God" is found eleven times (all in the prologue), while the designation "the LORD" appears twenty-four times. Within the dozens of chapters of poetry between the prologue and epilogue that recount the speeches among Job and his friends, however, the term "the LORD" (*Yahweh*) is used only once (12:9).[20] This difference in distribution is another point in favor of viewing the poetry and the prose sections as two separate sources that have been brought together to form the book as we have it.

---

18. For an example of how a single verse of the poetry in Job is difficult to decipher, see Aron Pinker, "A New Interpretation of Job 19:26," *Journal of Hebrew Scriptures* 15 (2015): *http://www.jhsonline.org/Articles/article_205.pdf*.

19. An interesting discussion of *hapax legomena* can be found in Hellen Mardaga, "*Hapax Legomena*: A Neglected Field in Biblical Studies," *Currents in Biblical Research* 10, no. 2 (2012): 264–74.

20. The word "LORD" appears several times late in the poetry section when God speaks (38:1; 40:1, 3, 6; 42:1).

Several other words are used to refer to the deity in the poetry. *'El* and *'eloah* are related terms that are usually translated into English as "God," and the latter is the more interesting for our purposes. *'Eloah* is found fifty-seven times in the Hebrew Bible, with forty-one of those occurrences coming in the book of Job. It is found most frequently in late texts, another factor that has a bearing on the dating of the poetry in Job, and its high frequency in the book could be attributed to the setting of the story. Because it is very close to an Aramaic word commonly used for God (*'elah*), it is likely that it became associated with foreign areas like the area of Edom/North Arabia in which Job is set.

An additional title for God that is commonly found in Job is *shadday*, an abbreviated form of *'el-shadday*, which is usually translated "the Almighty." The shorter version is found thirty-eight times in the Old Testament, with thirty-one of them in Job. It has been found in personal names in the ancient Near East from as early as the second millennium BCE, so in all likelihood it is being used in the book of Job as an archaism that is meant to evoke the earlier time period in which the story is set. These three titles for the deity—*'el*, *'eloah*, and *shadday*—only appear in the poetic portion of Job and are never found in the prose.[21] This exclusive use of the three titles only in the poetry is another strong argument for viewing the prose and poetry as originally independent of one another.

A couple of sections of the poetry appear to be later insertions into the text. One is the speech by Elihu in chapters 32–37, the longest in the book. The previous chapter ends with the statement "The words of Job are ended" (31:40), which appears to bring an end to the conversation among Job and his friends and to signal the beginning of God's response. Instead, Elihu launches into an extended lecture that breaks the flow of the action. This disruption points to the secondary nature of Elihu's speech as an insertion, as does the fact that he was not mentioned in the prologue when Job's other three friends were introduced (2:11).

Chapter 28 is likely an insertion as well. It is a magnificent composition that offers a reflection on the elusive nature of wisdom and how difficult it is for human beings to attain, and it is one of the most powerful sections of the entire book. It is also clearly out of place, since it comes out of the blue and does not smoothly follow after what comes before

> According to Job's twenty-eighth chapter, what is wisdom and why is it so difficult for humans to attain?

it. While it could be the continuation of the speech that Job was giving in the previous chapter, the shift in tone and content makes that highly unlikely. In addition, the next chapter begins with the statement "Job again took up his discourse and said" (29:1), which are the very words that begin chapter 27. These are the only two times that phrase is found in the book, and its repetition serves

---

21. The eleven references to "God" in the NRSV's prologue all translate the Hebrew word *'elohim*.

to mark chapter 28 as an interlude that is not spoken by Job. We therefore have quite a few clues within the text that indicate that the book of Job as we have it is the final result of a process of editing and reshaping.

Life as Litmus Test

As they seek to understand and make sense of his situation, Job and his friends adopt a theological perspective on life that is common throughout the Old Testament. It is often associated with the book of Deuteronomy, with its emphasis on following the law that God gave to Moses. This theology teaches that if you obey the law, you will be rewarded; but if you do not obey the law, punishment ensues. This is the interpretive lens through which the history of Israel is presented in the books that comprise the Deuteronomistic History (Joshua through 2 Kings), which presents an account of what took place from the time the Israelites entered the Promised Land until the Babylonian invasion and the beginning of the exile in the sixth century BCE. In that theologized retelling, at each step along the way the Israelites prosper as long as they remain faithful to the law, but as soon as they stray from it misfortune and tragedy come upon them.

This Deuteronomic perspective is found in much of the wisdom literature of the Hebrew Bible. For example, some of the sayings in the book of Proverbs adopt a tit-for-tat view of things by observing that how a person lives his or her life determines their fate: "The perverse get what their ways deserve, and the good, what their deeds deserve" (Prov. 14:14). Some of the Psalms that stem from Israel's wisdom tradition deliver a similar message: "For the LORD loves justice; he will not forsake his faithful ones. The righteous shall be kept safe forever, but the children of the wicked shall be cut off" (Ps. 37:28). So when Job and his friends appeal to a certain logic in the world whereby the good prosper and the bad suffer, they are standing very much within the conventional viewpoint found throughout the Hebrew Bible, including in the wisdom writings.

It is a view based on the principle of cause and effect that allows one to anticipate and predict the outcome with a great deal of confidence. All you have to do is determine how closely an individual or community is conforming to God's will as expressed in the law, and you will know whether they will flourish or fail. In this way, your actions and behavior become a litmus test by which you can gauge what fate awaits you around the corner.

Job and his friends believed that your answer to that litmus-test question would make you or break you, but they discovered that things were not as cut and dry as they had imagined. Even though he dotted every "i" and crossed every "t" when it came to observing the law, the rug was pulled out from under Job and his life fell apart. Job's friends

> What are some of the advantages and disadvantages of a litmus-test view of life?

tried to explain this turn of events by adhering to their way of thinking and claiming that Job must have done something to deserve it. Job, however, maintained that was not the case.

The technical term for the central theme of the book of Job is "theodicy," which attempts to address God's role in common human experiences like suffering, especially when the sufferer is innocent and the suffering is undeserved. If God is all-powerful and all-good, why does he permit people to suffer and experience tragedies that they do not deserve? This is particularly an issue for those who have a litmus-test view of life, because they believe that, even though they have done everything God wants, they are not reaping the reward that should be theirs.

The book of Job challenges this way of thinking, and so it calls into question one of the main theological tenets of the Old Testament. It suggests that God does not apply a litmus test to determine reward and punishment, but uses another standard. But what is that standard? God's lengthy speech to Job at the end of the book is the turning point that enables Job to change his mind, but what does he learn from God that makes possible his shift in perspective? With his onslaught of questions, God puts Job in his place and tells him that he can never understand the deity's ways. The response to Job's question about why he is suffering is, "Because I'm God and you're not." In effect, God overwhelms Job and reminds him of the vast chasm that exists between the two of them. Perhaps somewhere in that gap can be found a more satisfying answer to Job's question, but it remains permanently beyond his grasp.

But the Fool on the Hill Sees the Sun Going Down, And the Eyes in His Head See the World Spinning Round

Qohelet starts out in the place where Job ends up. He is well aware of the distance between God and humanity from the outset, and he is convinced that the deity is playing by a set of rules that is different from the one he is using. As he surveys the scene, Qohelet detects a curious blend of sameness and unpredictability in life that simultaneously suggest to him a rhythm and randomness within creation. Things are both cyclical and capricious. On the one hand, "The sun rises and the sun goes down, and hurries to the place where it rises" (1:5). But then again, "In my vain life I have seen everything; there are righteous people who perish in their righteousness, and there are wicked people who prolong their life in their evildoing" (7:15).

Just as in Job, this outlook clashes with the more orderly and predictable understanding of the cosmos and humanity that characterizes much of the rest of the Old Testament. It challenges a mainstream view in the Bible, but there are clues that suggest that Qohelet is a relative newcomer to the conversation. Certain linguistic features of the text point in that direction, with the book's vocabulary and content indicating that it likely comes from sometime in the third century BCE. Like Job, Qohelet contains a number of Aramaisms, words influenced by the Aramaic language that are typical of a later stage in the development of Hebrew. In addition, there is evidence of the use of Persian, which also supports a later dating. The clearest example of this borrowing of Persian terms is the term *pardes* (2:5), which is translated as "park" and is the basis of the English word "paradise."

Editor(s) at Work

Indications of an editing process are evident in the text of Qohelet, and they suggest that it was the work of multiple hands. The superscription in the book's opening verse, which identifies the author as "the Teacher, the son of David, king in Jerusalem," is probably a later addition meant to help establish the work's connection to Solomon. This is a feature occasionally found in other biblical books, and in some cases the superscriptions attempt to associate the writing with David or Solomon. In the book of Psalms, almost one-half of the one-hundred and fifty psalms begin with a superscription that makes a reference to David. Similarly, three of the seven sections that make up the book of Proverbs include superscriptions that mention Solomon (1:1; 10:1; 25:1). Such superscriptions are commonly viewed as secondary additions to a text, and they often serve the purpose of trying to establish a link between it and a famous person from the past.

At the other end of the book, the epilogue is also considered to be a later add-on to Qohelet. As noted earlier, it is possible that two separate epilogues have been attached to the original work, resulting in one longer coda. The first one repeats the title *qohelet* from the opening verse of the book and explains how the author is a typical wise man who instructs his audience to take his words to heart. The reference to his investigation of proverbs is likely a subtle allusion to Solomon, who is associated with that literary genre in the Old Testament (1 Kings 4:32): "Besides being wise, the Teacher also taught the people knowledge, weighing and studying and arranging many proverbs. The Teacher sought to find pleasing words, and he wrote words of truth plainly" (12:9–10).

The second epilogue (12:11–14) is a bit longer and is the more important of the two. In particular, the book's final two verses are an intriguing and perplexing conclusion to the work; they have generated much scholarly debate and discussion: "The end of the matter; all has been heard. Fear God, and keep his commandments; for that is the whole duty of everyone. For God will bring every deed into judgment, including every secret thing, whether good or evil" (12:13–14). If you have worked your way through the whole book and carefully paid attention to what you have been reading, those last three sentences come out of nowhere. There is a sneak-attack quality to them because they start off innocently enough but gradually veer from the script until Qohelet is singing an entirely different tune at the very end. The first sentence does not present any problems since all it seems to be saying is that the book is winding down. The second sentence begins with an admonition to fear God, which is not a red flag since this is a standard bit of advice in wisdom literature. But then things start to get strange. Where did the reference to following God's commandments come from? There is only one other use of the word translated "commandments" in the entire book, and there it urges obedience to the command of a king (8:5). God's commandments are not mentioned anywhere else, and it does not make sense for Qohelet to say this, since he does not think following the commandments is important because God does not take them into account when judging a person.

As odd as the command to keep the commandments is, its incongruity pales in comparison to Qohelet's closing message in the final sentence of the book, when he states that God will judge every action, both good and bad, whether done in the open or privately. It is a complete shift in tone, and nothing you have read up to that point prepares you for it. It also raises suspicions that the author of those words was not the same person who wrote the rest of the work. Throughout almost the entire book Qohelet has taken the exact opposite position and has argued that it does not matter whether one is good or bad because everyone experiences the same fate when they die and so your actions are inconsequential. With his last words he does an about-face that leaves the reader tempted to think that his book is as absurd as its author claims life to be.[22]

A logical way to resolve the quandary is to posit that Qohelet did not write the epilogue and that it is the work of one or more other hands. An advantage of this theory is that, if the epilogue is viewed as a later addition, the original ending of the book was in 12:8, where the repetition of the words "vanity/vanities" and the mention of the title "the Teacher" echo the book's second verse. This creates a nice bookend effect in which the work's central theme is mentioned at both the beginning and the end, and Qohelet's final words perfectly capture his main message: "All is vanity."

In a couple of places earlier in the book there are other comments that could be interpreted as contradicting its dominant teaching, and these might also be the work of a later editor. For example, God is presented as an arbiter in a text that suggests one's actions determine one's fate (3:17). It is also possible to see this as simply another expression of Qohelet's belief that there is a time for everything, as articulated in his poem in 3:1–8. Another example of possible inconsistency can be seen in 11:9, where the *carpe diem* attitude that characterizes much of the book is found in the first half of the verse, but is then followed by a caution that God is keeping score and there will be an ultimate price to

---

22. For a discussion of issues related to the epilogue, see Choon Leong Seow, "'Beyond Them, My Son, Be Warned': The Epilogue of Qohelet Revisited," in *Wisdom, You Are My Sister: Studies in Honor of Roland E. Murphy on the Occasion of His Eightieth Birthday*, ed. Michael L. Barré (Washington: Catholic Biblical Association of America, 1997), 125–41.

pay. These multiple voices and perspectives could be evidence of the growth and development of the book as it was reworked by editors who were attempting to respond to the needs of changing times and circumstances.

Another factor motivating those editors could have been a desire to put the book more in line with the Old Testament's prevailing theology that teaches that God will reward or punish each person based on his or her conformity to the law. That is clearly the message of the epilogue, and so it is the note on which the book ends. It is quite likely that the presence of this more mainstream theology, particularly in the epilogue, helped to tip the scales and led to Qohelet's inclusion in the Hebrew Bible canon. According to tradition, there were many debates about the book's worthiness, with some claiming it was objectionable and others viewing it more favorably. By the second century CE, it was well accepted within the Jewish community and was being read each year during the Feast of Booths, or Sukkoth, a practice that continues into the present day. Within Christianity, Qohelet was accepted as canonical early on, but as late as the fifth century objections were still being voiced over its legitimacy as a sacred text. The presence of the epilogue undoubtedly played an important role in its acceptance as a work of scripture.[23]

Echoes of Qohelet, Ancient and Modern

A number of ancient Near Eastern texts express sentiments similar to those found in Qohelet. One interesting example from Egypt comes from a set of writings referred to as "harper's songs," which are sometimes found on tomb walls and take their name from the blind harpists who are often portrayed in the tomb drawings and likely sang the words for the deceased. These compositions offer observations on life and death. They trace their roots back to the Old Kingdom period, but the Middle Kingdom song for the Pharaoh Intef (twenty-second century BCE) is the closest parallel to Qohelet. Its opening lines offer wistful reflections on the passing of time and the transitory nature of wealth that the biblical author could have written himself.

> A generation passes,
> another stays,
> since the time of the ancestors.
> The gods who were before rest in their tombs,
> blessed nobles too are buried in their tombs.
> Those who built tombs,
> their places are gone.
> What has become of them?

---

23. It is less likely that the book's tenuous connection to Solomon was instrumental in Qohelet's achieving canonical status. As already noted, he is not mentioned by name in the text. In addition, other works, like the Wisdom of Solomon and the Odes of Solomon, are clearly attributed to him but were not granted canonical status within Judaism.

The author follows up with instruction that Qohelet would also have approved, some practical you-can't-take-it-with-you advice in light of the fleeting and unpredictable nature of human existence.

> Hence rejoice in your heart!
> Forgetfulness profits you,
> follow your heart as long as you live!
> Put myrrh on your head,
> dress in fine linen,
> Anoint yourself with oils fit for a god.
> Heap up your joys,
> let your heart not sink!
> Follow your heart and your happiness,
> do your things on earth as your heart commands![24]

Another Egyptian composition similar to Qohelet from around the same time, and one which also shares certain features with the book of Job, is titled *The Debate between a Man and His Soul*. Despite its title, it might be better to think of this work as the account of an argument a man is having with himself as he ponders the absurdity of life. He is despondent over his lack of good fortune even though he has behaved in an upright and moral way. He considers the possibility of suicide, but then fears that someone who takes his or her own life will not be able to enjoy the benefits of the afterlife. The man ultimately decides to stop trying to measure up to society's rules and to simply live in a way that will allow him to enjoy himself. Qohelet never entertains suicide as the solution to his plight, but the connections between this Egyptian text and his book are obvious.[25]

As striking as the similarities between these (and other) ancient Near Eastern texts and Qohelet might be, we should not jump to the conclusion that he was borrowing from earlier works. The situation here is similar to what we saw with the book of Job, which also addresses a universal experience. Since we first developed the capability to know that we all eventually die, humans have struggled with their mortality. Countless authors have expressed their views and fears about death by composing works that explore these issues, and those writings are a running record of our efforts to come to terms with a mystery that lies beyond our comprehension. Qohelet is but one of many such literary works found throughout the ancient Near East and beyond.

> Can you think of any modern works of literature or art that address human mortality?

---

24. For the full text, see William W. Hallo, ed., *The Context of Scripture: Canonical Compositions from the Biblical World* (Leiden: Brill, 2003), 1:48–49.

25. The text of *The Debate between a Man and His Soul* can be found in Hallo, ed., *The Context of Scripture*, 3:321–25.

A Wise Choice

So which of the views espoused by these two biblical books seems more plausible or accurate? That of Nowhere Man, or that of the Fool on the Hill? Is life more like a litmus test or a lottery? Is there a coherent logic and order to the way of the world? Does the way we live determine what happens to us, or is human existence nothing but a string of random events that occur one after another with no causal relationships between them? And where does God fit into the whole scheme of things?

> Who offers a more plausible view of life, Job or Qohelet?

Despite the differences between them, Job and Qohelet agree on one fundamental thing: life sometimes does not make sense. The sticking point for Job is undeserved or innocent suffering, which raises for him the theodicy question as he seeks to understand how and why God would allow him to go through the hell on earth he is experiencing. Despite his friends' suspicions, Job is certain that he has done nothing to merit the anguish he is forced to endure. For Qohelet, it is life itself that troubles him and not just one particular aspect of life. He does not take things quite as personally as Job does because it is clear to him that he is in the same boat that everyone else is in, even if they do not realize it. In his view, life is one big free-for-all with no rules and an outcome that is completely up in the air and outside our control. Sometimes the right person comes out on top, but there are no guarantees, so it is best to make the most of things while we are in the game. If we were to put them in the same room and have them share their notes, Qohelet and Job would agree that life can be unfair.

> Compare Job's and Qohelet's views of God. Is one more in line with your own thinking than the other?

At the end of his book, God says that Job has "spoken of me what is right" (42:7). What would God say about Qohelet? The text does not say, and if it did it would undercut its primary view of the deity as a distant and uninterested supreme being. Their contrasting notions of God are a key difference between the two books and the figures associated with them. Job sees God as a conversation partner he can talk *to*, while Qohelet prefers to talk *about* God since there is, in his view, no chance for a dialogue between them. Job demands and expects answers from the deity; he wants his day in court. The case does not quite go the way he had hoped it would, but at least he has his hearing. Qohelet is resigned to serving his time without an appeal—after all, there is a time for everything—because of his view of God.

It is an interesting coincidence that each book ends by flipping its protagonist's way of seeing things on its head. After God's barrage of questions, Job comes to realize that his understanding of the world was mistaken because life is not always a litmus test and there is more to it than an imperfect human being like him can ever know or imagine. For his part, even if the epilogue comes from a later time, Qohelet wraps things up by second-guessing himself and doing a one-eighty with his recommendation to follow the commandments because God the judge is watching. He concedes that life is more than just a lottery because sometimes our actions do have consequences that determine our future. It is almost like they've swapped places; at the end of their books Job starts to look a bit like Qohelet and Qohelet is doing his best Job impersonation. So if both books contain elements of both perspectives, what is the takeaway? Are they being wishy-washy and can't make up their minds?

Perhaps Qohelet and Job are both guilty of what looks like doublespeak because that is the most honest and plausible way of treating the issues they explore. They are being authentic, not evasive. There is an element of truth in each book, because when all is said and done life is both/and rather than either/or. At times the world makes perfect sense. Things are orderly and as they should be, and everything is just humming along. But then the bottom falls out, and suddenly all that harmony and stability fly out the window and chaos ensues. We can go from Job to Qohelet in an instant, or vice-versa. One minute, life is a litmus test, and the next, it is a lottery. If we are to survive and thrive, we have to learn how to accept and live through the contradictions. Our lives shift constantly back and forth between different modes of existence, and so it would be wrong to say that life is one way or the other. The author F. Scott Fitzgerald once claimed that a mark of intelligence is the ability to hold two contradictory ideas in one's mind and still be able to function. Job and Qohelet suggest that it is also a mark of wisdom, and the presence of contradictory perspectives in their books reminds us that life is much more than anyone can fathom.

Implications and Applications

1. How has your understanding of the Bible changed after reading this chapter?
2. How has your understanding of the human condition and life changed after reading this chapter?
3. How is God presented in Job and Qohelet? Identify the main qualities and features of the deity in these books and explain how they contribute to the portrait of God that emerges from the Hebrew Bible.
4. How is humanity presented in Job and Qohelet? Identify the main qualities and features of human beings in these books and explain what they suggest about the human condition.
5. Does the presence of conflicting views in the Bible about life and the human condition trouble you?

6. Should ancient texts like the Bible be used as resources to help formulate modern views on life and the human condition?

7. What are some other ways of thinking about life in addition to seeing it as a litmus test and as a lottery?

8. What are some other ways of thinking about God's role in innocent human suffering beyond those mentioned in this chapter?

9. Do the texts discussed in this chapter play a role in shaping your views about life and the human condition? If so, how? If not, why not?

The Devil Who Displays Wisdom
Ellen White[*]

"The Devil made me do it," is an excuse given for bad behavior, but, as noted in this text, this idea does not come from scripture. The Satan (aka Satan, the devil, Lucifer, Lord of Lies, the Morningstar, and a host of other names) in the Hebrew Bible is always connected to questions of justice and the human condition, and thus to explore the character of the Satan biblically is to raise questions about fairness and free will. This is often true in modern presentations as well. In January 2016, Fox Television Network premiered a new series entitled *Lucifer*. This section will explore the ways this series uses the character of Lucifer to wrestle with the themes of Job and Qohelet in relation to predestination versus free will. To do this it will be important to be familiar with the contents of the corresponding chapter on Job and Qohelet, and the major themes in both of those books. After viewing some scenes from the series with these themes in the forefront of our minds, we will compare the show to the Bible to discover similarities and differences. Following that, we will turn to some other voices for insight. Finally, we will reflect on all of this within the context of our own lives. At the end of this exercise, we will see how contemporary culture can be a bridge between the Bible and modern life.

John P. Fleenor / © Fox / Courtesy Everett Collection

Lucifer (played by actor Tom Ellis) is torn between Jobian free will and Qohelet's predestination.

continued

* Ellen White holds a PhD in Hebrew Bible from the University of St. Michael's College and is a former senior editor at the Biblical Archaeology Society. She has taught at five universities across the United States and Canada.

The Devil Who Displays Wisdom *continued*

The lead character, Lucifer Morningstar, is not based on the biblical characters the Satan, the devil, or even Lucifer, but rather a character from Neil Gaiman's extremely successful Vertigo/DC Comics flagship series, *Sandman*, which ran for seventy-five issues from January 1989 to March 1996. Gaiman originally based Lucifer after the character in English poet John Milton's *Paradise Lost*, combining the seventeenth-century English portrayal with the modern rock image of David Bowie. The premise of both the comic and television show is that Lucifer has gotten bored with ruling hell and thus he closes the gates and retires. This is a Satan that Milton would relate to: not evil incarnate, but grossly misunderstood and troubled with serious daddy issues. He is not a character that Dante Alighieri would recognize or one that would fit within evangelical Christian interpretations nor the expectations of the general public; no one makes a deal with this Devil.

Plot Summary

Tired of being the ruler of hell, Lucifer Morningstar decides to take a vacation and become the owner of the nightclub Lux in Los Angeles. He is joined by the sultry female demon Mazikeen, Maze for short, who is less than pleased with working as a bartender while Lucifer has the divine equivalent of a midlife crisis. While enjoying his R&R, Lucifer witnesses the murder of Delilah, a former employee, and her unjust punishment for minor crimes sets him off on a crusade for proper justice. This quest brings him into contact with Detective Chloe Decker, who despite being immune to his charms becomes his crime-solving partner. Like all good heroes (or perhaps anti-heroes) Lucifer has a nemesis, an archangel named Amenadiel, who represents the idea of predestination in contrast to Lucifer's fixation on free will.

Watch *Lucifer*, season 1, episode 1: *https://www.hulu.com/watch/897236*.[26]

When watching the episode keep the following questions in mind:

- What is Lucifer's goal when he uses his powers? Is it always the same?
- Which events in the episode were just? Which were unjust? How did you evaluate these actions? Was anything both just and unjust?

continued

---

26. Hulu is a subscription website, but it offers a free 2-week trial. If you do not already have a membership to the site, signing up for this trial will allow you to watch the links in this bridge legally. You are under no obligation to continue with a paid membership after your trial has expired.

The Devil Who Displays Wisdom *continued*

- Think about who knows what when (don't forget to include yourself) and how the author uses knowledge to influence you.
- When do you see examples of the "litmus test" worldview? Can you list examples of the "lottery" approach to life?

Below the Surface

Despite an apparent lack of interest in the Bible, the show is actually a form of modern-day wisdom literature that wrestles with the same issues as Job and Qohelet. Let's explore several scenes from the first season that focus on the theme of justice from perspectives similar to Job and Qohelet.

Delilah's death is the focus of the Jobian theology of the first episode. Before Delilah died, Lucifer told her, "Pull yourself together. You are wasting your talent, your life." It was the show's equivalent to a priest saying, "Go and sin no more!" In other words, Lucifer is telling her that she can choose to be good and by so choosing affect her destiny. This is the mantra of Job. The last words Lucifer says to Delilah ("What happens next is up to you") are immediately followed by the drive-by assassination. These few seconds of film juxtapose Job and Qohelet in an extreme and vivid way. Job (Lucifer) says, "You have control," and Qohelet (the shooter) says, "No way!" Lucifer arises from this scene full of posh rage that his Jobian perspective has failed in this instance and thus begins his quest to set it right; to extract a punishment on the perpetrator befitting his crime. This accounts for his anger when Chloe shoots Jimmy and Lucifer exclaims, "Why did you do that?! . . . Noooo nooo nooo, you just let him off too easy. He needs to pay, he needs to suffer, he needs to feel the pain, not escape it!" Lucifer, like Job's friends, wants the punishment to match the crime.

You also watched the conversation between Lucifer and Amenadiel where Lucifer refuses to return to hell and Amenadiel implies that if Lucifer does not decide to follow God's plan soon, of his own accord, then God will step in and make him. Lucifer is expressing free will in this scene. He is trying to see if he has control over his own destiny. Simply put, he is attempting to choose to be something other than the evil ruler of hell. If he can, then he will bear the personal responsibility of the actions that he takes. This is the worldview of Job. But Qohelet is not absent from this scene. Amenadiel does leave and permits Lucifer his freedom, but threatens that this freedom might not last, that God might overrule his freedom to accomplish his own unknowable purposes; this is the worldview of Qohelet.

continued

The Devil Who Displays Wisdom *continued*

Watch *http://www.hulu.com/watch/919868* (37:32–38:23) and *http://www.hulu.com/watch/911416#i0,p4,d0* (3:25–4:41).

This scene from season 1, episode 9, "A Priest Walks into a Bar," comes after Lucifer experiences an unexpected death of someone that he could only characterize as good. He sees the priest in much the same way as God sees Job at the beginning of the book. Lucifer desires a world where the good are rewarded and the bad are punished. A world where there is a clear right and a clear wrong and one's choices for right or wrong directly affect the outcome of their lives. In a nutshell, he wants the retributive justice of Job. However, we saw that faced with the circumstances of Job, he does not react the way that Job's friends did and assume some sort of wrongdoing on behalf of the priest. Rather, he responds like Qohelet would with the charge that God's plan has no justice and a person's actions cannot alter her or his lot in life. Life is predestined no matter what one does with it.

We saw Lucifer come to this conclusion in the opening scene of the series, albeit in a much more lighthearted way. You will remember that the scene begins with Lucifer cruising through Los Angeles in a fancy sports car whipping past a cop who immediately gives pursuit. As you saw, Lucifer encourages the officer to give into his desires (taking the bribe, breaking the law) because, "Why wouldn't you?" Under the surface of this scene is the worldview of Qohelet; life is a crapshoot so why not do what you want. Even Lucifer's comment, "You people are funny about your laws aren't you?" fits within Qohelet's dominant theme. It doesn't matter if you obey the law, your fate is just random happenstance.

Trixie, Chloe's daughter, clearly enjoys Lucifer. He makes her laugh and she takes him seriously. The character is often used to demonstrate the more Qohelet-like side of Lucifer. At the beginning of episode 6, "Favorite Son," she has clearly been caught sneaking a piece of chocolate cake, the evidence is literally all over her face and at first she refuses to admit her guilt. However, in a devil-made-me-do-it (something that Lucifer insists he never does throughout the series) move she responds, "Lucifer said it was ok. He said if you really want to do something, you should!" This attitude that Lucifer projects is reminiscent of Qohelet 8:15, and provides an interesting dichotomy within the character between his "eat, drink, and be merry" Qohelet side and his measure-for-measure, Jobian desire to see justice done.

The character of Lucifer is complex, and it is mostly through his eyes that the viewer gets a glimpse of God. Lucifer is a combination of the litmus-test thinking in Job and the lottery worldview of Qohelet. In episode 6, he refers to himself as "a walking paradox," and this paradox comes from

continued

The Devil Who Displays Wisdom *continued*

combining elements of Job and Qohelet. The God we see through Lucifer is one who has a plan (Job), but is quite distant from humanity (Qohelet). One whose actions are unexplained even to Lucifer, who is constantly battling with what God wants him to do (Job) and how unjust he believes God to be (Qohelet).

Viewers' Reactions

After only four weeks on the air, googling the show resulted in more than three million hits. Despite the Hollywood flare and the blatant deviations from the Bible, the underlying theology has much more in common with the Bible than one sees on the surface, especially in relation to the themes of free will and predestination presented in Job and Qohelet.

Those closest to the series see a variety of theological themes played out each week. Joe Henderson of *White Collar* fame and show runner for *Lucifer* remarks, "[It is] a show that I think has a very Christian message to it . . . anyone can be redeemed." This is another way of looking at what we explored in the previous section. The way in which Lucifer wrestles with free will versus predestination is in essence him trying to determine whether he can in fact be redeemed.

On *Hollywood Today*, the actor who plays Lucifer, Tom Ellis (who comes from a long line of pastors) explains that his character's *raison d'etre* is to answer the question, "Am I the devil because I am intrinsically evil or am I just because my dad decided I was." Ellis highlights the theology that runs beneath the surface of his character: what is the role of free will in a person's destiny and how much control does one have over what happens? You saw this struggle in the first episode when Lucifer asked Amenadiel if he was really evil or if "dear old dad" (i.e., God) made him so. This is the theological question at the heart of both Job and Qohelet. Is a person able to make her or his own decisions, and thus bear the consequences of the actions chosen (Job), or has it all been decided according to a divine master plan so that humans have no control over their fates (Qohelet)?

Henderson notes traces of Job and Qohelet beyond the character of Lucifer: "The thing about Mazikeen is she's the devil on the Devil's shoulder," said Henderson "So you've got Chloe who is like the angel on his shoulder. The one fighting for justice and to take out bad guys and Mazikeen who represents Lucifer's old life, which is 'embrace your desire and have fun.'" As we have seen, these external influences play out within Lucifer and he ends up being a mixture of both, with Chloe standing in the role of Job and Mazikeen bringing Qohelet to the mix.

continued

The Devil Who Displays Wisdom *continued*

Daniel Fienberg of the *Hollywood Report Review* finds the show lacks theology in the early episodes and that "it's only the fifth episode in which the show begins to make any real acknowledgement that the idea of the Devil on Earth ought to have theological ramifications and that if the Devil is going to bother going to a shrink, he ought to have some issues, daddy issues in particular." Feinberg points out that the theological elements are more subdued in the earlier episodes and that the introduction of the "shrink" gives Lucifer the platform to wrestle with his own internal struggles with the "What is life?" question, and to explore God's (his daddy's) role in all that undergirds living.

Kate O'Hare, a Catholic entertainment reporter, sees it differently, saying, "At minimum, while it can hardly be considered theologically accurate, it doesn't insult God or belief—and, as Lucifer points out, people are answerable for their own sins." Here O'Hare points to one area, Jobian theology, where the show is theologically accurate. While many struggle with the way in which the Satan has been portrayed, O'Hare demonstrates that the show is not theologically bankrupt even though it deviates from certain textual elements. By exploring beneath the surface, she is seeing the undergirding theology of free will. Brandon Ambrosino of the Huffington Post concurs with these observations, calling the show "theological food for thought." He observes the tension between the personal responsibility mentioned by O'Hare and the detachment inherent in predestination that plays out in each episode.

This tension is discussed in detail by Andrew A. Smith of the Tribune News Service: "Lucifer quitting his job is more than just Creation's proudest angel once again refusing to do what he's told. Instead, he brings up the two words religious scholars have been arguing about since there were religious scholars: free will . . . here's the devil discussing predestination. In his mind, he isn't bad—rather, God made him bad." Smith goes on to state his opinion that Lucifer is merely trying to pass the buck, which reveals Smith's personal belief in free will over predestination. Author of *Jesus Potter Harry Christ*, Derek Murphy takes the opposite position when he says, "Heaven needs Lucifer to play devil or God's whole system doesn't work." This clearly reflects the view that God's plan reigns over the will of lower beings.

Lisa Schmeiser of Previously.tv sums up the various views on the theology of *Lucifer*: "Lucifer [was] outraged that someone who had faith in God suffer[ed] the consequences of other people's bad decisions—both because it offends his sense of vengeance and because it confirms his worst

continued

The Devil Who Displays Wisdom *continued*

---

thoughts about his dad. . . . I sort of enjoy Lucifer's brand of punishment. It's proportionate to the crime and it doesn't equivocate. . . . The game is rigged, and it's codswallop that God should seek to punish both the players and the entities who try to sit it out."

Reel to Real

Like wisdom literature, the crime genre on television often raises difficult questions surrounding justice and the way the world works. For example, the guilty party often goes unpunished, sometimes on a technicality, sometimes because they are really good at being bad. (Do you think this is why there are so many crime shows on television? Do you like to watch them? Do you ever think about the philosophies that lie beneath the surface?) The cases presented quite often raise murky issues, especially when it seems that the outcome of the case will be unjust. Sometimes it concludes in a way that allows viewers to make their own decisions regarding what would be just, but other times it is more directive, especially at the end of the episode, much like the conclusion of Job.

So what? Well, as Kaltner points out, the Bible is not univocal. There is diversity in the text and different answers are given for the same question, the same characters are presented in different ways in various texts. Do you think there can be more than one answer to questions of life? Can life be just and unjust at the same time? Are some things guided by free will and others predetermined? Can you think of an example from your own life where this would be true? Can you think of an example where you got what you deserved, and one where you did not? What we see here is precisely this phenomenon.

In the end, both Job and Qohelet have elements within them that seem to contradict their main point. (Have you ever felt this way? Can you think of a time where you faced the inner conflict that we have seen in Lucifer?) Kaltner suggests that this might actually reflect beauty in the design, a literary means of reflecting experienced reality, rather than a flaw in the writing. Perhaps the most poignant part of the entire *Lucifer* series is the title character's internal battle between the *laissez faire* attitude of Qohelet and the unequivocal battle for justice in Job. It does produce a character that seems inconsistent and lacking in direction, but it also draws to the surface the inconsistency that one actually experiences in life. There are times when your world might seem to be fair and just (you studied hard and got an A, someone hurts you and is punished for it, you worked hard and earned

continued

The Devil Who Displays Wisdom *continued*

enough to buy yourself a car) and others when randomness seems to rule (someone you love gets very sick, an act of nature damages your property, you get rear-ended waiting at a stop sign, your partner cheats on you). At the end of the day, the questions at the foundation of wisdom literature (Do I have control over my fate? Is there any point to living a good life? What does it mean to live a good life?) are still being asked, and Fox's *Lucifer* comes to the same mixed conclusions that Job and Qohelet did.

Further Exploration

Examine contemporary culture through the lens of chapters 4's discussion of insights found in Job and Qohelet. Watch the movie *Patch Adams* (1998, time: 1:55:00) while keeping the major biblical themes in mind. Look for similarities and differences. Explore the reactions and theological reflections of others. Reflect on your own experience and determine your own responses to the theologies present.

Questions to keep in mind while viewing *Patch Adams*:

- Unlike the television show *Lucifer*, *Patch Adams* is based on a true story. Do you respond differently to true stories and fictional stories? If so, how was this manifest in your viewing of *Lucifer* and *Patch Adams*? If not, explain why.

- Do you see elements from Job in Patch Adams' life? What were they? Name the similarities and differences.

- Does *Patch Adams* reflect a Qohelet-like philosophy? In what ways do you see reflections of the lottery approach in the movie? Can you name a particular scene where this is prevalent?

After watching the film and reflecting on the above questions, analyze Adams's rant to God in light of the various wisdom perspectives from both Job and Qohelet. Include similarities and differences. Then argue for which one, Job or Qohelet, Adams would have most related to, making sure to provide specific details. Turn to the internet to find reactions of others to the theological themes found in the film. Detail the various responses and reactions. Identify which are convincing and which are not. Finally, put yourself into the place of Adams and explore your thoughts and feelings. Do you see yourself as more of a Job or a Qohelet? Would that change if you faced the same circumstances as Adams?

Perspectives on the Other

This book was written as a presidential campaign was revving up in the United States. In fact, this chapter was started on the day of the first of a series of debates that would help determine the Republican candidate for the 2016 election. That coincidence of timing could not be more appropriate because political campaigns are always designed and run in a way that pays careful attention to the topic that is the focus of the chapter—the differences that exist among people. People running for office have to set themselves apart from the field by identifying and highlighting how they are different from their opponents. Those who are locked in a one-on-one battle for the big prize must convince enough people that they are better than the other person in the race, or they will likely suffer the ignominy of having to return to their normal humdrum existence and therefore not be subjected to the scrutiny and probing that comes with holding public office.

In order to define oneself or one's side over against the other, demonization of the opponent is a frequent approach. For example, some critics will call attention to tactics of their foes that they claim are meant to exclude or disenfranchise others, like restrictive voter registration laws, suspicious redrawing of district boundaries, or defunding of services. Hurling such allegations is a common strategy that takes place across the political spectrum, and it can sometimes have a big effect on the outcome of an election.

Like the candidates themselves, those who cast the votes can also get caught up in identity politics because they are often defined by the distinctions and differences among them. Polls that attempt to handicap an election and predict its likely outcome sometimes divvy up the population into smaller segments that are at odds with one another. A majority of those living in the cities endorse a particular issue, while a majority of those in the suburbs are opposed to it. Two-

> Do you think people's tendency to categorize and label one another has a primarily positive or negative effect?

thirds of those under thirty-five favor a certain candidate, but the same percentage of those over that age would never vote for the bum. Most black voters support Amendment 2, most white voters reject it, and most Latino voters are undecided. Sometimes it can seem like the entire electoral process is built on a single principle: divide and conquer.

It might be that the political system is arranged with an eye toward difference because it reflects how we tend to go about things even when there is no election on the horizon. The French expression *vive la différence* ("Long live the difference!") is commonly used in reference to relations between men and women, but it could easily be extended to describe modern life in general. Difference is alive and kicking in all sorts of ways, because we tend to identify, classify, and rank one another based on a host of factors. Race, ethnicity, gender, sexual orientation, age, religion, and socio-economic status are just a few of the more common categories that we employ to label ourselves and others. Sometimes this type of categorization serves a useful purpose, as when it helps us better recognize that certain groups within society are in need of help because they are being mistreated. But at other times it can be harmful because it separates us and splits us up into disparate entities that can prevent us from appreciating the common humanity we all share. This chapter looks at an often harmful way of drawing differences that is sometimes found among religious people: making a distinction between those whom God approves of and those he does not.

In all likelihood, the knowledge of difference has been with humanity ever since self-awareness developed; with that came the ability to recognize that people are not all the same. By the time the biblical authors came along, this notion was well-ingrained in the human psyche, and some of the texts they wrote are nearly obsessed with the question of how to relate to and treat "the other." The Old Testament deals with difference the same way it treats many topics: with a variety of voices that do not present a consistent message. Some passages embrace otherness, while others have been cited by white supremacist groups that call for complete separation between the races. Since so many people turn to the Bible for guidance on how to relate to those who are different from themselves, it is very important that the various ways it treats the topic be recognized. This chapter considers Ruth and Jonah, two short biblical books that reflect the Bible's diverse perspectives on diversity and therefore raise important questions about what role the Bible can play in informing modern views about how we should relate to those who are different from ourselves.

The Book of Ruth

Ruth is a work of literature that demonstrates what great story-tellers ancient writers could be. It is a real page-turner that contains all the elements you would expect in a story that you can't put down: natural disaster, death, birth, marriage, trickery, sexual intrigue, and reversal of fortune. And it packs all that into four brief chapters that contain a total of just eighty-five verses, so it gets right to the point with a minimum of unnecessary details. And that point is that even out-siders have a seat at God's table.[1]

First Impressions

READ: Ruth 1–4

At its heart, the book of Ruth is a survival story about two women who hit rock bottom but then overcome the odds and end up on top through a com-bination of personal ingenuity, hard work, luck, and perhaps a little help from above. The two protagonists are Ruth and her mother-in-law Naomi. They are the only people in the story mentioned in all four chapters. The first five verses of the book, which cover a period of more than a decade, explain how Naomi and her husband Elimelech, along with their two sons, leave their hometown of Bethlehem because of a famine and settle in the land of Moab on the eastern side of the Dead Sea. Sometime after they arrive, Elimelech dies and Naomi is left with her sons, Mahlon and Chilion, who marry two local women. About ten years after their relocation, both sons die, leaving the Israelite widow Naomi alone with her two Moabite daughters-in-law, Ruth and Orpah.

Much of the remainder of chapter 1 describes Naomi's decision to make a solo return trip to Canaan and her attempt to convince Ruth and Orpah to remain in Moab, where they can remarry and have a good life. Orpah consents, but Ruth refuses. In her first words in the book, she declares,

> Do not press me to leave you
> or to turn back from following you!
> Where you go, I will go;
> where you lodge, I will lodge;
> your people shall be my people,
> and your God my God.
> Where you die, I will die—
> there will I be buried.
> May the LORD do thus and so to me,
> and more as well,
> if even death parts me from you! (1:16–17)

---

1. The following commentaries offer full analyses of Ruth from different perspectives: André LaCocque, *Ruth: A Continental Commentary* (Minneapolis: Fortress, 2004); Tod Linafelt, *Ruth* (Collegeville, MN: Liturgical Press, 1999); Kirsten Nielsen, *Ruth: A Commentary* (Louisville: West-minster John Knox, 1997); and Jeremy Schipper, *Ruth: A New Translation with Introduction and Commentary* (New Haven: Yale University Press, 2015). A fine overview of the ways that the book of Ruth has been studied is given by Jennifer Koosed in *Gleaning Ruth: A Biblical Heroine and Her Afterlives* (Columbia, SC: University of South Carolina Press, 2011).

These are the best-known verses from the book of Ruth, not least of all because they have been read at countless wedding ceremonies as an expression of the commitment the newlyweds make to one another. The first chapter concludes with a scene that describes Naomi and Ruth returning to Bethlehem, where the local women greet them, but Naomi asks them to call her by another name. The significance of that passage will be discussed below.

> What do you think might have motivated Ruth to stay with Naomi?

A new character is introduced in chapter 2 who will continue to play a major role throughout the rest of the book. A relative of Elimelech named Boaz is a wealthy landowner, and Ruth shows up at his field to take part in a practice that was common at the time known as "gleaning." This was a custom that allowed the more vulnerable members of society, such as poor people, widows, and foreigners, to gather produce from the harvest that was left behind by those working the land. Throughout her time with him, Ruth is unaware of the fact that Boaz is Elimelech's relative, and she learns of it only when she returns home to Naomi and tells her how her day went.

Chapter 3 describes a very strange encounter between Ruth and Boaz that will be discussed more fully below. At Naomi's suggestion, Ruth bathes, dresses in her finest clothes, and makes her way to the threshing floor where Boaz has been winnowing barley and is now asleep. After uncovering his feet, she lies down next to him until he awakens around midnight and finds her there. Several aspects of the scene are difficult to interpret, but their words suggest that Ruth asks Boaz to exercise his duty as a relative by providing for Naomi and her. Boaz agrees to do so, but he informs Ruth that there is another man who is more closely related and who needs to be consulted before anything can be done.

The other relative makes his appearance at the beginning of chapter 4 when Boaz meets him at the city gate and informs him that he has the first claim on a parcel of Elimelech's land that Naomi is selling. The man is eager to complete the transaction until Boaz tells him that it is a package deal and he will also acquire Ruth along with the land. Upon hearing this, the man relinquishes his claim and Boaz then announces that as the next nearest kin he has acquired the land and will take Ruth as his wife. As the book ends, Ruth gives birth to a son named Obed; a listing of the child's lineage ends with Jesse, the father of King David.[2]

Good Neighbor Policy

The opening of the book of Ruth clues us in to the important role that geography will play in the story. In fact, the first two verses appear to violate

---

2. Chapters 2 and 3 have a similar outline that features an encounter between Ruth and Boaz that is preceded and followed by a brief conversation between Naomi and Ruth. Jerome Walsh has discerned a complex set of similar patterns throughout the entirety of the book in his *Style and Structure in Biblical Hebrew Narrative* (Collegeville, MN: Liturgical Press, 2001), 88–89.

the basic rule of writing that says we should avoid repetition because they each contain the same information that Elimelech and his family were from Bethlehem and had to settle in the country of Moab. (As we will see, the author of Ruth likes to use repetition in order to draw attention to important themes in the book.) This double reference to their journey anticipates an important aspect of the work: this is a story that explores what happens when borders are crossed and people from different backgrounds interact. By the sixth verse Naomi is at the border and heading back where she came from, but with Ruth the Moabite in tow she has someone with her who does not belong there.

Moab is a curious place for this Israelite family to settle based on how the area is portrayed elsewhere in the Hebrew Bible. It is commonly presented as the quintessential land of the other that was often at odds with the people of Israel, and so perhaps their choice to head there indicates just how desperate Elimelech and his household were to leave Canaan. The first mention of Moab in the Bible tells you all you need to know about what the biblical writers thought of the place. Genesis 19 describes the destruction of the cities of Sodom and Gomorrah, a story in which Abraham's nephew Lot plays a key role. To avoid the conflagration, he and his two daughters literally head to the hills and live in a cave. Thinking that they are the only human beings left alive, the daughters conspire to have sexual relations with their father when he is in a drunken state in order to perpetuate the human race. The chapter ends by identifying the son of the firstborn daughter as Moab, the ancestor of the Moabites (Gen. 19:30–38).[3] This is generally held to be an etiology, or origin story, that is meant to be a put-down of the Moabites as the product of incest. Although there is probably no basis in fact for the story in Genesis 19, it gives us some insight into the tense relationship the Israelites often had with their neighbors on the other side of the Dead Sea (cf. Deut. 23:3–6; Isa. 15–16; Jer. 48; Amos 2:1–3).[4]

For this reason, it is striking that the author of Ruth often draws attention to her status as a Moabite—a despised foreigner. This is another example of the author's fondness for repetition that was mentioned earlier. When we first meet her, she is described as a Moabite wife (1:4). When she and Naomi go to Bethlehem, there is a double reference to her

> What effect do the reminders of Ruth's foreign status have on you as a reader?

homeland (1:22a). When Ruth speaks with Naomi in chapter 2 about going to the field to glean, she is referred to twice as "the Moabite" (2:2, 21). When Boaz

---

3. The younger daughter bore Ammon, the ancestor of the Ammonites, who were another people often portrayed as Israel's enemies. The name "Moab" is actually a pun because it resembles two Hebrew words that mean "from the father."

4. For an overview of the Moabites and their land, see Gerald L. Mattingly, "Moabites," in *Peoples of the Old Testament World*, ed. Alfred J. Hoerth, Gerald L. Mattingly, and Edwin M. Yamauchi (Grand Rapids: Baker, 1994), 317–33.

inquires about her, his worker notes her foreign background twice (2:6). In his conversation with the other next-of-kin, Boaz refers to Ruth as a Moabite when he informs the man that she will also be part of the transaction (4:5). Once the deal falls through and he can get what he wants, Boaz announces that he has acquired Elimelech's land and Ruth "the Moabite" (4:10). It should also be noted that Ruth herself refers to her outsider status when, during her meeting with Boaz in the field, she says, "Why have I found favor in your sight, that you should take notice of me, when I am a foreigner?" (2:10b).

With these frequent reminders of her place of origin, the author does not want the reader to forget about Ruth's social position as an outsider. Everything that she says and does in the story should be interpreted in light of that fact. Descriptors and titles usually matter in the Bible, and literature in general, and they can aid in our understanding of what is happening within the narrative.[5] The repeated references to Ruth "the Moabite" work in the same way. Her for-

> Are there other ways of interpreting the response of the women of Bethlehem besides seeing it as xenophobic?

eign status is at the core of who she is, and the fact that she is one of those reviled people from Moab increases the amount of baggage that comes along with her character. The effect of that baggage can be seen in a subtle way in the scene that describes the return to Bethlehem (1:19–22). Both Naomi and Ruth enter the town, but the local women inquire only about the former: "Is this Naomi?" Perhaps they cannot tell it is their old friend because it has been ten years since Naomi left and one's appearance can change in that time. But it is also possible that they are not sure it is Naomi because of the company she keeps. The last time they saw her she was with her husband and two sons, but now here she is with this stranger from somewhere else. A point in favor of the latter interpretation is that the text says, "When they came to Bethlehem, the whole town was stirred because of *them*" (1:19). It is not just Naomi that has them buzzing, but the pair of them. It may be that there is an element of xenophobia to the scene, as the local folks have a hard time accepting that one of their own might be associating with someone who is not from Bethlehem.

Naomi's surprising response to their query comes close to "Yes and no. I am who you think I am, but then again I'm not." Her words remind us that issues of identity loom large in this story.

---

5. A powerful example of this can be seen in the account of how Amnon, King David's son and the crown prince, rapes his half-sister Tamar in 2 Samuel 13. It is a tragic and painful story to read because it describes one of the most despicable acts imaginable, which is compounded by the fact that the rapist and his victim are related by blood. In order to keep that aspect of the story front and center in the reader's mind the author does not just refer to the characters by name, but repeatedly uses terms and titles that underscore their familial relationship. In the twenty-two verses it takes to tell the story, the word "sister" is found eight times and the term "brother" appears ten times. That repetition helps to highlight the truly horrific nature of the events being recounted.

> Call me no longer Naomi, call me Mara,
> for the Almighty has dealt bitterly with me.
> I went away full, but the LORD has brought me back empty;
> why call me Naomi when the LORD has dealt harshly with me,
> and the Almighty has brought calamity upon me? (1:20–21)

There is a nice wordplay at the beginning of the passage that works only in Hebrew and cannot be duplicated in translation. The name "Naomi" means "pleasant," but she is rejecting it because of all the hardship she has experienced in her life. She now prefers to be called "Mara," which means "bitter" and better reflects her current situation. Despite her request, though, Naomi continues to go by her given name throughout the rest of the book.

Naomi leaves no doubt as to who she thinks is responsible for her bitterness, as four of the five lines quoted above place the blame squarely on God. She does not specify what exactly the deity has done to her, but her words suggest that she thinks God is the one behind the deaths of her husband and sons. The third line offers an ironic assessment of both her departure from and return to Bethlehem.

> Is Naomi being a little hard on God by blaming him for all her troubles?

She claims that the Lord sent her away full, likely a reference to the other members of her family who departed with her, but in fact the reason they left was a famine that left them anything but full, literally speaking. She also says that she now returns empty, probably an allusion to the absence of the men in her life, when in fact she is not alone at all. Ruth is accompanying her, and the birth of Ruth's child will be the means by which Naomi's emptiness will be filled.

Given Naomi's negative assessment of God as the cause of her problems, it is interesting that Ruth never reconsiders her vow made earlier in chapter 1 that Naomi's God will be hers as well (1:16). If Naomi's God is responsible for the death of Ruth's husband Mahlon, should she not reconsider that promise? In addition, why would she follow a deity who has been the source of so much pain and anguish for her mother-in-law? Perhaps it would have been smarter to have taken Orpah's lead as Naomi had advised her when she said, "See, your sister-in-law has gone back to her people and to her gods; return after your sister-in-law" (1:15). The text remains silent about

> Why do you think Ruth continues to follow Naomi's God after Naomi blames God for her difficulties?

whether or not Ruth ever wavered, and this is in keeping with the image of her the author wishes to project—an image of an upright foreigner who has decided to follow the God of Israel.

Throughout the rest of the book, Ruth is a model citizen who puts the lie to the negative views of Moabites found elsewhere in the Old Testament. She obeys her mother-in-law and provides for her, interacts respectfully with Boaz and his workers, and is eventually rewarded by marrying a prominent member of society with whom she has a child who will be an ancestor of the great King David. Not bad for someone who was born on the wrong side of the tracks.

A Stranger in a Strange Text

An interesting aspect of the book of Ruth is that it mentions a number of social practices and customs that often strike modern readers as odd and therefore help to remind us of the cultural divide that separates our world from that of the book's original audience. One that has already been mentioned is gleaning, whereby vulnerable members of society were allowed to go to the fields and help themselves to the fruits of the harvest that had been left behind by workers. It was a

> What is your reaction to the practice of gleaning? What might be some ways of implementing this practice in the modern world?

type of welfare program that provides the context for what takes place in chapter 2, when Ruth and Naomi receive the sustenance they need. There are several references to gleaning in legal texts, and so the Bible presents it as a law given by God to Moses. The relevant texts all describe gleaning as something meant to assist the downtrodden within the community: "When you reap the harvest of your land, you shall not reap to the very edges of your field, or gather the gleanings of your harvest; you shall leave them for the poor and for the alien: I am the LORD your God" (Lev. 23:22; cf. Lev. 19:9–10; Deut. 24:19–22). Women who have lost their husbands are also often included in the list of those who may glean, so these laws appear tailor-made for a poor, foreign widow like Ruth.

Two other unusual social customs mentioned in Ruth are found in chapter 4, in the scene involving Boaz and the next-of-kin that determines who acquires the land and marries Ruth. One is related to the episode's setting at the city gate, which was the place in ancient Israel where legal cases were heard and justice was decided. The description of what takes place there has many of the elements of a court proceeding as Boaz first asks the man to sit in a particular place, assigns seats to the ten elders of the city who will serve as witnesses, and then proceeds to argue the case in a way similar to what might take place in a formal hearing (4:1–6).

Ani Nirni / Tel_Dan_Canaanite_Gate.JPG / Wikimedia / CC0 1.0

This example from Dan in northern Israel (ca. 1500 BCE) is typical of ancient Israelite city gates, where elders gathered to decide legal cases; in Ruth 4:1, Boaz meets with the elders at the gate to decide Ruth's fate.

City gates have always been centers of commerce and social life because of the many people who pass through them and congregate near them, and a number of biblical texts indicate that they also functioned as the equivalent of courtrooms in ancient Israel (Deut. 21:18–21; 22:13–15; Josh. 20:1–4; Isa. 29:21; Amos 5:10–15).

The other strange element in this scene is a rather curious ritual that is explained by the narrator: "Now this was the custom in former times in Israel concerning redeeming and exchanging: to confirm a transaction, the one took off a sandal and gave it to the other; this was the manner of attesting in Israel" (4:7). The text then goes on to describe the exchange of a sandal, but it is a bit ambiguous because after the other man tells Boaz he can have the field it says, "He took off his sandal." Who is taking off his sandal, Boaz or the other man?

Perhaps the oddest aspect of the book of Ruth from the modern perspective is its connection to an ancient Near Eastern practice known as "levirate marriage," which takes its name from the Latin term for a husband's brother (*levir*). The details of this practice are laid out in Deuteronomy 25:5–10, which stipulates that if a married man dies without having had a son his brother should marry the dead man's widow and their first-born son would be the legal offspring of the deceased. There were several reasons for such an arrangement. In the first place, it provided security for the woman, who otherwise would be a widow without anyone to look after her. It also guaranteed that the deceased man's property would not be lost to the family if the widow were to remarry. Finally, it allowed for the dead man's name and memory to live on through the offspring his brother would be able to provide.[6]

The clearest example in the Bible of how levirate marriage works is found in Genesis 38, which features Judah's daughter-in-law Tamar (not the same Tamar from 2 Samuel 13 who was mentioned above). After her husband, Judah's oldest son Er, dies without having a son, his brother Onan marries her but fails to act in accordance with the levirate law; instead, he spills his semen on the ground whenever he has sexual intercourse with Tamar.[7] Onan is put to death by God because of this, which makes Judah reluctant to give son number three to her. She eventually resorts to trickery by disguising herself as a prostitute and having sex with Judah, who fathers the child (twins, actually) that his sons were unable or unwilling to produce. Upon sentencing his daughter-in-law to death for engaging in improper sexual relations, the tables are turned on Judah when Tamar produces evidence that he is the father of her children. He ends up exonerating her and admitting his own guilt for not following the law of levirate marriage.

---

6. An interesting discussion of how levirate marriage is presented in the biblical literature is available in Dvora E. Weisberg, "The Widow of Our Discontent: Levirate Marriage in the Bible and Ancient Israel," *Journal for the Study of the Old Testament* 28, no. 4 (2004): 403–29.

7. This story is the reason masturbation is sometimes referred to as "onanism." It is important to note, however, that in this story the actual reason for God's anger was not because Onan engaged in a reputedly forbidden sex act, but because he refused to do his duty toward his deceased brother and the widow he left behind.

The book of Ruth exhibits awareness of the custom of levirate marriage, but it does not entirely follow the letter of the law as laid out in Deuteronomy 25.[8] Naomi seems to be familiar with it when she asks Orpah and Ruth, "Even if I thought there was hope for me, even if I should have a husband tonight and bear sons, would you then wait until they were grown? Would you then refrain from marrying?" (1:12b–13a). But the hypothetical scenario she describes would not technically be levirate marriage because her new sons would be the offspring of another man and not full brothers of Mahlon and Chilion. Similarly, in chapter 4, in regard to the determination of who will acquire the property and marry Ruth, neither Boaz nor the other man is Mahlon's brother, so strictly speaking it would not be an example of levirate marriage. The difference between what the book of Ruth says about levirate marriage and how it is outlined in Deuteronomy might suggest that the details of the practice changed over time or that different forms of it existed simultaneously. It is also possible that the book of Ruth is not describing levirate marriage at all, but is rather providing an account of how widows were taken care of at the time the text was written.[9]

> What is your initial reaction to the practice of levirate marriage?

Exactly what takes place on the threshing floor in chapter 3 is not completely clear, but the scene has strong sexual undertones. Naomi instructs Ruth to uncover Boaz's feet and lie down (3:4), which is precisely what she does (v.7). Boaz is shocked to find a woman lying at his feet when he wakes up at midnight (v.8), and she stays there until the morning hours, when she departs (v.14). In the Hebrew Bible and in other ancient Near Eastern literature, a foot is not always a foot; it can be a euphemism for the genitals, and that appears to be the case here (see, for example, Exod. 4:25 and 2 Sam. 11:8). If so, then in following Naomi's advice Ruth is taking the bold move of uncovering Boaz's private parts. Did they, or didn't they? The text does not tell us that Ruth and Boaz engaged in sexual relations, but it does not exclude that possibility either, so it is left up to the reader's imagination. Ruth's request that Boaz spread his cloak over her echoes a passage in the book of Ezekiel that uses the same image to talk about the covenant between God and Israel as a type of

> Do you think it is more likely that Ruth and Boaz had sexual relations on the threshing floor, or that they did not?

---

8. The same thing can be said of the story of Tamar in Genesis 38 mentioned above, since it is her father-in-law and not her brother-in-law who provides her with a child.

9. The description of levirate marriage in Deuteronomy 25 also explains what should happen if a man refuses to marry his deceased brother's widow. The passage has an interesting connection with the Ruth story in that the widow is to go to the city gate and make her case to the town elders, who will then question the man. A sandal plays a role in what happens if he still refuses, but it appears to be unrelated to the sandal-swapping ritual mentioned in Ruth that seals the deal. In this case, the woman pulls off the man's sandal and spits in his face, and his family is forever known as "the house of the one whose sandal was pulled off."

marriage, so perhaps Ruth is proposing that Boaz should marry her (Ezek. 16:8). If so, that enhances the sexual nature of the scene while challenging the gender norms of the time.[10]

Boaz and Ruth do end up tying the knot, so maybe what takes place on the threshing floor is meant to anticipate that outcome. With the birth of their child, the plot is resolved; Elimelech's family line continues and Naomi's problems are solved. The last line of dialogue in the book comes from the women of Bethlehem, who proclaim, "A son has been born to Naomi" (4:17). As with the first time they spoke (1:19), they do not mention Ruth, but just prior to this they acknowledge the critical role her daughter-in-law played in reversing Naomi's fortune (4:15). For her part, Naomi acknowledges that reversal by letting them know that she is now able to live up to her name and return to being "pleasant."

That happy outcome is only possible thanks to Ruth, who is the agent of Naomi's transformation. She serves as an intermediary between Boaz and Naomi, who never meet or speak to one another a single time in the book. But Ruth brings them together nonetheless as the culmination of a journey that takes her from her homeland, across the border into Israel, on to Bethlehem, to Naomi's house, into Boaz's field, and onto the threshing floor. Ruth the Moabite probably had no idea what she was getting herself into when she told her mother-in-law, "Where you go, I will go."

Second Opinions

Just like its two main characters, the book of Ruth tends to wander. Depending on what kind of a Bible you are reading, it could be located toward the beginning of the Old Testament or it might be among the last books of the collection. In the Christian canon it is situated between Judges and 1 Samuel, in a section called the "Historical Books." This is also where it is in the Septuagint, the Greek translation of the Hebrew Bible that was begun in the third century BCE and has been influential within the Christian community. A likely reason for Ruth's placement there are its opening words—"In the days when the judges ruled"—which suggest it is a follow-up to the book of Judges.

In Jewish Bibles Ruth is found much later, in the final section of the Bible that is known as the "Writings," where it comes between the Song of Songs and Lamentations. That third section is sort of a catch-all category that includes works written in many different styles and genres. Ruth is also part of a sub-category of biblical writings that are referred to as the Megillot, a Hebrew term that means "scrolls." These are five texts—the others are Esther, Song of Songs, Qohelet, and Lamentations—that are each read on a particular feast day in the Jewish calendar.

---

10. Alternative interpretations of what takes place in this episode are discussed in Shadrac Keita and Janet W. Dyk, "The Scene at the Threshing Floor: Suggestive Readings and Intercultural Considerations on Ruth 3," *The Bible Translator* 57, no. 1 (2006): 17–32.

Ruth is read on the feast of Shavuot, or Weeks, which celebrates the harvest, the time of year in which most of the story is set.

The reference to the judges in its opening verse might support its placement after the book that goes by that name, but Ruth is still something of an interloper in the Christian order of the canon. Its presence between Judges and 1 Samuel puts it right in the middle of a set of books (Joshua, Judges, 1 and 2 Samuel, and 1 and 2 Kings) that together are referred to as the "Deuteronomistic History." They are given this designation because they recount the history of Israel from the entry into the land until the fall of the kingdom, and they do so from the perspective of the book of Deuteronomy and its emphasis on the law that was given to Moses.[11] According to the way that history is told, when the Israelites follow the law, all goes well for them; but when they disobey it, things fall apart. The book of Ruth does not share that perspective, and so it is as much of a fish out of water in the Deuternomistic History as its namesake is among the people of Bethlehem.

Uncovering the Real Ruth

Wordplay and irony are found frequently within the book of Ruth. Much of this is apparent only in the Hebrew original, and so it usually escapes the notice of most readers, but awareness of it can add to one's enjoyment of the story and call attention to the artistry that went into writing it.

Playing with Words

As noted, Naomi's name change contains a wordplay that signals a shift in her mood as she goes from "pleasant" to "bitter" and then back again. Her sons are chips off the old block because their names also have meanings, and they are among the funniest in the entire Bible. The soon-to-be-no-more Mahlon and Chilion have names that literally mean "sickly" and "weak." Boaz's name means something along the lines of "in him there is strength," which could be a comment on his physical power or his personal integrity. The way he is consistently presented as an upright person who takes the moral high ground makes the latter possibility especially appealing.

> How much of a disadvantage is it for the reader who does not know Hebrew and so cannot recognize the wordplays and repetition that are often lost in translation?

Even the unnamed can be referred to in interesting ways, as we see when Boaz greets the next-of-kin at the city gate (4:1). English translations tend to render the Hebrew phrase Boaz uses when he calls out to him as "friend" or "sir," but it is actually an unusual colloquialism that is more like "what's-his-face" or

---

11. See Steven L. McKenzie, "Deuteronomistic History," in *The New Interpreter's Dictionary of the Bible*, ed. Katharine Doob Sakenfeld (Nashville: Abingdon, 2007), 2:106–7.

"so-and-so." It is strange that Boaz does not call him by his given name. They were relatives after all, so he must have known it. Maybe his anonymity is the author's way of dismissing him as someone who is not capable of doing the right thing by acquiring the land and Ruth along with it.

Sometimes biblical place names, not just personal names, can be examples of wordplay or can function ironically. The best instance of this in Ruth is Bethlehem; the name of the town Elimelech's family flees from because of a famine literally means "house of bread." The use of euphemism is another form of playing with words, and we saw an instance of it in Ruth's uncovering of Boaz's feet and how the term is probably a polite way of referring to his genitals.

Another type of wordplay found in Ruth entails the repetition of similar sounds, words, or phrases. This is usually done to create a certain auditory effect or to make connections between different parts of the story. Here, too, familiarity with Hebrew is often required in order to catch how this literary technique is being employed. Ruth's final words to Boaz in 2:10 as they talk in the field exhibit a fine example of the repetition of the same sounds. In English she says, "That you should take notice of me, when I am a foreigner." What requires twelve words in English is said in only three in Hebrew, which makes repeated use of the letters "n," "k," and "r" to create a pleasant effect: *lehakireni we'anoki nokriyya.*

There are several good examples of the repetition of terms or phrases that establish links between different parts of the story and therefore help to unify it. When they are on the threshing floor and Ruth asks Boaz to spread his cloak over her (3:9), the word she uses for his garment is the same one that he used in the previous chapter in reference to God's wings (2:12). This adds a theological dimension to her request that suggests Ruth is placing her trust in the God of Israel by asking Boaz to take care of her.

When Boaz is first introduced to us he is described in Hebrew as an *'ish hayil,* which the NRSV translates as "a prominent rich man" (2:1). The word *hayil* has a wide range of possible meanings that can connote power, wealth, competence, or bravery. However it is translated, it is meant to present Boaz's social standing in a very positive light. Boaz uses a similar term when he refers to Ruth as an *'eshet hayil,* which is translated as "a worthy woman" (3:11). This use of the term *hayil* in two phrases that are virtually identical links the two characters in the reader's mind and invites us to view them as mirror images of each other.

Another example of repetition can be seen at the end of the third chapter when, in the last words she speaks in the book, Ruth reports to Naomi that Boaz had told her, "Do not go back to your mother-in-law empty-handed" (3:17). The Hebrew word translated here as "empty-handed" was used by Naomi herself in the first chapter when, upon their arrival in Bethlehem, she complained, "I went away full, but the LORD has brought me back empty" (1:21a). Here, too, the repetition of the term encourages the reader to interpret the scenes in light of one another. Boaz's words to Ruth recall the crucial problem around which the entire plot revolves—Naomi's emptiness—and they anticipate the role that Ruth (and he) will play in solving that problem through the birth of their child.[12]

Now You See Him, Now You Don't

Trivia time—what character is mentioned by name in all four chapters of the book of Ruth but never speaks a single time? If you guessed Mahlon and Chilion (aka, "sickly" and "weak"), guess again. Those two frail lads are identified in the first and last chapters, but not in between. Their father Elimelech comes pretty close to winning the prize, but he is mentioned in only three of the four chapters.

The answer will likely surprise you; it's God. That's right. The deity pops up repeatedly throughout the tale, but he never speaks a word.

A close examination of the passages in which God is mentioned reveals some interesting facts. It has already been noted that in a few places Naomi singles out the deity as the one responsible for her situation when she complains about God's role in her troubles early in the story (1:13, 20, 21). The vast majority of the rest of the references are in the context of a blessing or a wish on the part of one character that God might be with

> Why do you think God does not do much and does not speak at all in the book of Ruth?

another (1:8, 9, 17; 2:4, 12, 20; 3:10; 4:11, 12, 14). In each of these cases, God does not do anything, but is instead called upon by a person to intervene or be present in the life of another individual. In other words, God is a relatively passive figure in the story; he is mentioned frequently, but does not do much.

The two exceptions to that pattern form bookends that open and close the story. The only places where God is the active subject of a verb are the first time and the next-to-last time he is mentioned. In the initial scene, Naomi decides to head back home to Bethlehem because she hears that "the LORD had considered his people and given them food" (1:6). At the tail end of the story, the narrator explains that Ruth and Boaz are able to have a child because, "when they came together, the LORD made her conceive, and she bore a son" (4:13). Those are the only two actions God undertakes in the book, and note how similar they are to one another. In each case, the deity is a provider who gives something to someone that solves a crisis and allows the plot to advance to its next stage. In the first instance, Naomi and Ruth can return to Israel because God has made food available there. Toward the end, God makes possible the pregnancy that helps

---

12. A detailed discussion of how repetition functions in the Old Testament is provided in Meir Sternberg, *The Poetics of Biblical Narrative: Ideological Literature and the Drama of Reading* (Bloomington, IN: Indiana University Press, 1985), 365–440.

transform bitter Naomi to pleasant once again. Bread and baby, newborn and nourishment—two symbols of life and hope from God.

Twists of Fate, or Something Else?

Is that the extent of God's involvement, or is it possible to see the divine hand at work at other points in the story beyond these two? The frequent references to the deity throughout the book make him ever-present, even if not overly active, and that might be the author's way of suggesting that God is busy working behind the scenes. Take the reference to God ending the famine, for example. If he solved the problem, could he not have been the cause of it in the first place? In the ancient world, it was commonly believed that the deity who was associated with a particular place had authority over what happened there. By that logic, if Israel experienced a famine, would that not mean that the God of Israel was somehow involved? The mention of God removing the famine tends to support this idea. In addition, elsewhere in the Old Testament, God is given (and sometimes takes) credit for inflicting hunger and starvation on various groups, including his own people. In Jeremiah 24:10, God says, "I will send sword, famine, and pestilence upon them, until they are utterly destroyed from the land that I gave to them and their ancestors" (cf. Lev. 26:19–20; Deut. 28:23–24; Jer. 24:10; Ezek. 6:11–12; Joel 1; Amos 4:6–10).

And then there is the way that some things seem to happen a little too conveniently in the book. When she goes out to glean in the beginning of chapter 2, Ruth just happens to end up in the portion of the field that is owned by Boaz, the person who will shortly play such a pivotal role in her life (2:3). The NRSV translation reads, "As it happened, she came to the part of the field belonging to Boaz," giving the impression that she is an active agent who is responsible for where she ends up. But the Hebrew text literally says, "Her chance (or luck) came to the field," which downplays her agency and suggests that something else was involved in getting her there.[13] And when she arrives on the scene, guess who just happens to show up in the very next verse. None other than Boaz! His entrance is heralded with the Hebrew particle *hinneh*, which is commonly translated "Behold!" and is sometimes used to express surprise at some unexpected turn of events.

The same sense of fate guiding a character's steps might also be present in the threshing floor scene, when Ruth is able to find her way in the darkness to the spot where Boaz has decided to bed down for the night. It is certainly apparent at the beginning of chapter 4 when Boaz sits down by the gate and immediately runs into the other relative, the very man he is looking for (4:1). The

---

13. The Jewish Publication Society translation does a nice job of conveying this sense when it renders the phrase, "As luck would have it."

telltale term *hinneh* is also found in this scene, underscoring Boaz's astonishing good fortune in bumping into the exact person he needs to have a chat with.

It could be that all of these things are just fluky coincidences that we should not read too much into. On the other hand, we should not be too quick to dismiss the possibility that something else is afoot here. Some people interpret what others consider to be happenstance as divine intervention, and perhaps that is a possibility the author wants us to enter-

> What do you think of the idea that the seemingly random coincidences in Ruth are actually God's work?

tain for the book of Ruth. It looks like Naomi does exactly that in chapter 2 when Ruth comes back from working in the field and tells her that she ran into Boaz. Naomi does not say, "What luck!" or "How weird!" Rather, she exclaims, "Blessed be he by the LORD, whose kindness has not forsaken the living or the dead!" (2:20). She is sure that Ruth's encounter with Boaz is not due to chance because she believes that God brought the two of them together in order to take care of her and Ruth in their time of need and to honor the memories of her deceased husband and sons.

Once the notion of God working the strings and levers behind the scenes becomes part of the equation, all kinds of interpretive possibilities are opened up. We are never told how Elimelech, Mahlon, and Chilion met their demise, but maybe the deity was responsible for their untimely deaths that set the whole plot in motion. The belief that God has supreme control over life and death is a central biblical teaching—as seen in his being the cause of Ruth's pregnancy—so the idea that he is a widow-maker in the story is not as far-fetched as it might seem.

Speaking of Ruth and her baby, if we bring God into the picture an interesting interpretation of her status becomes possible. The text tells us that she and Mahlon may have been married for as long as ten years (1:4–5), and yet they did not have children. A common motif in the Old Testament is that of the barren wife, which centers on a woman who is unable to have children until God intervenes and makes it possible. The stories of Sarah (Gen. 11:30), Rebekah (Gen. 25:21), Rachel (Gen. 29:31), Samson's mother (Judges 13:2), and Hannah (1 Sam. 1:5) all describe this situation. It may be that the book of Ruth presents a subtle version of this motif. Unlike those other texts, hers does not call direct attention to Ruth's barrenness from the begin-

> Is Ruth another example of a biblical barren wife? If so, how does it affect how the story should be interpreted?

ning, nonetheless the length of her marriage to Mahlon points in that direction. But like those other women, she becomes pregnant through God's intervention, which supports her inclusion among their ranks. This would make Ruth the only once-barren wife in the Bible who is a foreigner, a distinction that is in keeping with the book's positive evaluation of her despite her status as a non-Israelite.

All in the Family

The children, all boys, who were born to those once-barren women grew up to become prominent men; Isaac, Jacob, Esau, the sons of Jacob, Samson, and Samuel are all Bible luminaries whose stories are popular and well-known. The same thing cannot be said about Ruth's son Obed, whose name means "servant," because his biblical career was pretty much a one-off. He is born and then is never mentioned again in the Old Testament except in a genealogical list that identifies him as Boaz's son (1 Chron. 2:12). That might brand him as an under-achiever compared to his more accomplished counterparts, but sometimes great-ness skips a generation . . . or two.

Twice in the book's final verses we are told that Obed was the father of Jesse, who was the father of King David, which would make Ruth David's great-grandmother.[14] In light of what the Old Testament says about the Moabites (remember the story of Lot and his daughters?), having one in the family tree of the most revered ruler in Israelite history was bound to be a source of tremendous embarrassment. According to one legal text, having that kind of pedigree is enough to get you expelled from the ranks of the chosen people: "No Ammonite or Moabite shall be admitted to the assembly of the LORD. Even to the tenth generation, none of their descendants shall be admitted to the assem-bly of the LORD" (Deut. 23:3). The math is easy to do; David is only two gener-ations removed from Ruth, which puts him well within the ten-generation hot zone. Actually, even if David were a more distant relative, it would not help his case because the English translation softens the force of the Hebrew original of the verse, which ends with the word "forever."

Should the entire line of David, which includes virtually every king who ruled in Judah, be considered pretenders to the throne because they can all be traced back to Ruth the Moabite? Probably not, because that would only create a whole new set of problems. More likely, the association it makes between David and Ruth gives us an indication of the true agenda that drives the book. The author's interest is in Ruth, not David.[15] The book was likely written to expand the understanding of what, or who, constitutes the people of God. In doing so, it is diametrically opposed to the message in Deuteronomy 23 about Moabites being despised to the tenth generation. It is a biblical precedent for setting aside other biblical texts for the sake of inclusivity. It challenges the idea some people have that the Bible gives them the right to reject the other. Although Ruth is a foreigner, she embraces the God of Israel as her own, relocates to Israel to start

---

14. David is not the only prominent biblical figure whose lineage is traced to Ruth. According to the Gospels of Matthew (1:5) and Luke (3:32), she and Obed are also part of Jesus' family history. Those are the only other references to them in the Bible outside the book of Ruth.

15. It is likely that the final verses of the book that give Obed's genealogy and mention David were a later addition to the original story; the original story apparently was meant to enhance Ruth's character and establish her legitimacy in the eyes of the Israelites.

a new life, is recognized for the good things she does, and eventually gives birth to a child whose own offspring will play a key role in the future history of the Israelite people. Should not such a person be deserving of membership within the community?

The book of Ruth challenges the insider/outsider dichotomy sometimes found in the Hebrew Bible that disparages and demonizes non-Israelites as inferior to Israelites. Nowhere is this more clearly seen than in texts that describe what the Israelites are to do to the other peoples they encounter as they make their way to the Promised Land. In no uncertain terms, they are commanded to completely wipe them off the face of the earth (see Deut. 7:1–2; 13:15–17; 20:16–17).

That view is challenged by the book of Ruth, which suggests that if one of the Moabites can be great-grandmother to the great King David, then maybe they are not so bad after all. Ruth's character is presented in a way that is meant to challenge stereotypes and assumptions (and even biblical prohibitions) that help to perpetuate the idea that foreigners are not a part of God's purposes and plans. This inclusive understanding of God's relationship with humanity is in tension with those biblical passages that speak of God's election of Israel as the Chosen People, as well as others that will be treated below that call for the removal and elimination of those who are not part of the covenantal community. The alternative perspective it offers undoubtedly developed in response to the context out of which the book of Ruth originally emerged.

It is likely that the book was written at a time when the Israelites' relationships with non-Israelites were an important issue that they were wrestling with; the early post-exilic period of the fifth century BCE is probably when it was composed. Passages from other biblical texts of that time, like Ezra (9:1–4, 12) and Nehemiah (13:23–27) criticize Israelite men who had married foreign women while living in exile, and Ezra even demands that they should divorce those wives before returning to the land because their marriages are a sin in God's eyes (10:10–17). The book of Ruth the Moabite says, "Not so fast!" It calls into question that attitude, and it puts forward a different understanding of interpersonal relations by proposing that God's seeming absence from the life of the other might simply be presence of a different sort.

> How might someone argue for and against the book of Ruth's view of foreigners and outsiders?

The Book of Jonah

Another text that provides insight into biblical views of the other is Jonah, which has much in common with Ruth. It is also a short narrative that holds the reader's attention, and it is even a quicker read than Ruth because its four chapters contain only forty-eight verses. Like Ruth, it relates a story in which people from different backgrounds encounter one another, but there is an interesting twist. Ruth is set in Israel, where she is a lone foreigner who finds herself in a strange land. In Jonah's story the roles are reversed, as he is now the lone foreigner who has journeyed to another place. Another important difference between the two books can be seen in how God is portrayed. The deity plays a much more active and visible role in Jonah than in Ruth, where we often have to read between the lines and infer his presence in the story.

First Impressions

READ: Jonah 1–4

Jonah is one of a dozen relatively short works that are commonly referred to as the "Minor Prophets" or, in the Hebrew Bible, "the Book of the Twelve." In the Bible these writings are found immediately after those of the three Major Prophets, Isaiah, Jeremiah, and Ezekiel, whose books are much longer.

> Since he is never described that way in his book, should we avoid calling Jonah a prophet?

Although he is grouped with those other books, Jonah is the odd man out among his prophetic comrades for a number of reasons. In the first place, its style sets his work apart from theirs. While the writings of the other prophets are full of oracles from God that are usually written in poetry, only one verse of Jonah can reasonably be considered to be an oracle. In effect, we read more *about* Jonah in his book than we read *from* him (or from God). Another anomaly is that Jonah is never referred to as a prophet in the entire book. It is stated twice that the word of the Lord came to him (1:1; 3:1), which is one of the defining features of the biblical prophets, but he is never given the title "prophet." Perhaps this is so because, as will become apparent, Jonah does very little to deserve that designation.

Before going any further, we should probably address the elephant in the room—or, to be more accurate, the whale in the tale. Is any biblical character more closely identified with a particular animal than Jonah is associated with his whale? Daniel and the lions would probably give them a run for their money, but for many people Jonah and his fishy friend are an inseparable duo that is the Bible's answer to Dorothy and Toto. There is only one problem, though: the story never mentions a whale. It just refers to a "big fish" without identifying the type. We are not sure exactly how the great fish morphed into a whale, but that is how it is described in the King James Version of the New Testament from the early seventeenth century, in which Jesus mentions Jonah and the whale (Matt. 12:40).[16] The only other whale sightings in the King James Bible are found in Ezekiel 32:2 and Job 7:12, but those two verses contain a word that is usually

---

16. The King James Version describes it as a "great fish" in the book of Jonah, and not as a whale.

The Metropolitan Museum of Art, New York, Purchase, Joseph Pulitzer Bequest, 1933

Jonah and the whale? The Hebrew text identifies the creature that swallows Jonah as a *dag* ("fish"). Jonah is swallowed by a fish in this fifteenth-century Iranian manuscript.

rendered as "sea monster" or "dragon" in other translations. The book opens with God commanding Jonah to go the Assyrian city of Nineveh, in modern-day Iraq, where he is to tell the inhabitants that the deity is displeased with them because of their evil ways. Jonah instead does an about-face and heads in the opposite direction by hopping on a boat bound for Tarshish. He does not get far, though, because God sends a storm that almost causes the crew to abandon ship, until they discover that Jonah is the cause of their problems. At Jonah's suggestion, they throw him into the sea and the storm subsides. God then causes a large fish to swallow Jonah, and he remains inside it for three days. Virtually all of chapter 2 is comprised of a prayer Jonah utters while inside the fish. The prayer both describes his misfortune and expresses confidence that God will rescue him. That is what comes to pass when God orders the fish to spew out Jonah and he is returned to dry land.

The third chapter starts the same way as the first one, with God telling Jonah to go to Nineveh and speak to its residents. This time Jonah heeds the deity's command and goes to the city, where the people express their belief in God through rituals associated with repentance like fasting and wearing sackcloth.[17] Even the ruler of the city joins in by expressing his remorse and ordering that all of Nineveh's inhabitants, including the animals, must don sackcloth and refrain from eating. That strategy has its desired effect; the chapter ends with God having a change of heart and deciding not to destroy the city.

---

17. Sackcloth is rough material that is made from animal hair. It is often worn by people in the Bible to indicate that they are in a state of mourning or repentance.

That outcome doesn't sit too well with Jonah, who complains that God is too merciful and loving. In fact, Jonah wishes the deity would put him out of his misery by killing him. Jonah goes outside the city and builds a booth, where he can rest in comfort and see what awaits Nineveh. God then provides a bush for Jonah that gives him even more shade, but it is soon taken away when God sends a worm that causes the bush to shrivel up. As the sun beats down on Jonah, he again expresses a death wish (4:8). At that point the story ends abruptly when the deity chastises the prophet for failing to recognize that God has every right to be concerned about the many citizens of Nineveh.[18]

There's Something Fishy about This Story

Much about the book of Jonah suggests it is a humorous, even absurd, story that is not meant to be taken literally. All of the human characters are presented as parodies of themselves who act in ways we would not expect them to behave. The "hero" is a prophet who is told by God to go somewhere, and then flees in the opposite direction (1:3). He meets up with a group of sailors who head back to land when a storm breaks out at sea (1:13). Any fisherman worth his salt knows that is the last place to go, because his boat could be smashed to pieces on the shoreline. Then an entire city of people come to believe in a foreign god based on one line of dialogue uttered by a stranger (3:5). They are ruled by a king who is so easily swayed that he puts aside the symbols of his power and follows that foreign god, even though he has not heard for himself what the stranger has to say (3:6–9).

All of these characters are playing against type by conducting themselves in unexpected ways, and that pattern extends to the non-human actors in the story as well. The most obvious example are the animals of Nineveh, who obey the king's command to refrain from food and water, get dressed in sackcloth, cry out to God, and turn from their evil ways (3:7–9). But the anthropomorphisms do not end there, since even the boat carrying Jonah and the sailors takes on a human-like quality. The literal translation of the Hebrew verb used in the description of the storm says that the ship was "thinking about" breaking up (1:4). This story is full of characters and events that defy logic and ask the reader to accept the unimaginable. And speaking of

How do its satirical and exaggerated elements affect how we should interpret the Jonah story?

18. Among the many studies on the book of Jonah are Kenneth M. Craig Jr., *A Poetics of Jonah: Art in the Service of Ideology* (Columbia, SC: University of South Carolina, 1993); James Limburg, *Jonah* (Louisville: Westminster John Knox, 1993); Phyllis Trible, *Rhetorical Criticism: Context, Method, and the Book of Jonah* (Minneapolis: Fortress, 1994); and Yvonne Sherwood, *A Biblical Text and Its Afterlives: The Survival of Jonah in Western Culture* (Cambridge: Cambridge University Press, 2001).

things that are hard to swallow, we have not yet mentioned Jonah's three-day sojourn inside the belly of a gigantic fish.[19]

It is also a well-constructed tale whose two halves contain many similar elements. The first and third chapters begin in the same way by stating that the word of the Lord came to Jonah, and then God tells him to get up and go to the great city of Nineveh to deliver a message to its inhabitants (1:1–2; 3:1–2). The shared vocabulary in the opening lines of the two chapters causes the reader to think that the second time he is called, Jonah will respond as he did the first time—by fleeing from God—and this impression is reinforced through the repetition of the same verb in the third verse of each chapter: "And Jonah arose." But lightning does not strike twice; Jonah wises up the second time and heads in the right direction—to Nineveh.

A group of foreigners is then introduced in each half of the book, the sailors in chapter 1 and the Ninevites in chapter 3. In both cases, the group ends up acting in a way that expresses its fear and belief in Jonah's God, as the sailors sacrifice and make vows to the Lord (1:16) and the Ninevites fast and put on sackcloth (3:5). One person is singled out as the leader in each group and expresses hope that Jonah's God will rescue them. Upon finding Jonah asleep in the hold of the ship the captain says, "What are you doing sound asleep? Get up, call on your god! Perhaps the god will spare us a thought so that we do not perish" (1:6). The king of Nineveh hopes for the same outcome in a statement that ends with similar language: "Who knows? God may relent and change his mind; he may turn from his fierce anger, so that we do not perish" (3:9).

There then follow interactions between Jonah and God in each half of the book. In chapter 2 this takes the form of a prayer from Jonah to God about his fate, prayed from inside the fish (2:1–9). The prayer is preceded by God controlling an element from nature (the fish) as a demonstration of divine authority (1:17). That monologue by Jonah

> What do the similarities between its two halves suggest about the composition of the book of Jonah?

becomes a dialogue in the second half that begins as a prayer (4:2–11), when he and God engage in a lengthy conversation about his fate that is interspersed with three references to the deity once again demonstrating authority by controlling natural elements (a bush, a worm, the wind).

By the end of the second verse, God has already spoken more in the book of Jonah than he does in all of Ruth. After that, though, God does not utter another word until the beginning of chapter 3. Between those two lines of dialogue the deity still continues to be an important character in the story, but in

---

19. On the presence of satire in the text, see John C. Holbert, "'Deliverance Belongs to Yahweh': Satire in the Book of Jonah," *Journal for the Study of the Old Testament* 21 (1981): 59–81. The role of irony in Jonah is discussed in Mona West, "Irony in the Book of Jonah: Audience Identification with the Hero," *Perspectives in Religious Studies* 11, no. 3 (1984): 233–42.

a non-verbal way. Unlike in Ruth, where he is the subject of only two verbs throughout the entire book, God in Jonah is responsible for many of the key events that occur throughout the narrative. In the first chapter, the deity both sends the wind upon the sea to prevent Jonah from fleeing (1:4) and appoints the large fish that will restrict his movements even further (1:17). The Hebrew verb that is used to describe God sending the fish becomes a key term later on in the story because it will be repeated three other times in rapid succession in chapter 4, where God appoints a bush (4:6), a worm (4:7), and an easterly wind (4:8). Once again, this is a way of demonstrating the deity's complete control over the created world.

God will find his voice again in chapter 3, but only partially so. At the beginning of the book, God's first words are, "Go at once to Nineveh, that great city, and cry out against it; for their wickedness has come up before me" (1:2). And then, as noted above, after a period of silence that extends through the rest of the first chapter and all of the second, the deity says almost the exact same thing to Jonah: "Get up, go to Nineveh, that great city, and proclaim to it the message that I tell you" (3:2). What is especially interesting here is what God does not say; he mentions the message that he will give to Jonah, but not its exact words. This means that when Jonah goes on to deliver his message to the Ninevites two verses later the reader has to assume and trust that it is, in fact, the very same one that God communicated to him. The message Jonah goes on to convey to the Ninevites, the only time he speaks like a real prophet in the entire book, is a model of brevity: "Forty days more, and Nineveh shall be overthrown!" (3:4).

Whether or not Jonah spoke the actual words God told him to say, they prove to be very effective. In fact, he has more success than any prophet on record as all the people (and animals) in Nineveh heed his message and mend their ways. And that outcome, too, is not without its irony, because the citizens of Nineveh and their furry friends, just like the foreign sailors he encountered earlier, exhibit a level of faith in the God of Israel that even Jonah cannot muster. In a final parodic twist, Jonah is so disillusioned by how successful his preaching has been that he calls God out for being too compassionate toward the Ninevites, sets up camp outside the city, and wishes he were dead (4:2–9). With that final tantrum, Jonah pulls off a double distinction that really sets him apart—he is simultaneously the Bible's most successful prophet and its biggest pouter.

Second Opinions

Jonah is mentioned one other time in the Old Testament outside the book that bears his name. A passage in 2 Kings describes how Jeroboam II, a ruler of the northern kingdom, was able to expand the borders of Israel and thereby return them to the dimensions they were some two centuries earlier under King Solomon: "He restored the border of Israel from Lebo-hamath as far as the Sea of the Arabah, according to the word of the LORD, the God of Israel, which he spoke by his servant Jonah son of Amittai, the prophet, who was from Gath-hepher" (2 Kings 14:25). This is not some other Jonah because his father Amittai is also mentioned in the prophetic book (1:1). It is interesting that the verse from 2 Kings refers to Jonah as a prophet, something that is never explicitly stated in the book that

> Why might it be that the book's author refrains from calling Jonah a prophet?

is named after him. Another tidbit present here but not in the book is the reference to his hometown of Gath-hepher, a place that was probably located somewhere near the town of Nazareth in Galilee that is associated with Jesus in the New Testament.

It could be that the book of Jonah contains traditions concerning the prophet mentioned in 2 Kings, but the precise origin of the story about him, the fish, and his trip to Nineveh remains a mystery. It is highly unlikely that the book of Jonah was composed during the reign of Jeroboam II in the eighth century BCE; most probably it comes from a much later time.[20]

An aspect of Jonah that has a bearing on the date of the book is the way it sometimes shows familiarity with other biblical writings, especially prophetic texts. In some places this is seen in allusions to other passages, and elsewhere the similarities are more obvious and apparent. For example, the reference in 3:10 to God relenting and changing his mind about destroying Nineveh after he sees how its people have left behind their evil ways appears to play out a scenario that God puts forward in the book of Jeremiah: "But if that nation, concerning which I have spoken, turns from its evil, I will change my mind about the disaster that I intended to bring on it" (Jer. 18:8). Similarly, the description of the king of Nineveh getting up from his throne, removing his robe, putting on sackcloth, and sitting in ashes (3:6) echoes a verse in Ezekiel (Ezek. 26:16).

The most striking connection between Jonah and another prophetic writing can be seen in Joel 2:13, which states, "Rend your hearts and not your clothing. Return to the LORD, your God, for he is gracious and merciful, slow to anger, and abounding in steadfast love, and relents from punishing." This passage is quite similar to what Jonah says in 4:2b, where he explains why he first tried to escape

> Are there any other ways of explaining the similarities between Jonah and other prophetic writings besides borrowing and literary dependence?

God's presence: "That is why I fled to Tarshish at the beginning; for I knew that you are a gracious God and merciful, slow to anger, and abounding in steadfast

---

20. See, for example, George Landes, "A Case for the Sixth Century BCE Dating for the Book of Jonah," in *Realia Dei: Essays in Archaeology and Biblical Interpretation in Honor of Edward F. Campbell Jr. at His Retirement*, ed. Prescott H. Williams Jr. and Theodore Heibert (Durham, NC: Duke University Press, 1999), 100–16.

love, and ready to relent from punishing." The two passages use the same adjectives to describe God, in the same order. The presence in Jonah of the Hebrew term that is translated "steadfast love" is particularly striking because it usually has the connotation of covenant faithfulness. Jonah has taken a word that is normally reserved for Israel's relationship with God and has applied it to all people's relationship with God. These three texts are found in relatively late books— Jeremiah, Ezekiel, and Joel—that date to the exilic or post-exilic period. The similarity between them and Jonah suggest that its author was likely familiar with them, which in turn makes a postexilic date for Jonah in the fifth or fourth century BCE plausible.

The story of Jonah does not appear to be a pastiche that was put together from different sources. The only section that breaks the narrative flow somewhat and slows things down a bit is Jonah's lengthy prayer from inside the fish in 2:2–9. Those verses could be removed and the story would still make perfect sense, because the reference to Jonah praying to God in 2:1 would then be immediately followed by God speaking to the fish and telling it to spit out Jonah onto dry land. For this reason, it has been suggested that Jonah's prayer in chapter 2 is a later addition and not part of the original composition.

> Which possibility is more likely to you: that Jonah's prayer from inside the fish in chapter 2 was a later insertion, or that it was part of the original story?

An argument in favor of seeing the prayer in chapter 2 as a work that predates Jonah is the fact that nothing in it relates directly to the story that surrounds it. The reference to the speaker being cast into the water fits the narrative somewhat, but in the prayer it is God who throws him into the sea, while in the story it is the sailors (2:3). Also, there is no reference to the large fish. The prayer begins with a reference to the speaker crying out to God from "the belly of Sheol," which is an allusion to the underworld or land of the dead, but if it were composed with the surrounding story in mind one would expect the belly of the fish to be mentioned. Most likely, the prayer was composed before the Jonah narrative was written and was later incorporated into it because its themes resonated with the story.[21]

Prophet Margins

As is the case with the book of Ruth, a number of aspects of the story of Jonah can be easily missed because they are subtle or because they require familiarity with biblical Hebrew and the wider cultural context of the Old Testament. One is Jonah's name (*yonah*), which means "dove" in Hebrew. In a few

---

21. An overview of how the prayer in chapter 2 relates to the rest of the book of Jonah is found in Amanda W. Benckhuysen, "Revisiting the Psalm of Jonah," *Calvin Theological Journal* 47 (2012): 5–31.

places in the Bible, doves are presented as foolish and timid birds that fly away in fear, and perhaps Jonah is given that name because he exhibits those traits through his unwillingness to accept both God's call and the divine decision to let the Ninevites live: "And I say, 'Oh that I had wings like a dove! I would fly away and be at rest; truly, I would flee far away; I would lodge in the wilderness" (Ps. 55:6–7; cf. Hos. 7:11; 11:11). If you substitute Jonah's name for the words "a dove" in that verse—they are identical in Hebrew—it provides an apt description of Jonah's state of mind at the end of his book as he struggles to come to terms with God's mercy toward the people of Nineveh.

Speaking of Nineveh, it was the capital of the Neo-Assyrian Empire until it was destroyed in 612 BCE by a coalition of Babylonians and Medes. Its ruler is referred to as the "King of Nineveh" in Jonah (3:6), but that title is not found in the historical record and is another point in favor of dating the story to a later time period when the Neo-Assyrian Empire was no longer around. Located in northern Mesopotamia, Nineveh was one of the major metropolitan areas of the ancient Near East, and it had been around since the sixth millennium BCE. The book of Jonah acknowledges this status by referring to it as a "great city" (1:2; 3:2) and calling attention to its size as "an exceedingly large city, a three days' walk across" (3:3). According to ancient sources, Nineveh was surrounded by a double wall that was more than a mile wide and about three miles long. Consequently, the book's claim that it would have taken three

Ancient Nineveh, with a wall seven miles in circumference, was much smaller than Jonah 3:3 indicates. Such exaggerations were probably the author's way of alerting the reader that he is telling a tall tale with a message, not a literal history.

days to traverse the city is a clear exaggeration since Jonah probably could have passed through Nineveh in a couple of hours.[22]

Tarshish, on the other hand, is another matter because very little is known about the place to which Jonah tried to run from God. We are not even sure where it was. Whatever its location, according to the book of Ezekiel it was

---

22. Issues related to the size of Nineveh are discussed in Charles Halton, "How Big Was Nineveh?," *Bulletin of Biblical Research* 18 (2008): 193–207.

a mineralogical paradise that had silver, iron, tin, and lead for the taking (Ezek. 27:12; cf. 38:13; Jer. 10:9). It was a seafaring area whose ships were celebrated, and 1 Kings 10:22 mentions that it contained gold, along with exotic animals like apes and peacocks that were sometimes exported by boat to Israel (cf. 1 Kings 22:48; Ezek. 27:25). The only problem is that we do not know exactly where those boats were coming from, since the location of Tarshish remains a mystery.[23]

While we do not know precisely where Jonah was heading, we do know how he intended to get there. His mode of transport was a boat, but there is an interesting thing about the way the vessel is identified in the story. It is referred to four times in the first five verses of the book, but two different words are used to describe it. The first three times the Hebrew word *'oniyya* is used (1:3, 4, 5), but the fourth time it is called a *sepina* (1:5). The first word is a common term in the Bible for a boat, but this is the only occurrence of *sepina* in the entire Old Testament. The reason for this shift in terminology is unclear, but it could have to do with the Hebrew root that *sepina* comes from. It can mean "to cover," and it is sometimes used in reference to the roof of a building or the ceiling of a room. Perhaps it is used here to identify the ship as one that has a deck and therefore a lower compartment that is covered. This fits the details of the story very well, because the term is found in the description of Jonah going down into the lower level of the boat, where he proceeds to fall asleep (1:5).

Jonah's retreat into the bowels of the boat continues a descent that he has been undertaking since he first heard God's call to go to Nineveh. In response, he "went down" to Joppa (1:3), where he "went on board" a ship heading to Tarshish (1:3), only to "[go] down" into the lower level of the vessel (1:5). In each case a verb from the Hebrew root *yarad* is used to convey Jonah's downward motion, capped off with a nice wordplay at the end of verse 5 when the word translated as "fast asleep" contains the same consonants in the same order (*yeradam*). The sailors then toss him into the sea and he sinks like a brick, only to be swallowed by the big fish whose belly is reminiscent of the hold of the ship he was sleeping in not so long ago.

That fish is like the boat for another reason as well—it is referred to in two different ways in the text. Twice in 1:17 and once in 2:10 it is identified as a male fish (*dag*), but in 2:1 its gender briefly switches and it is a female (*daga*). Some medieval commentators tried to explain this by suggesting that there were actually two fish in the story, one male and one female, and Jonah went back and forth between them. In this reading, his discovery that he has to share the female fish's belly with her unborn babies is more than he can bear and he utters his prayer in desperation due to the cramped quarters.[24]

---

23. Most scholars think that Tarshish was located somewhere in the Mediterranean Sea basin, with southern Spain and Carthage in North Africa as possible candidates.

24. A discussion of the fish's gender can be found in Lena-Sofia Tiemeyer, "A New Look at the Biological Sex/Grammatical Gender of Jonah's Fish," *Vetus Testamentum* vol. 67 (2017): pp. 307–23.

Like the book of Ruth, Jonah sometimes repeats key terms to call the reader's attention to important themes or for other literary purposes. An example of this is the frequent use of the term "great," which can also be translated "large" or the equivalent. It occurs fourteen times in the story, where it describes the city of Nineveh (1:2; 3:2, 3; 4:11), the wind God sends (1:4), the storm (1:4, 12), the fear of the sailors (1:10, 16), the fish (1:17), some of the people of Nineveh (3:5), the king's nobles (3:7), Jonah's displeasure (4:1), and Jonah's happiness (4:6).

Another frequently used term is "evil," which is found nine times. It describes the wickedness of the city (1:2), the misfortune the sailors experience (1:7, 8), the evil ways of the citizens of Nineveh (3:8, 10; 4:2), the punishment God was going to send on Nineveh (3:10), and Jonah's anger (4:1 [2x]). Many of these occurrences are used in reference to the wickedness of the people of Nineveh, and the continual reminder of their evil nature underscores for the reader the depths of God's mercy and forgiveness that Jonah is unable to accept.

A third repeated term is the Hebrew verb *manah*, briefly mentioned above; since it is often translated differently in the four places it appears, its frequent use can escape notice. Each time God is the subject of the verb, which the New Revised Standard Version translates twice as "appointed" (4:6, 7) and once each as "provided" (1:17) and "prepared" (4:8). Its first use is at the end of chapter 1 to describe how God sends the great fish to swallow Jonah (1:17). In the final chapter of the book it occurs in three consecutive verses to explain how God provides a bush to shade Jonah (4:6), only to send a worm that leads to the bush's drying up (4:7), followed by God's sending a scorching wind on the sunbaked Jonah that causes him to wish he were dead (4:8). In each instance the deity exercises control over an aspect of the created world that is sent to Jonah and has some effect on his state of mind. The repetition of this verb may be related to the theme of universalism that is at the heart of the story. Just as God cares for all people and gives them the opportunity to repent, so too does the deity have authority over all the elements of the natural world.

> Do you think the repetition of words and phrases in a story is an effective literary device? What effect can it have on the reader?

A final subtle detail worth pointing out has to do with Jonah's only prophetic utterance in the book: "Forty days more, and Nineveh shall be overthrown!" (3:4). The final word of the sentence is ambiguous in Hebrew because it can mean either "destroyed" or "changed." The latter meaning sometimes conveys the sense of a change of heart or a conversion to a new way of thinking or being. This means that the message from God delivered by Jonah is either a warning that the city of Nineveh will soon be destroyed, or a prediction that its inhabitants will repent and mend their ways. The term Jonah uses makes

> How do the two possible ways of translating the verb in 3:4 affect the way we evaluate Jonah's character in the story?

it unclear if he is delivering good news or bad news. Either or those outcomes could have been described in a more clear-cut way by using other Hebrew terms, so it is likely that the author intentionally used ambiguous language to increase the dramatic tension in the story.[25]

Dealing with Difference

The book of Jonah is read every year in synagogues during the afternoon prayer service on Yom Kippur, which is the holiest day of the Jewish calendar. Also known as the "Day of Atonement," Yom Kippur focuses on repentance through prayer and fasting. Jonah is an ideal text to read on such an occasion, because repentance is a central theme of the book. It is curious, though, that the only Israelite character in the story—Jonah himself—never actually repents. In fact, he does just the opposite, and by the end of the story his relationship with God is severely strained. Rather, all of the non-Israelite characters in the book— the sailors, the Ninevites, and their animals—either repent or somehow express belief in Jonah's God. The only one who does not explicitly do so is the large fish, but it nonetheless twice obeys God's will by first swallowing Jonah and then spitting him out.

The basic message of Jonah is similar to that of Ruth: in both stories, non-Israelites are viewed positively and become a part of God's community. Ruth the Moabite has a child through an act of God, and ends up becoming the great-grandmother of King David. Similarly, the anonymous Ninevites acknowledge the power of God and repent in sackcloth and ashes. In these two books, non-Israelites are not stigmatized or denigrated as they sometimes are in other parts of the Old Testament. For example, the stories that recount the Israelites' entry into the land describe in graphic terms how, at God's command, they completely annihilated the local population (Josh. 6:20–21; 8:24–29; 10:28–43; 11:1–23).[26]

> What is your reaction to biblical passages that call for the complete annihilation of groups of people?

As much as such divinely sanctioned bloodbaths might cause Bible readers to squirm, these texts are not describing actual occurrences. Rather, they are attempting to support a particular theological perspective and agenda through the reporting of allegedly historical events that never really happened. The Israelites are presented as a group of outsiders who are numerically outnumbered by the people already living in the land, but they are able to overcome that obstacle and dominate the local population through a combination of able leadership,

---

25. For an analysis of Jonah's words in 3:4, see R. W. L. Moberly, "Preaching for a Response? Jonah's Message to the Ninevites Reconsidered," *Vetus Testamentum* 53, no. 2 (2003): 156–68.

26. A classic study of violence in the Old Testament is Susan Niditch, *War in the Hebrew Bible: A Study in the Ethics of Violence* (New York: Oxford University Press, 1993).

clever military strategy, and divine intervention. In reality, the origin of the Israelites was a lot more complicated than that narrative suggests, and it is quite likely that many of them were actually Canaanites.[27]

Questioning God

The books of Ruth and Jonah take a more positive and inclusive view of relations with outsiders, and so they offer an alternative to the "take-no-prisoners" mindset of works like Joshua. At the same time, though, Jonah's character seems to distance himself from the tolerant message of the book that is named after him, because of the xenophobic streak he possesses. That trait is most clearly seen in the final chapter of the book, but perhaps there is evidence of it at the beginning of the story when Jonah responds to God's command to go to Nineveh by fleeing in the opposite direction. The first chapter does not divulge his motivation for heading to Tarshish, but maybe Jonah does not want to make the trip to Nineveh because he refuses to have anything to do with foreigners whom he considers to be unworthy recipients of a message from the God of Israel.

Jonah finally does acquiesce and obey God's order to go to Nineveh, but his heart does not seem to be in it and the reader cannot help but wonder if he is just going through the motions. It takes three days to walk across the city—an exaggeration of its size, as noted above—but Jonah gets only a third of the way through it when it appears he has had enough. After one day's walk, he blurts out a single line, only five words in Hebrew, to no one in particular. As far as we know, those are the only words he ever says to the people of Nineveh. Did he keep on walking to the other end of the city? The text does not tell us. As already noted, the message Jonah delivers to the Ninevites is ambiguous; does it mean that the city will be destroyed, or that it will be changed? If that ambiguity is intentional, it would be in line with the half-hearted

> Could Jonah's reluctance to accept his mission be rooted in something other than xenophobia?

way he has executed his mission so far. There is a passive-aggressive dimension to Jonah's response that could be rooted in his xenophobia and unwillingness to accept God's concern for the Ninevites.

That xenophobia fully manifests itself in chapter 4. Here the book's message of inclusivity is sharply contrasted with its main character's exclusivity. Immediately after the reference to God's change of heart, the fourth chapter opens by describing Job's response: "But this was very displeasing to Jonah, and he became angry" (4:1). Jonah then comes clean about why he tried to skip town

---

27. For a discussion of issues related to the origin of the Israelites, the historicity of the stories in Joshua, and ethnicity in the Bible, see the chapter titled "The Race Card" in John Kaltner and Steven L. McKenzie, *The Back Door Introduction to the Bible* (Winona, MN: Anselm Academic, 2010).

when God first commissioned him to go to Nineveh: "That is why I fled to Tarshish at the beginning; for I knew that you are a gracious God and merciful, slow to anger, and abounding in steadfast love, and ready to relent from punishing" (4:2b). Jonah cannot handle the idea of a compassionate and forgiving God whose mercy extends beyond the borders of Israel, and it is so much more than he can bear that three times in the next few verses he says that he wishes he were dead (4:3, 8, 9).

Jonah personifies those who find it difficult or impossible to accept others who are different from themselves, and who then try to justify that attitude by appealing to God for support and validation. He never identifies the problem he has with the Ninevites, but it could be based on differences of geography, ethnicity, religion, or some combination of the three. However he defines those differences, the people of Nineveh are not like Jonah, and so he is incapable of accepting the idea that God will save them.[28]

His inability to accept the mercy God shows the Ninevites causes Jonah to challenge and question the deity. He concludes that if this is the way God really is, then he would rather be dead than alive. With that as the solution to his dilemma, Jonah is up to his old tricks again. Wishing he were dead is just a more extreme way of trying to flee from God, this time without a ticket for the next boat heading west. Jonah finds himself in this life-or-death situation because he is unwilling to accept who God is, and he admits as much when he explains the reason why he tried to run away earlier: "I knew that you are a gracious God and merciful" (4:2b).

This time God adopts a different strategy in response to Jonah's insolence. Instead of a three-day ride in the belly of a giant fish, God gives Jonah a taste of his own medicine. The deity answers Jonah's questioning with questions of his own. After not saying a word since the beginning of chapter 3, God finds his voice again in the fourth chapter by speaking three times, and each of those utterances contains a question that is directed to Jonah. Immediately after the prophet first announces his desire to die, God asks him, "Is it right for you to be angry?" (4:4). Jonah does not verbally respond to that query, but his actions speak volumes. He leaves Nineveh and sets up shop outside it by building a booth where he can escape the sun and wait "to see what would become of the city" (4:5).

But it is the petulant prophet, not the foreigners he despises, who receives God's attention. The deity first makes Jonah more comfortable by giving him a large plant that will provide him with additional shade, but then sends a worm that destroys the plant and follows that up with a scorching wind that gives Jonah heatstroke-like symptoms and again causes him to wish he were dead.

28. A discussion of how the book of Jonah challenges exclusivism is found in Ryan Patrick McLaughlin, "Jonah and the Religious Other: An Exploration in Biblical Inclusivism," *Journal of Ecumenical Studies* 48 (2013): 71–84.

This leads to God's second question: "Is it right for you to be angry about the bush?" (4:9). Like the English translation, in Hebrew this question is identical to the one God first asked except for the added reference to the bush. This time Jonah does verbally respond to God's question, but he does not advance the conversation very far because all he does is reiterate his death wish (4:9). As with the other two times Jonah expressed his desire to die, this response elicits a question from God, but this time it is preceded by a statement: "You are concerned about the bush, for which you did not labor and which you did not grow; it came into being in a night and perished in a night. And should I not be concerned about Nineveh, that great city, in which there are more than a hundred and twenty thousand persons who do not know their right hand from their left, and also many animals?" (4:10–11).

Once Jonah admits that his care for something as trivial as a bush has become a matter of life and death, God is able to turn the tables and point out that human beings are much more worthy of concern and compassion.

The book of Jonah ends with a question from God. To put it another way, this means something is missing: Jonah's response. We do not know whether or not he thinks God should care about Nineveh. Based on its wording, it is clearly a rhetorical question that anticipates an affirmative answer: "And should I not be concerned about Nineveh . . . ?" But the conversation is cut off in mid-stream, and Jonah does not pronounce or denounce the "Yes" that is implied in God's question. It just hangs there in mid-air, waiting for a reply that never comes. Did Jonah have a change of heart like that of the Ninevites and gain new insight into the true nature of God, or did he get his wish and die, a xenophobic exclusivist who could not come to terms with a merciful God? Did he leave his booth, walk into the city, and proclaim a new message, or did he turn on his heels, look for another boat heading for parts unknown, and cease to be God's spokesperson? We will never know.

Maybe the book does not give Jonah the last word because that would tie things up too neatly. If he were to answer God's final question, then the plot would be resolved and the story would be nothing more than an entertaining tale that relates the adventures of someone who lived "once upon a time." To have it

> How do you think Jonah would have answered God's final question?

end that way would rob the text of its modern-day relevance and meaning by making it harder to see ourselves in it. In fact, Jonah's story is our story, and, because it remains open-ended and unanswered, Jonah's question is our question. We live in a world of diversity and difference in which we constantly encounter and rub elbows with the other, an otherness that can be rooted in gender, race, religion, ethnicity, sexuality, politics, or any number of other things. There are many challenges in such a world, and Jonah's story describes two of the ways people sometimes respond to those challenges: by fleeing or fighting. But the book's unresolved ending reminds us that there is a third way: rather than fight or flee, we can listen for and be open to the questions that come with living in a world of difference and diversity. When we ponder those questions carefully and try to answer them honestly, we fill in the silence at the end of Jonah's story and we make it possible to begin to think about God and others in a new way.

A MODERN TAKE ON THE OTHER

The song "Imagine," written by John Lennon in 1971, issues a simple but powerful call to break down the walls that divide people from one another. Read the lyrics of the song (*http://www.azlyrics.com/lyrics/johnlennon /imagine.html*), and view the video of Lennon performing it (*https://www. youtube.com/watch?v=yRhq-yO1KN8*).

1. According to the song, what are some of the things that cause divisions between people?
2. Is the world that Lennon envisions in "Imagine" possible or will it remain just that, a figment of our imagination?
3. Can you think of other examples of contemporary art that address issues related to the other?

Implications and Applications

1. How has your understanding of the Bible changed after reading this chapter?
2. How has your understanding of the other changed after reading this chapter?
3. How is God presented in Ruth and Jonah? Identify the main qualities and features of the deity in these books and explain how they contribute to the portrait of God that emerges from the Hebrew Bible.
4. How is humanity presented in Ruth and Jonah? Identify the main qualities and features of human beings in these books and explain what they suggest about the human condition.
5. Does the presence of conflicting views in the Bible about how to relate to the other trouble you?
6. Should ancient texts like the Bible be used as resources to help formulate modern views on how to interact with those who are different from us?
7. Attitudes and views about differences between people (such as race, religion, gender, and sexuality) pose the greatest threat to society today.

Do the books of Ruth and Jonah provide any insight on how to confront that threat?

8. What are some other ways of thinking about and relating to the other beyond those mentioned in this chapter?

9. Do the texts discussed in this chapter play a role in shaping your views about those who are different from you? If so, how? If not, why not?

6

Perspectives on Social Justice

I n his "Letter from Birmingham City Jail," one of the most influential pieces of correspondence in American history, the Reverend Dr. Martin Luther King Jr. attempted to explain to his fellow clergy members why he and others were engaged in the struggle to gain civil rights for African Americans during the 1950s and 1960s. Early in the letter he penned a breathtakingly simple sentence that elegantly articulated what motivated them to put up with the abuse and hardships they were forced to endure for the sake of their cause: "Injustice anywhere is a threat to justice everywhere." King went on to describe the interconnectedness that exists among all people in what he called our "single garment of destiny," and he said that whenever someone is directly affected by something, everyone else is also affected by it indirectly. King and those who shared his vision believed that if even only one person is experiencing oppression, the entire human race is at risk.[1]

It has been more than half of a century since MLK wrote his letter, and the wisdom of that brief eight-word sentence composed in his jail cell continues to reverberate into our own day. Our "garment" has sometimes been tailored to meet the changing fashion standards of later times, but there's no denying that we're all in it together and that we share a common destiny that continues to be shaped by what happens to any of us. Many of the most significant social changes that have taken place in recent decades have come about in response to certain injustices that needed to be rectified because they directly affected the well-being of some people and therefore indirectly affected the well-being of all. People throughout the world have gained rights that were previously denied to them in virtually every area of human experience and engagement, including politics, religion, race, physical ability, age, gender, sexuality, health care, and marriage, to name some of the most prominent examples.

Despite those advances that have improved the lives of countless people, we still have a long way to go and so we should not be too quick to pat ourselves on the back. To put the matter bluntly, our "single garment of destiny" is a bit frayed in places and is not quite as attractive as it could be. For example, more than 20

---

1. The original copy of King's letter can be seen at the following link; the sentence quoted here is on the second page: *http://okra.stanford.edu/transcription/document_images/undecided/630416-019.pdf.*

Martin Luther King Jr. stands with other modern-day martyrs in this grouping in Westminster Abbey. With his unrelenting call for justice, King continued the tradition of the ancient Israelite prophets, whom he often quoted in his speeches.

percent of all children in the United States live in families with incomes below the federal poverty level.[2] Similarly, nearly twenty-five million Americans live in food deserts that lack supermarkets and other resources that would give them access to fresh and affordable food.[3] Those harsh realities highlight the stark inequalities that exist within our society. Pages and pages of similarly depressing statistics could be cited *ad nauseum*, despite the fact that the United States is one of the wealthiest and most prosperous nations on the planet. Following King's logic, those of us who live comfortable lives had better wake up and realize we are all being threatened because injustice is out there lurking.

Martin Luther King Jr. and his supporters were articulate voices for the cause of justice, but they were by no means the first to sound the alarm and speak out on behalf of the most vulnerable members of society. He remarked on more than one occasion that "the arc of the moral universe is long, and it bends toward justice." This chapter illumines the great length of that arc by exploring the biblical roots of King's commitment to equality and fairness. Like other ancient writings, the Bible acknowledges that inequities exist among people, and in places it offers solutions that attempt to address those imbalances. The prophetic writings of the Old Testament books are particularly critical of the ways that marginalized groups can be mistreated by the powerful within society. These writings bear the names of people like Amos, Micah, and Isaiah, who spoke out against the injustice of their time and challenged it within the context of their belief in the God of Israel. The prophets of the Hebrew Bible were well

---

2. See the website of The National Center for Children in Poverty at Columbia University for statistics and information, *http://www.nccp.org/topics/childpoverty.html*.

3. The United States Department of Agriculture has studied the devastating effects of food deserts on poor people in America. See their website at *https://www.ers.usda.gov/data/fooddesert/*.

aware of our "single garment of destiny," even if they did not use the phrase, and through the ages their books have inspired Martin Luther King Jr. and many others who have lived and lost their lives in the struggle for peace and justice.

First Impressions

Biblical stories occasionally depict the great disparity that existed between the rich and the poor in ancient Israel, but such narratives hardly ever offer a critique of how the wealthy wronged those who were below them in the social pecking order. For that type of negative assessment of the rich/poor divide we usually have to go to works like the prophetic books mentioned above. These writings do not mince words or pull any punches when they turn their attention to the guilty parties (i.e., the well-to-do).

A Biblical Power Couple

READ: 1 Kings 21

One narrative that does tell such a story is that of Ahab and Naboth in 1 Kings 21. It is one of the Bible's clearest illustrations of the old adage, "Power corrupts, and absolute power corrupts absolutely." Ahab ruled over the northern kingdom of Israel for about twenty years in the middle of the ninth century BCE. The Bible gives more attention to him than to any other king of the north, mainly because he is universally panned in the text as an absolutely awful monarch. When we first meet him, we are told that "Ahab son of Omri did evil in the sight of the LORD more than all who were before him" (1 Kings 16:30) and "Ahab did more to provoke the anger of the LORD, the God of Israel, than had all the kings of Israel who were before him" (1 Kings 16:33). He is viewed that way mainly because of his association with the two other people who are mentioned by name in this story: his wife Jezebel and a man named Naboth, who had the misfortune of owning a vineyard that was located right next to Ahab's palace.

Judging from the way he treated Naboth, Ahab was one lousy neighbor. Not satisfied with the palace he occupied and all the royal trappings that went along with it, he decided he had to expand his footprint; he settled on Naboth's vineyard as the additional acreage he just could not live without. Like his namesake in the famous novel, he became a man obsessed. He desired the property next door as fiercely as Captain Ahab pursued Moby Dick. Ahab the king, unlike his fictional counterpart, eventually got his wish, as Naboth lost both his land and his life.

King Ahab actually had very little to do with his successful land-grab, because it never would have happened if his wife Jezebel had not stepped in to grease the wheels. Jezebel is one of the most despised people in the Hebrew

Bible. As with her husband, the first reference to her in the text tells us all we need to know about Jezebel: "And as if it had been a light thing for him [Ahab] to walk in the sins of Jeroboam son of Nebat, he took as his wife Jezebel daughter of King Ethbaal of the Sidonians, and went and served Baal, and worshiped him" (1 Kings 16: 31). This verse suggests that marrying Jezebel might have been a bigger mistake than all the other sins Ahab committed. The reason for this assessment is pretty clear: she was a foreigner from Sidon, a city north of Israel, who convinced Ahab to follow her god, Baal.

As Ahab's story unfolds over the next five-plus chapters in 1 Kings, repeated references to Jezebel present her in a most unflattering light. She engages in a campaign to kill off all the prophets of the Lord (18:4) while simultaneously supporting eight hundred and fifty prophets of foreign deities (18:19). She threatens to assassinate the prophet Elijah, causing him to flee for his life to the southernmost part of the land (19:1–3). She convinces Ahab to engage in idol worship, thereby sealing his fate as the most reviled ruler of the north in the eyes of the biblical authors (21:25–26). Jezebel goes on to suffer a gruesome death when she is hurled out a window, trampled on by horses, and eaten by dogs until all that remains of her are her skull, her feet, and the palms of her hands (2 Kings 9:30–37).[4]

It's Good to Be King, But Sometimes It's Better to Be Queen

That bloody end seems only fitting in light of the amount of mayhem and carnage that Jezebel caused during her reign as queen of Israel, and the story in 1 Kings 21 shows her at her duplicitous and deceitful best. After unsuccessfully attempting to pry Naboth's vineyard from him, Ahab returns to his palace a dejected and defeated man who is described in terms that would be more fitting for a petulant child than a mighty ruler: "He lay down on his bed, turned away his face, and would not eat" (21:4b). Upon learning the reason why he is "so depressed" (her words), Jezebel springs into action and devises a plan that is meant to cheer up Ahab. She convinces a group of prominent citizens to falsely accuse Naboth of cursing God and the king—charges that result in Naboth's death.

> How is the bias of the southern-based author of the text seen in the way the story of the northern king Ahab and his wife Jezebel is presented?

The episode paints a fascinating picture of the relationship between Ahab and Jezebel as she takes the bull by the horns and gets for him what he is incapable of acquiring on his own. And she does it by pretending to be him. She convinces some of the important members of society to agree to her plan by sending to them letters in Ahab's name that have been signed with the king's

---

4. A treatment of Jezebel's role in the Bible can be found in Patricia Dutcher-Walls, *Jezebel: Portraits of a Queen* (Collegeville, MN: Liturgical Press, 2004).

royal seal. At every step along the way, Ahab is passively compliant and behaves in a very un-kingly way. When Jezebel tells him to eat and cheer up because she is going to get him Naboth's vineyard, he does not ask her how she intends to do it. She does not bother to alert him about her plan, and when Naboth is killed, Ahab never asks her how such a lucky coincidence could have occurred. In fact he does not say anything at all, but remains strangely silent and simply follows her command to take possession of the dead man's property (21:15–16). Because modern notions of marriage are typically more egalitarian than ancient ones, it is easy to miss the fact that Jezebel is playing against type when she is presented as anything but a quiet, submissive, stay-at-home wife. This is something that would have been evident to the author's original audience, and it is possible that one of her "sins" was that she was a strong woman.

Despite this intriguing portrayal of how they interact with one another in the story, of more interest for our purposes is the relationship that Ahab and Jezebel have with Naboth. This chapter presents the king and queen as a biblical "power couple" in the worst sense of that term, and it provides a tragic example of how absolute authority and unlimited political clout, if left unchecked, can run roughshod over the

> Why do you think the relationship between Ahab and Jezebel is presented the way it is?

rights of those who are powerless. We know nothing about Naboth other than that he was from an area known as Jezreel and that he owned a vineyard near the king's palace.[5] The fact that he had property near where the king lived could suggest that he was a person of some means, just as in today's world your zip code can be an indicator of your social status. On the other hand, Naboth refers to the vineyard as his "ancestral inheritance" (21:3), which could mean that he is just a rank-and-file member of society whose family has owned a vineyard for a long time that happens to be in the plot of land adjacent to the royal palace.

It is striking that when Ahab talks to Jezebel about his encounter with Naboth he does not describe the plot of land that way. When she asks the king why he is so glum, "He said to her, 'Because I spoke to Naboth the Jezreelite and said to him, "Give me your vineyard for money; or else, if you prefer, I will give you another vineyard for it"; but he answered, "I will not give you my vineyard"'" (21:6). Three verses earlier Naboth described it to Ahab as his "ancestral inheritance," but when Ahab reports that conversation to Jezebel it is simply a vineyard. It is a subtle but significant change in terminology because there is a world of difference between the two. Naboth was not telling Ahab "I *won't* give you my vineyard." He was saying, "I *can't* give you my vineyard because it isn't mine to give." As an ancestral inheritance, the land has been in

---

5. Jezreel is a fertile valley in the northern part of Israel that occupied a strategic position for both trade and travel routes in ancient times.

Ancient Israelite vineyards were usually equipped with winepresses, like this first-century example from Nazareth. Naboth's vineyard probably included a similar press.

the family for generations and Naboth is merely its current caretaker until it passes into the hands of the next relative in line. In keeping with their less-than-honest communication style, Ahab withholds key information from Jezebel by redefining the ancestral inheritance as just a vineyard. That slight change serves to implicate the king, because it suggests that he is prepared to get what he wants at all costs, even if he has to misrepresent the facts and trample on the rights of a family that does not have the social standing that his does.

A Web of Deceit

Jezebel falls into the trap set by Ahab and then she constructs one of her own that results in Naboth's demise. It is a slimy story of corruption that begins at the highest levels of government and then seeps down into society until everyone has been infected by it. Ahab gets the ball rolling when he misrepresents what Naboth said to him and then does not bother to ask Jezebel how she intends to get him the vineyard. The queen then shows that unethical behavior is not just a guy thing, and outdoes her husband by passing herself off as the king and sending forged letters to some of the prominent citizens of the area, who set up a kangaroo court in which Naboth never has a chance and is stoned to death for something he did not do.

> In its depiction of how the various characters relate with one another, what is the story of Ahab and Naboth suggesting about political authority?

The ones who cast those stones might have been victims of the power dynamics of the time, but they too were not without blame. Had they refused to do what the letter requested, they knew that there would likely be a few rocks hurled in their direction as well. So, in that sense, they had no choice but to obey the royal orders. On the other hand, they had to know it was all a set-up that was meant to take out Naboth because he had done something to anger the king. The very wording of the note they received would have clued them in to that likelihood because of the way it describes the two men who are to falsely accuse Naboth of cursing God and the king. The NRSV translates the Hebrew term (*beney beliya'al*, literally "sons of wickedness") as "scoundrels," but perhaps something like "lowlifes" or "dirtbags" would better capture the intended meaning (21:10, 13). It should have been crystal clear to everyone who received a letter that the whole trial was a fraud and that Naboth was being framed.

This means that all the people who received the letters, and not just the two "scoundrels," were willing accomplices in Jezebel's plan to do away with Naboth. It was a complete travesty of justice from top to bottom, conceived in the royal palace and carried out by the ones who should have been most committed to fairness for all people. Those to whom Jezebel wrote letters are described as the "elders" and "nobles" of the city. These two groups were among the most respected members of society in ancient Israel, and the elders in particular are often identified in the Bible as the ones responsible for ensuring that laws were obeyed and individuals were treated fairly. The nobles and elders were supposed to be the guardians of justice throughout the land, but in the Naboth story they fail to discharge their duty because they're in the back pocket of the king (and queen) and they blindly follow the royal command to send an innocent man to his death. What makes their actions even more despicable is the way their relationship with Naboth is highlighted in the text. Twice they are described as "the elders and nobles who lived . . . in his city" (21:8, 11), calling attention to the fact that they knew him personally and were his neighbors. Obviously, there were more than two scoundrels present when Naboth was thrown under the bus.

> Is there any way that the actions of the elders and nobles in the story can be defended?

Immediately after Naboth's death and the report that Ahab is now the proud owner of a new vineyard, God instructs the prophet Elijah to deliver a word to the king that announces his own imminent demise: "You shall say to him, 'Thus says the LORD: Have you killed, and also taken possession?' You shall say to him, 'Thus says the LORD: in the place where dogs licked up the blood of Naboth, dogs will also lick up your blood'" (21:19). The message is clear: because of the way he abused his power and allowed his greed to rule him, the ruler of Israel will suffer a fate similar to that of the man who was guilty of nothing more than having something the king wanted. Through its description of the misuse of authority and the tragic effect such misuse can have on the innocent, the story of Ahab, Jezebel, and Naboth is a disturbing reminder that the long arc of the moral universe sometimes bends toward injustice.[6]

Voices for the Voiceless

It is no coincidence that Elijah was pressed into action in response to what had been done to Naboth. The Bible depicts prophets playing a number

---

6. For an alternative interpretation that argues Ahab was within his rights to take Naboth's vineyard, see Stephen C. Russell, "The Hierarchy of Estates in Land and Naboth's Vineyard," *Journal for the Study of the Old Testament* 38, no. 4 (2014): 453–69.

of important roles within Israelite society, but perhaps the most significant was that of the whistleblower who would speak truth to power. This is clearly seen in the way Elijah goes after Ahab and tells him in no uncertain terms that he will be punished for the way he mistreated the previous owner of the vineyard. The verse quoted above is just one part of a lengthy tirade he directs at the king. In addition to informing him that he will die in the same ignominious way that Naboth did, Elijah goes on to accuse Ahab of doing so many evil things in God's sight that his entire family line will suffer the consequences of his actions (21:24).[7]

Another example of a prophet who confronts a ruler who has been involved in something shady can be seen in the encounter between Nathan and King David (2 Sam. 12). After David arranged to have a soldier named Uriah put to death to cover up the fact that David is the father of the child that the man's wife Bathsheba is carrying, the prophet Nathan visits the palace to let him know that God is not too happy about what the king has done. Nathan delivers the message in a roundabout but very effective way by telling David a story about a rich man who treats a poor man unfairly when he takes the man's only lamb, even though he himself has many flocks. David unwittingly condemns himself when he criticizes the rich man's actions, and Nathan then spells out the consequences for the king's involvement in Uriah's death. This story and the one involving Ahab and Naboth are the two clearest examples of Old Testament narratives that criticize the wealthy for mistreating the poor, and the similarities between them should be apparent. In each case a rich person takes something he wants from someone who cannot afford to lose it, and is then held accountable.[8]

An important thing to keep in mind about prophets is that they did not speak on their own authority but functioned as mouthpieces for God. In other words, they were intermediaries who conveyed the divine will to human beings. Prophets like Elijah and Nathan do this in stories where they are presented as characters who are part of the plot, but most of the biblical prophets are not mentioned in narratives. Rather, their messages are found in books named after them that contain primarily divine oracles and not stories.[9]

> Can you identify any additional similarities and differences between the story of Ahab and Naboth and the message that Nathan delivers to David?

---

7. The classic work on the role of prophets in biblical times is Robert R. Wilson, *Prophecy and Society in Ancient Israel* (Philadelphia: Fortress, 1980).

8. A comparative study of the two passages from an attorney's point of view can be seen in Herbert Rand, "David and Ahab: A Study of Crime and Punishment," *Jewish Bible Quarterly* 24, no. 2 (1996): 90–97.

9. A thorough discussion of prophecy in the Hebrew Bible is found in Joseph Blenkinsopp, *A History of Prophecy in Israel* (Louisville: Westminster John Knox, 1996).

Many of the prophetic writings are concerned about the plight of the poor, but several of them are especially tuned in to issues related to social justice. Those prophets who were living in times when such problems were particularly acute tend to spend more time addressing them, and so the context of each book plays a key role in determining how much attention it gives to the theme of societal injustice. No biblical prophet speaks out more forcefully against the inequalities he saw around him than Amos, who can be considered the Hebrew Bible's preeminent defender of the poor. We therefore begin our study of the prophetic literature by considering his book before turning to some other works that come to the defense of society's most vulnerable members.[10]

A Man of Woe (and Whoa!)

READ: Amos 1–9

Amos lived during the first half of the eighth century BCE, and his book is one of the earliest prophetic writings.[11] Assigning a date to it does not entail any guesswork on our part because, like many of the other prophets, Amos does the work for us by identifying who was on the throne when he was prophesying. According to the first verse in the book, King Uzziah (r. 785–733 BCE) was ruling the southern kingdom of Judah, and King Jeroboam II was his counterpart in the northern kingdom of Israel (r. 788–747 BCE). He also throws in the additional information that his book can be traced to "two years before the earthquake." It is a tantalizing reference even though we cannot date the earthquake with any precision, but it must have registered pretty high on the Richter scale because they still knew about it centuries later when the book of Zechariah was written (Zech. 14:5).

A distinction is commonly made between northern and southern prophets based on the audience to whom the message is directed. Amos is a clear example of a northern prophet because he addresses the kingdom of Israel, but he does so as an outsider who is actually from the southern kingdom of Judah. In the opening verse his hometown is identified as Tekoa, which was a small village about ten miles south of Jerusalem. That verse also provides information about his livelihood as a herder, or perhaps an owner, of flocks of sheep. Later in the

---

10. Overviews of how the biblical literature addresses social justice can be found in John R. Donahue, *Seek Justice That You May Live: Reflections and Resources on the Bible and Social Justice* (New York: Paulist Press, 2014) and Bruce V. Malchow, *Social Justice in the Hebrew Bible* (Collegeville, MN: Liturgical Press, 1996).

11. The following works discuss the theme of social justice in Amos: Robert Coote, *Amos among the Prophets: Composition and Theology* (Philadelphia: Fortress, 1981); Carol J. Dempsey, *Hope amid the Ruins: The Ethics of Israel's Prophets* (St. Louis: Chalice, 2000); William Doorly, *Prophet of Justice: Understanding the Book of Amos* (New York: Paulist Press, 1989); and Joseph Jensen, *Ethical Dimensions of the Prophets* (Collegeville, MN: Liturgical Press, 2006).

book it is stated that he also held down a second job as someone who helped speed up the ripening process of a particular type of fig tree called a sycamore. That passage claims he had no prior experience in the prophetic role when God recruited him to be a prophet (Amos 7:14–15).

After that standard opening, the book begins with a collection of passages that are often referred to as "oracles against the nations" (chapters 1–2). These are messages that typically express God's anger and displeasure at foreign countries and areas that are enemies of Israel. A listing of the country's sins and offenses is often given, followed by the punishment that God will send their way because of what they have done. Most prophetic books contain these oracles against the nations, so it is not surprising that they are be found in Amos. What is strange, though, is their location. In every other case the oracles come much later in the book. Amos is the only work that begins with them. Another oddity is the inclusion of Israel and Judah as the areas toward which two of the oracles against the nations are directed. Here, too, it is fairly common in prophetic works for Judah and Israel to be on the receiving end of God's wrath, but it is quite unusual that they would be lumped in with their neighbors like this. Perhaps their placement at the end of the list is Amos's way of saying they are no different from their neighbors in God's eyes and so they should forget about any special treatment they might be expecting.

> Can you think of any other reasons why Amos would include Judah and Israel in his oracles against the nations?

No Justice, No Peace

The first words of the oracle against Israel leave no doubt as to what has God so upset as Amos zeroes in on the theme that will dominate much of the rest of the book: the shameful ways some people are violating the rights of others.

Thus says the LORD:
For three transgressions of Israel,
and for four, I will not revoke the punishment;
because they sell the righteous for silver,
and the needy for a pair of sandals—
they who trample the head of the poor into the dust of the earth,
and push the afflicted out of the way;
father and son go in to the same girl,
so that my holy name is profaned (2:6–7).

Amos's opening salvo against the Israelites identifies crimes against humanity as their main offense. They are guilty of exploiting the needy and innocent among them in order to line their own pockets. Righteous people are sold for money, and those most in need are traded in for better footwear. The images used in the passage are disturbingly graphic and they reflect the cruel nature of people who ignore the plight of those who most need their assistance. This total disregard of human life is possible because the mistreatment of other people, especially the impoverished, is seen as nothing more than an opportunity for the fat cats of Israel to prosper and grow richer. "They do not know how to do right, says the LORD, those who store up violence and robbery in their strongholds" (3:10). Such oppression is just another coin of the realm that allows the powerful to pad their bank accounts and widen the gap between the haves and the have-nots.

> What are some of the main reasons why poor people are often mistreated or ignored?

Amos returns to this topic later in the book when, in a passage that draws upon similar vocabulary and imagery, he calls attention to the questionable ethics and shady practices of some of the local merchants.

> Hear this, you that trample on the needy,
> and bring to ruin the poor of the land,
> saying, "When will the new moon be over so that we may sell grain;
> and the sabbath, so that we may offer wheat for sale?
> We will make the ephah small and the shekel great,
> and practice deceit with false balances,
> buying the poor for silver and the needy for a pair of sandals,
> and selling the sweepings of the wheat." (8:4–6)

Some shopkeepers were so interested in turning a profit that they could hardly wait for the holy days and feasts to be over so they could reopen their stores and get back to making a buck. And much of the effort of these hustlers involved swindling the poor and engaging in fraud. The *ephah* was a unit of dry measure for items like grain and the *shekel* was a unit of weight tied to the local currency, so the reference to making the former small and the latter great is an allusion to the age-old art of ripping off the customer through a business scam. The one mentioned specifically here—practicing deceit with false balances—was an ancient form of doctoring the weight of the merchandise. Selling the sweepings along with the wheat was another con whereby the chaff, which is the husk that surrounds the grain and is normally removed and disposed of, was mixed in with the good stuff and sold to the unsuspecting consumer. Human beings cannot digest chaff but livestock can, so these crooks were passing off fodder as food. As someone who made his living in the animal and agriculture sectors himself, Amos must have found these practices to be appalling.

Amos derides the prominent citizens of his time for their luxurious ways. His criticisms drip with sarcasm and mockery: "Alas for those who are at ease in

Zion, and for those who feel secure on Mount Samaria, the notables of the first of the nations, to whom the house of Israel resorts!" (6:1). Here he goes after the bigwigs who are the movers and shakers in society. In particular, he sets his sights on the politically influential through his references to the capital cities of both the northern and southern kingdoms: Samaria and Zion (another name for Jerusalem).

A few verses later he delivers a withering assessment of the lifestyles of the rich and famous and their distorted priorities. The disdain in his voice, the shaking of his head, and the pointing of his finger are easy to imagine as he describes a way of life that would make any self-respecting blue-blood squirm in discomfort.

> Alas for those who lie on beds
>   of ivory,
> and lounge on their couches,
> and eat lambs from the flock,
> and calves from the stall;
> who sing idle songs to the sound
>   of the harp,
> and like David improvise on
>   instruments of music;
> who drink wine from bowls,
> and anoint themselves with the finest
>   oils,
> but are not grieved over the ruin
>   of Joseph! (6:4–7)

The Metropolitan Museum of Art, New York, Rogers Fund, 1962

Amos calls them out for their opulent lifestyle that includes exquisite furniture, an overabundance of leisure time, too much fine dining and wining, and other creature comforts. He also makes a subtle reference to religious abuses, since the Hebrew term for "bowl" usually describes a cultic vessel that is only supposed to be used when offering a sacrifice to God.[12]

Only the wealthiest ancient Israelites could have afforded furniture decorated with ivory like the beds to which Amos refers. This ivory inset panel from the ancient Israelite city of Samaria dates roughly to the time of King Ahab.

The name "Joseph" is sometimes used in the Hebrew Bible to refer to the northern kingdom of Israel, and so here Amos is saying that the wealthy of the land have been so self-absorbed living in the lap of luxury that they have not

---

12. The Hebrew word is *mizraq*, which is mentioned in reference to the Temple more than two dozen times in the Old Testament (see, for example, Exod. 27:3; 38:3; Num. 4:14; 1 Kings 7:40; Jer. 52:18).

bothered to notice that society is crumbing all around them. He closes the section by letting them know that they will be the ones leading the parade out of the land: "Therefore they shall now be the first to go into exile, and the revelry of the loungers shall pass away" (6:7). The Hebrew word in Amos 6 that the NRSV translates twice as "Alas" (vv. 1, 4) is also sometimes rendered into English as "Woe." It could be said that Amos was a man of both "Woe!" and "Whoa!" because he directed a message of despair toward those who would be punished for making the lives of the poor more difficult while, at the same time, telling them that enough was enough and things had to stop.[13]

Showy Piety versus Right Action

But that appeal to mend their ways probably fell on deaf ears, if it was heard at all by the upper crust of Israelite society, because they suffered from a condition that often plagues the affluent: they took their privileged status as a sign of divine favor that indicated God's approval of what they were doing. This attitude can lead to a sense of entitlement and arrogance that hinders the ability to be self-reflective and open to change. There is no greater threat to

> If God approves of what people are doing, isn't it natural to assume that they would be successful? If so, why shouldn't we infer that those who are successful are the people God approves of?

righteousness than self-righteousness, and Amos suggests that the latter was not in short supply in Israel. He is especially critical of the way the people make a spectacle of their piety through public expressions of their faith. Referring to two popular shrines in the northern kingdom, the prophet rebukes them for their showy displays.

Come to Bethel—and transgress;
to Gilgal—and multiply transgression;
bring your sacrifices every morning,
your tithes every three days;
bring a thank offering of leavened bread,
and proclaim freewill offerings, publish them;
for so you love to do, O people of Israel!
says the LORD God. (4:4–5)

They believed that their frequent sacrifices, gifts, and offerings at Bethel and Gilgal were making them right with God, but those things actually had the

---

13. The Hebrew word translated "alas" in the NRSV (*hoy*) is actually found only in the first verse, but the translator includes it in the fourth verse because its meaning is continued there. English translations of the Bible that translate the term as "woe" include the King James Version, the Revised English Bible, and the New American Bible.

opposite effect.[14] Because of their misdeeds, these showy acts of piety were nothing but transgressions in God's eyes, and they were too blind to see it. The things they "love to do" (the sarcasm of that phrase is palpable) were motivated by self-love, not love of God. The same point is expressed more dramatically in another passage that lets them know that their rituals do not have the desired effect.

> I hate, I despise your festivals,
> and I take no delight in your solemn assemblies.
> Even though you offer me your burnt offerings and grain offerings,
> I will not accept them;
> and the offerings of well-being of your fatted animals
> I will not look upon.
> Take away from me the noise of your songs;
> I will not listen to the melody of your harps. (5:21–23)

These harsh words from God must have stopped the self-satisfied people of Israel dead in their tracks. They considered their feasts, sacrifices, and hymns of praise to be a form of payback for all the good things God had sent their way and, more importantly, a guarantee of more of the same in the future. With a stinging string of verbs, the deity says that is not the way he sees things, and he completely rejects their overtures: "I hate," "I despise," "I take no delight," "I will not accept," "I will not look upon," "I will not listen to." In the very next verse—the most famous line in the book—God tells them that the problem is not what they did, but what they did not do.

> But let justice roll down like waters,
> And righteousness like an ever-flowing stream. (5:24)

All their songs and gifts and special holidays don't amount to a hill of beans in God's eyes because they are nothing more than empty rituals and pious platitudes that make the wealthy feel good about themselves and perpetuate the status quo. God does not want actions that are motivated by self-interest, but actions that are done on behalf of others that will shake things up and completely transform society. That new reality is possible only if justice and righteousness are present everywhere and at all times, and not just in certain moments and places. Such a change is possible only if the wealthy citizens of Israel reconfigure their lives in a way that treats those less fortunate than themselves with the dignity they deserve.

> Do you think Amos would have objected to their elaborate forms of worship if the rich people of Judah had treated the poor better?

---

14. Bethel was a town in the southern part of Israel near the border with the kingdom of Judah. The location of Gilgal is less certain, with at least three different proposals having been put forward.

Seek good and not evil,
that you may live;
and so the LORD, the God of hosts, will be with you,
just as you have said.
Hate evil and love good,
and establish justice in the gate;
it may be that the LORD, the God of hosts,
will be gracious to the remnant of Joseph. (5:14–15)

Micah

Amos was not the only prophet to speak out against social injustices, and we now turn to a couple of examples of other writings in which this is an important theme. Micah came along a bit after Amos and was active in the late eighth century BCE, when he directed his message toward the southern kingdom of Judah. Some of the passages contained in his book are remarkably similar to what we saw in Amos, indicating that comparable abuses and violations were taking place in both kingdoms.[15]

Some greedy land barons during Micah's time were bilking unsuspecting citizens of their property and evicting them from their land. Micah lets them know that their plots and machinations are not acceptable to God.

Alas for those who devise wickedness and evil deeds on their beds!
When the morning dawns, they perform it, because it is in their power.
They covet fields, and seize them; houses, and take them away;
they oppress householder and house, people and their inheritance.
Therefore thus says the LORD:
Now, I am devising against this family an evil
from which you cannot remove your necks;
and you shall not walk haughtily,
for it will be an evil time. (2:1–3)

The description of these cheaters losing sleep because of their obsession with their illegal takeovers and foreclosures is an apt comment on how covetousness can become so all-consuming that it hijacks a person's life. Similarly, the reference to them carrying out the schemes they have hatched just because they can underscores how easily power can be abused when the ones holding it are unaffected by the consequences of their actions.

---

15. For discussions of the theme of social justice in Micah, see Juan I. Alfaro, *Justice and Loyalty: A Commentary on the Book of Micah* (Grand Rapids: Eerdmans, 1989); Kathleen A. Farmer, "What Does It Mean to 'Do Justice'?," *Journal of Theology* 108 (2004): 35–48; and Erin Runions, "Called to Do Justice? A Bhabian Reading of Micah 5 and 6:1–8," in *Postmodern Interpretations of the Bible: A Reader*, ed. A. K. M. Adam (St. Louis: Chalice, 2001), 153–64.

Another passage captures well the predatory practices of the rich and powerful by imagining them as cannibals who feast on their victims' bodies. The reference to their being ignorant of justice suggests that Micah is going after judges or other legal authorities who were taking advantage of their positions to defraud (and devour) the vulnerable.

> Listen, you heads of Jacob
> and rulers of the house of Israel!
> Should you not know justice?—
> you who hate the good and love the evil,
> who tear the skin off my people,
> And the flesh off their bones;
> who eat the flesh of my people,
> flay their skin off them,
> break their bones in pieces,
> and chop them up like meat in a kettle,
> like flesh in a caldron. (3:1–3)

A few verses later another oracle begins in a similar way and broadens its accusation to include other groups that had status and influence within society. Interestingly, prophets are singled out for criticism, and so Micah acknowledges that his fellow spokespersons for God were not above reproach and some of them were guilty of the very charges they were leveling at other people.

> Hear this, you rulers of the house of Jacob
> and chiefs of the house of Israel,
> who abhor justice and pervert all equity,
> who build Zion with blood and Jerusalem with wrong!
> Its rulers give judgment for a bribe,
> its priests teach for a price,
> its prophets give oracles for money;
> yet they lean upon the LORD and say,
> "Surely the LORD is with us!
> No harm shall come upon us." (3:9–11)

It is a picture of corruption run amuck—the building blocks of the city are "blood" and "wrong"—as all the leaders of society look to profit off those who seek their services by demanding a kickback or jacking up their fees. As was seen in the case of Amos, these "pillars of the community" have been blinded by their sense of self-worth, and they suffer from an inability to recognize that they are heading down the road to ruin. The next verse informs them that the whole system is about to come crashing down and the entire land will be reduced to rubble due to their shady dealings.

> Therefore because of you
> Zion shall be plowed as a field;
> Jerusalem shall become a heap of ruins,
> and the mountain of the house a wooded height.[16] (3:12)

Micah's solution to all these problems is pretty much in line with what Amos sees as the way forward. He advises his audience that all the rituals in the world will not matter much in God's eyes, and they need to reorient their lives in a way that puts people other than themselves at the center of things.

> "With what shall I come before the LORD,
> and bow myself before God on high?
> Shall I come before him with burnt offerings,
> with calves a year old?
> Will the LORD be pleased with thousands of rams,
> with ten thousands of rivers of oil?
> Shall I give my firstborn for my transgression,
> the fruit of my body for the sin of my soul?"
> He has told you, O mortal, what is good;
> and what does the LORD require of you
> but to do justice, and to love kindness,
> and to walk humbly with your God? (6:6–8)

The last sentence of the passage captures in a nutshell a central teaching of the prophetic literature. Getting back on the right track and being in God's good graces is as easy as one, two, three; justice, kindness, and humility are all it takes. That trio is the key because they cannot be done on one's own. There is nothing wrong with bowing down before God while beating your breast, or offering a sacrifice, or singing a hymn, but what good are they when injustice is raging all around you? Micah and the other prophets did not think those activities on their own would solve any problems or make the world a better place because they are just between a person and God without involving others. But justice, kindness, and humility are all relational and require that we interact with other people. The American writer and activist Eldridge Cleaver once said, "If you're not part of the solution, you're part of the problem." The prophets would say "Amen!" to that sentiment, because they believed that it is necessary to roll up your sleeves and get to work if the world is to become a better place. Without the presence

> Do you think Micah is right that prayer and other religious rituals alone are not enough to bring about change in the world?

---

16. This prediction would have been shocking to the people of Jerusalem in view of the many biblical passages that speak of God's dwelling place on Mount Zion (i.e., the Temple) enduring forever.

of justice, kindness, and humility it's just not going to happen because, in their absence, people tend to think of themselves rather than others.

Isaiah

The Minor Prophets like Amos and Micah were not the only ones calling for fairness and equity. These causes were near and dear to the hearts of the Major Prophets as well. The book of Isaiah is a case in point. It is a complex work that contains material covering a span of more than two centuries, and scholars generally agree that the bulk of chapters 1 through 39 comprise oracles that come from the time of the prophet Isaiah of Jerusalem, an eighth-century BCE contemporary of Micah and Amos. Like them, he was responding to a set of circumstances in which injustice was rampant and the perpetrators thought they could keep on bleeding the poor as long as they continued to masquerade as pious followers of God. Once again, the deity sniffs out their hypocrisy and tells them to stop the charade.[17]

> Hear the word of the LORD,
> you rulers of Sodom!
> Listen to the teaching of our God,
> you people of Gomorrah!
> What to me is the multitude of your sacrifices?
> says the LORD;
> I have had enough of burnt offerings of rams
> and the fat of fed beasts;
> I do not delight in the blood of bulls,
> or of lambs, or of goats.
> When you come to appear before me,
> who asked this from your hand?
> Trample my courts no more;
> bringing offerings is futile;
> incense is an abomination to me.
> New moon and Sabbath and calling of convocation—
> I cannot endure solemn assemblies with iniquity.
> Your new moons and your appointed festivals my soul hates;
> they have been a burden to me,
> I am weary of bearing them.
> When you stretch out your hands,

---

17. Many books have been written on the book of Isaiah. Some that discuss his concern for justice are the following: Walter Brueggemann, *Isaiah 1–39* (Louisville: Westminster John Knox, 1998); Mark Gray, *Rhetoric and Social Justice in Isaiah* (New York: T&T Clark, 2006); and Thomas L. Leclerc, *Yahweh Is Exalted in Justice: Solidarity and Conflict in Isaiah* (Minneapolis: Fortress, 2001).

I will hide my eyes from you;
even though you make many prayers,
I will not listen;
your hands are full of blood. (1:10–15)

The opening references to them as "rulers of Sodom" and "people of Gomorrah" would have let the audience know that God was angry with them. Sodom and Gomorrah were two cities on the Dead Sea near Jerusalem that are identified in the Bible with immorality because of events that occurred there (Gen. 18–19). According to Isaiah, God is chastising the people of Jerusalem because they are nothing but a bunch of phonies who think they can cover up their sins by reaching out to him with their prayers and offerings. Those very acts of supposed devotion betray them and reveal their true nature, because their extended hands are covered in the blood of those they have treated unfairly; they need to be cleansed.

Wash yourselves; make yourselves clean;
remove the evil of your doings from before my eyes;
cease to do evil, learn to do good;
seek justice, rescue the oppressed,
defend the orphan, plead for the widow. (1:16–17)

Like his prophetic colleagues, Isaiah sees acts of justice and mercy as the antidote for what ails the wealthy class. In the last line, he singles out orphans and widows as two sets of people who should be the beneficiaries of their acts of kindness. Those two groups, along with foreigners, are sometimes identified in the Old Testament as among the people most in need of protection and assistance because their lack of social support made it difficult for them to survive (cf. 10:1–2; Exod. 22:21–24; Deut. 10:17–18).

> Who are the modern-day equivalents to the way that widows, orphans, and foreigners are viewed in the biblical literature?

Isaiah uses graphic and arresting images to depict the unspeakable horrors the downtrodden of society must face on a regular basis, but he injects an element of hope with his characterization of God as an advocate and super-lawyer who will speak out on their behalf to ensure they get a fair hearing.

The LORD rises to argue his case;
he stands to judge the peoples.
The LORD enters into judgment
with the elders and princes of his people:
It is you who have devoured the vineyard;
the spoil of the poor is in your houses.

What do you mean by crushing my people,
By grinding the face of the poor?
says the Lord GOD of hosts. (3:13–15)

Many other passages could be cited to demonstrate that the prophets played an indispensable double role in Israelite society: they were simultaneously the thorns in the sides of the powerful ("Woe!") and the defenders of the underdogs ("Whoa!"). Speaking in God's name, they took on the powers that were to try to bring about a fairer and more equitable world. No influential segment of society—not judges, the merchant class, political leaders, priests, fellow prophets, or the king himself—was spared if they did anything to jeopardize the rights of others. The prophets may not have always succeeded, but they were never silenced. Their message has echoed down the centuries and has given voice to latter-day Elijahs who have confronted the Ahabs of their own times. In another section of his "Letter from Birmingham City Jail," Martin Luther King Jr. acknowledged that link and his indebtedness to his prophetic forbears when he wrote, "Just as the prophets of the eighth century B.C. left their villages and carried their 'thus saith the Lord' far beyond the boundaries of their home towns . . . so am I compelled to carry the gospel of freedom beyond my own home town." And on it goes, as the call for justice continues its unwavering march into the future toward parts unknown.

Second Opinions

Who Stands to Prophet, and How?

The Hebrew term for a prophet is *nabi'*, the meaning of which is not completely agreed upon by Bible scholars. The most likely possibilities are that it either refers to someone who has been called to do a particular task, or it identifies an individual who calls upon one or more of the gods. The English word "prophet" comes from the Greek *prophētēs*, which is found in the New Testament and describes someone who speaks on behalf of another. This meaning fits well with the Old Testament understanding of these figures because they often deliver messages to their audiences in the name of God. Other terms that are sometimes used in the Bible to refer to prophets include "man of God" and "seer." One passage indicates that the latter title was an older way of referring to a prophet (1 Sam. 9:9).[18]

---

18. A detailed study of the Hebrew term for prophet is found in Daniel Fleming, "The Etymological Origins of the Hebrew *nābi'*: The One Who Invokes God," *Catholic Biblical Quarterly* 55, no. 2 (1993): 217–24.

Female Prophets

As the title "man of God" suggests, the great majority of the prophets mentioned in the Old Testament are male, but five women are explicitly identified as prophets in the text as well. Miriam, the sister of Moses and Aaron, is described as a prophetess in Exodus 15:20 as she prepares to sing a song of praise to God after the Israelites have crossed the sea during the Exodus. Likewise, Deborah is called a prophetess in Judges 4:4, a verse that also states that she was judging Israel. As one of the judges, Deborah has the distinction of breaking through the ancient Israelite glass ceiling twice, since she is the only woman who bears two titles that are normally reserved for men only.

> What is your reaction to the fact that there are female prophets in the Bible?

Two other women mentioned by name also serve as prophets in the Old Testament. One is Huldah, who issued a warning to the people of Judah because they had abandoned proper worship of God. She is the only female prophet in the Old Testament who delivers a message that is similar to those of her male counterparts, and in her six-verse speech she uses the standard prophetic formula "Thus says the LORD" three times and speaks on God's behalf an additional time (2 Kings 22:14–20; cf. 2 Chron. 34:22–28). The other named prophetess is Noadiah, who is described by Nehemiah in his book as one of the prophets who made him fearful (Neh. 6:14). The final prophetess mentioned in the Hebrew Bible is an unnamed woman with whom the prophet Isaiah has sexual relations. God gives a symbolic name to the son of their union that alludes to the destruction of two allied forces of the north, Damascus and Syria, who were plotting against the Assyrian Empire (Isa. 8:1–4). It is generally held that this unnamed prophet was Isaiah's wife, and therefore the title probably does not mean that she was actually a prophet herself but that she was the spouse of one.[19]

Beyond these five references, there are two other passages in the Old Testament that allude to women acting as prophets. One of these texts evaluates their activity positively, while the other one is more critical of it. The first is found in Joel 2:28–29, which describes events that will occur on the Day of the Lord, when all of creation will live in harmony with one another and with God. It explains how both males and females will be prophets in that new age.

> Then afterward I will pour out my spirit on all flesh;
> your sons and your daughters shall prophesy,
> your old men shall dream dreams,
> and your young men shall see visions.
> Even on the male and female slaves,
> in those days, I will pour out my spirit. (Joel 2:28–29)

---

19. Issues related to gender and prophecy are treated in the essays found in Jonathan Stökl and Corrine L. Carvalho, eds., *Prophets Male and Female: Gender and Prophecy in the Hebrew Bible, the Eastern Mediterranean, and the Ancient Near* East (Atlanta: Society of Biblical Literature, 2013).

The other passage is in the book of Ezekiel, and it criticizes certain women who claim to be speaking in God's name when they are not. God relays to the prophet the scathing message that he should deliver to such pretenders: "As for you, mortal, set your face against the daughters of your people, who prophesy out of their own imagination; prophesy against them and say, Thus says the LORD: Woe to the women who sew bands on all wrists, and make veils for the heads of persons of every height, in the hunt for human lives! Will you hunt down lives among my people, and maintain your own lives?" (Ezek. 13:17–18). It is not clear exactly what sort of practices these women were engaging in, but the armbands and head coverings mentioned in the passage likely refer to accessories that they claimed had magical properties that enabled them to bewitch unsuspecting members of society. These texts, and others like them, give some sense of how complex and variegated prophecy was in ancient Israel by acknowledging the fact that women could fully participate in it and by calling attention to certain forms of it that were considered to be inauthentic because they were not in line with God's wishes.[20]

Truthsayers, Not Soothsayers

False notions of prophecy were not unique to the ancient world; many moderns continue to have a mistaken view of what being a biblical prophet entailed. One of the biggest misperceptions that people have is that prophets were nothing more than fortunetellers or soothsayers, persons who predicted what was going to happen in the future. According to this line of thinking, they possessed that power because they had a direct pipeline to God, who whispered into their ears about what was coming down the road that they then simply parroted back to the people to whom they had been sent.

This is not at all how the prophets functioned, but one reason why this image of them has endured through the ages and remains so common has to do with the contents of the biblical literature itself. As noted above, a phrase that is commonly associated with prophets in the Old Testament is "Thus says the LORD," which is usually followed immediately by a quote containing exactly what the Lord has said. The phrase occurs more than four hundred times in the Hebrew Bible, and in virtually every case it is spoken by someone who is identified as a prophet in the text. It is most often present in those books that are named after figures that many people

> What are some of the preconceptions you have about prophets and their role?

tend to identify as the classical biblical prophets. For example, the phrase occurs in the book of Ezekiel more than 125 times, and "Thus says the LORD" appears nearly 150 times in the book of Jeremiah. The high frequency of this formula

---

20. For an overview of the phenomenon of false prophecy, see David L. Peterson, "Prophecy, False," in *The New Interpreter's Dictionary of the Bible*, ed. Katharine Doob Sakenfeld (Nashville: Abingdon, 2009), 4:620–21.

that introduces divine speech can subtly reinforce the idea that the prophets' main job was to repeat what they were hearing from God, and this can create an impression of them as little more than ventriloquist dummies who sat on the divine lap and moved their lips in synch with what God was telling them to say. In other words, they were God's mouthpieces and nothing more. This image is supported by the relative lack of narrative material in the prophetic books, where the prophets speak a great deal but, with rare exceptions, really don't do much.

The inaccurate views that some modern people have about biblical prophecy are also partly due to the meanings that are occasionally associated with terms like "prophet" in our day and age. That word can sometimes describe someone who predicts events that will take place in the future that have nothing to do with what is going on at the moment. If ancient Israelite prophets had been asked to compare that job description to what they were actually doing, they would have dismissed anyone who claimed to have that ability as nothing but a sham and a con artist.

The reason why biblical prophets would have reacted that way is because their messages were always as much about current events as they were about coming attractions. They often pointed to what was looming on the horizon, but those warnings were usually based on the here and now. The typical biblical prophecy has a foot in both the present and the future, and it often connects the dots to posit a cause-and-effect relationship between the two. The prophets did not go around making predictions that had no basis in reality, but rather they saw the future as an inevitable outcome of what was going on around them.

In other words, prophetic books are texts that were formulated in response to particular contexts in the prophet's own day. Because it was part of a two-way communication, a prophet's message can be properly understood only when the context to which it was directed is properly understood. Without that information, our understanding of the big picture is as incomplete as when you listen in on one end of a phone conversation; you can glean a bit of information about the other party based on what one side is saying, but much remains unknown.

Amos's Context

The book of Amos, treated earlier in this chapter, provides an excellent example of the role that context plays in shaping a prophetic message. Amos lived in the eighth century BCE, when the Assyrian Empire was gathering strength in Mesopotamia and expanding its reach into other parts of the ancient Near East. Its efforts to grow its footprint proved so successful that it would ultimately become the largest empire the world had seen up to that point.[21] This was also a time

---

21. A description of the Assyrian Empire can be found in A. Kirk Grayson, "Assyrian Rule of Conquered Territory in Ancient Western Asia," in *Civilizations of the Ancient Near East*, ed. Jack M. Sasson (Farmington Hills, MI: Macmillan, 1995), 2:959–68.

of great prosperity for the wealthy members of society in the northern kingdom of Israel, many of whom had prospered by oppressing and exploiting the poor as described in the texts discussed earlier. Many of these upper-class citizens took their material success as a sign of divine favor, and they believed that God approved of what they were doing. Amos said, "Not so fast!" and warned the people that just the opposite was the case. He took those two key aspects of his context—the imminent threat of the Assyrian Empire, and the mistreatment of the poor by the rich—and interpreted them in theological terms, and the result was one of the most powerful appeals for social justice in all of literature, modern or ancient. In his view, the future invasion of the Assyrians was the work of God, who was going to punish the Israelites because he was fed up with the way the most vulnerable members of society were being abused by the most powerful.[22]

The aforementioned oracles against the nations that open his book establish Amos's theological and social justice agenda right off the bat. The section begins with six of Israel's neighbors being chastised for their behavior and then informed of the punishments that await them. The guilty half-dozen—Damascus, Philistia, Tyre, Edom, Ammon, and Moab—are told they will all be rebuked with fire from God because of their various crimes against humanity (Amos 1:3–2:3). Amos's intended audience in Israel would have undoubtedly felt smug and self-righteous as they listened to this litany of their rivals and enemies being reprimanded one-by-one by the God who was in their (the Israelites') corner. But things suddenly took an unexpected turn when God's attention was next directed at none other than Judah, which had actually been part of Israel in the not-too-distant past. Unlike the others, Judah is told that it will be sanctioned for religious reasons that include rejecting the law of God and not keeping his statutes (Amos 2:4–5).

What began as a celebration of its adversaries' misfortunes now starts to look like a cause of concern for Israel, and a glance at the map confirms that suspicion. The first six places mentioned are presented in no apparent geographical order, but their haphazard arrangement helps to create the impression that Israel is swimming in a sea of transgression and evil—Damascus (northeast of Israel), Philistia (southwest), Tyre (north), Edom (south), Amon (east), and Moab (southeast). When Judah (to the immediate south) is identified as God's next target Israel realizes that it is sitting in the bull's-eye. God then proceeds to bring the hammer down on Israel, and the amount of attention it receives indicates that this is the real focus of the divine wrath. While the oracles against the other

> Identify on a map the locations of the six neighbors of Israel that are mentioned in the oracles against the nations in Amos 1-2.

---

22. Other biblical prophets sometimes do a similar thing by presenting foreign rulers as pawns in the hand of the God of Israel. For example, Isaiah describes the Persian leader Cyrus (sixth century BCE) in this way in Isa. 45:1–7.

seven places are each two or three verses in length, the one against Israel goes on for eleven verses (Amos 2:6–16). That difference in length is matched by a difference in the infractions of the guilty party, as Israel is faulted for both social injustices against the poor, like pushing the afflicted aside (2:7), and religious improprieties, like preventing those who have dedicated their lives to God from fulfilling their vows (2:12).[23]

Although Assyria is not mentioned by name in the book, there are clear indications that Amos was aware of the threat it posed and he saw it as a tool that God would use to punish the Israelites. Immediately after they are criticized for violating the rights of the poor, the Israelites are told they will be invaded by an enemy who will overpower them (3:11; cf. 6:14). The Assyrians' preferred means of controlling the local populations of the areas they occupied was to send the leading citizens of the region into exile, and this is the very punishment the Israelites are to face (5:27; 6:7). The political reality of his time was one in which Amos saw the clear danger that the encroaching Assyrian Empire posed, and

In 701 BCE, Assyrian troops successfully attacked the city of Lachish in Judah, an event celebrated in this bas relief. In 720 BCE, the Assyrians returned and conquered the Kingdom of Israel; many Israelites were carried off to Assyria as slaves.

he interpreted that situation in theological terms that allowed him to address the social context of inequality and injustice that was plaguing Israel. In this way, as is typical in prophetic works, text and context worked hand-in-hand to deliver a powerful message to his audience.

A Problem with Several Solutions

Amos was concerned about the way that the most vulnerable members of society were being mistreated, and he pointed his finger at the wealthy as the ones responsible for the plight of the poor. He maintained that the system was rigged because it enabled powerful people to engage in corrupt practices and

---

23. John H. Hayes examines each of the oracles in his "Amos's Oracles against the Nations," *Review and Expositor* 92, no. 2 (1995): 153–67.

questionable dealings that exploited those who could not defend themselves. He railed against a flawed system that perpetuated the obscene lifestyles of the well-to-do at the expense of their fellow citizens.

Deuteronomic Theology

As legitimate and necessary as Amos's social critique might be for some, it is not the only perspective that the Old Testament provides on the vexing problem of poverty. The causes of economic inequality and how to respond to it are understood in a number of ways throughout the text, and those views are not always in complete agreement. The Deuteronomic theology that dominates much of the Hebrew Bible expresses a certain resignation about the existence of poverty because it considers it to be an ever-present fact of life. At the same time, it teaches that those who are well-off have a duty to make the lives of the poor as comfortable as possible: "Since there will never cease to be some in need on the earth, I therefore command you, 'Open your hand to the poor and needy neighbor in your land'" (Deut. 15:11). Forms of social support were sometimes put in place in ancient Israel in order to follow this command and thereby ease the burden that many labored under. An example of this is the practice of gleaning, mentioned in the previous chapter, whereby some of the produce of the land was left in the fields for the poor (Lev. 19:9–10). Because of its emphasis on obedience to the law, the Deuteronomic tradition also teaches that poverty could be wiped out if Israel were to remain faithful to God's commandments (Deut. 15:4–5). This idea is similar to the message of Amos and other prophets that social injustice and other problems result from the people turning their backs on God.

Wisdom Literature

A rather different view of poverty is put forward in the biblical wisdom literature, particularly the book of Proverbs. It agrees with Amos that the mistreatment of the disadvantaged members of society is an affront to God, and it also urges that they be treated with respect: "Those who oppress the poor insult their Maker, but those who are kind to the needy honor him" (Prov. 14:31; cf. 19:17). But Proverbs parts ways with the prophet by shifting the blame for the predicament of the poor from the wealthy to another party: the poor themselves. "A slack hand causes poverty, but the hand of the diligent makes rich" (Prov. 10:4). This verse identifies personal laziness as the primary reason why hard times come one's way, but Proverbs also singles out other character flaws that set you down the path to financial ruin. Among the other traits guaranteed to put you in the poor house, according to the book of Proverbs, are the following: being a person

> How can the Hebrew Bible's different views on poverty be explained?

of all talk and no action (14:23), a fondness for strong drink and too much food (23:20–21), poor decision-making skills (28:19), staying in bed too long (20:13; 24:33–34), and general pigheadedness (13:18).

These differing perspectives show that the biblical writers come down on both sides of an age-old debate that continues to swirl in our own time: are poor people victims or perpetrators? Have they been bilked by the system, or are they milking it? Are they blameless or blameworthy? The book of Proverbs favors the latter alternative because it was likely written as a how-to guide on life for up-and-coming young people who were going to be the shakers and movers of the future. The last thing the author(s) wanted to do was encourage them to be do-nothing slackers who slept until noon every day. Wisdom literature also often adopts a cause-and-effect understanding of life in which one's actions have consequences and determine the type of person one becomes. This is why the book of Proverbs understands poverty to be a personal choice of sorts that stems from the decisions one makes. But the message elsewhere in the Old Testament, like in Amos, is that the poor are not the ones responsible for their state in life, and the other members of society should do what they can to help those who are most in need of assistance. Despite their different views on the genesis of poverty, it is clear that the biblical authors are united in seeing it as something that is of human origin, not something that just suddenly pops up out of nowhere. The Bible leaves no doubt that poverty is a problem that begins with people.[24]

> Do any of the Bible's views on poverty strike you as more plausible than the others?

Identifying Poverty and How to Address It

Several different Hebrew terms are used in the Old Testament to refer to the poor, with the most common ones being 'ani, 'anawim, dal, and 'ebyon. The first two words are likely etymologically related, and they are found a total of nearly one hundred times in the Bible. They come from a Hebrew root that carries the sense of being bowed down or afflicted, and this suggests something of how they would have been perceived in society. Those who were most vulnerable to mistreatment would have been included in this category, like widows, orphans, foreigners, and people suffering from physical maladies, such as the blind, the deaf, and the lame. The term dal appears approximately fifty times, and it probably refers to a farmer who possessed a small plot of land and barely got by making a meager living. In Amos the dal is someone who is in a helpless situation because

---

24. A discussion of biblical attitudes toward poverty that includes the New Testament writings and a consideration of the implications for modern society can be seen in Robert Wafawanaka, "Is the Biblical Perspective on Poverty That 'There Shall Be No Poor among You' or 'You Will Always Have the Poor with You'?," *Review and Expositor* 111, no. 2 (2014): 107–20.

the wealthy are constantly exploiting him and trampling on his rights. The *'ebyon* is a person who is completely destitute and has been reduced to begging in order to survive. Appearing about sixty times in the text of the Old Testament, it is a term that is used to describe the neediest members of Israelite society.

The dire situations of the *'ani, 'anawim, dal, 'ebyon,* and other poor people in ancient Israel would have differed from person to person and from group to group, but the Old Testament leaves no doubt that the way out of their unfortunate circumstances was the same for all of them. A more just and fair society was the only thing that would alleviate their poverty and restore to them the dignity they deserved as human beings. Two different concepts are commonly found in the Bible to describe this transformed reality marked by fairness and equity for all people.

The first is *mishpat.* Appearing more than four hundred times in the Old Testament, this word is sometimes translated "justice." It comes from a verb that means "to judge," but it also carries the sense of working toward bringing about the proper result or resolution for a problematic situation. It therefore implies that when things are out of kilter and the status quo needs to be changed, effort

> What does the term "justice" mean to you?

must be undertaken to restore things to the way they are supposed to be. Justice therefore had a different connotation in ancient Israel than it does for many people today. Whereas we tend to think of it in legal terms as the application of laws and principles that we are supposed to live by that will bring about some ideal state we call "justice," they viewed it in a more interpersonal way; *mishpat* could be achieved only when the relationships among people were in good order. According to Amos and the other prophets, economic and social relationships that led to the oppression of the poor by the rich were an indication of the absence of *mishpat,* and it could only be restored by replacing those relationships with more equitable ones.[25]

The other concept is expressed in the word *tsedaqah* and related terms that all come from a Hebrew root that primarily means "to do the right or proper thing." It is commonly translated as "righteousness," and like *mishpat* it is relational in nature. According to the Old Testament, righteousness is a qual-

> What does the term "righteousness" mean to you?

ity that God possesses (Jer. 9:24), and people are urged to live righteously to fulfill their covenantal obligation to the deity. There is an active dimension to *tsedaqah*; it is not enough to just avoid doing *bad* things, but one must always strive to do the *right* thing in all one's relationships. In this way, to be righteous

---

25. For the practical dimensions of *mishpat,* see Kathleen A. Farmer, "What Does It Mean to 'Do Justice'?," *Journal of Theology* 108 (2004): 35–48.

is to be selfless because righteousness demands that one must place the needs and desires of others above one's own.[26]

The two terms *mishpat* and *tsedaqah* (or related words) are found together frequently in the Hebrew Bible, indicating their mutuality and interconnectedness. Justice and righteousness go hand-in-hand, and they combine to create the ideal environment in which all relationships can grow and prosper. The prophet Isaiah explains what such a world would look like when he writes, "Then justice will dwell in the wilderness, and righteousness abide in the fruitful field" (32:16). Earlier in the book, Isaiah describes the tragic outcome that results when these two key ingredients are missing from life: "For the vineyard of the Lord of hosts is the house of Israel, and the people of Judah are his pleasant planting; he expected justice, but saw bloodshed; righteousness, but heard a cry!" (5:7). This passage complains that the people have violated the terms of the covenant because the justice and righteousness that should be present in society have been replaced by evidence of violence and hostility. There is a clever double wordplay in the original Hebrew of the verse that adds more meaning to the prophet's message; the words for "justice" (*mishpat*) and "bloodshed" (*mispakh*) are quite similar, as are the words for "righteousness" (*tsedaqah*) and "cry" (*tse'aqah*). The related sounds of the two word pairs might be pointing to an important, though often subtle, fact of life. Sometimes what sounds or looks like one thing is actually something else, perhaps even its opposite. A person's perceived act of justice or righteousness might really be an act of bloodshed that causes a cry from the person on the receiving end. Through his wordplay, Isaiah issues a reminder to be aware that things are not always as they appear to be.[27]

The More Things Change . . .

It might seem like a strange question to pose about what is arguably the best-selling book of all time, but here goes anyway: How relevant is the Bible in today's world? With something in the neighborhood of five billion copies having been produced since Gutenberg chose it as the first book to arrive hot off the presses of his new contraption in the mid-fifteenth century, the Bible has been a fixture of the Western world that has been hard to avoid. As mentioned in an earlier chapter, according to a study conducted by the American Bible Society there are 4.4 Bibles in every American home. In addition, it is a regular part of the rituals that take place in every church, synagogue, and courtroom in the land,

---

26. How the concept of righteousness functions in the prophetic literature of the Old Testament is discussed in Nancy deClaissé-Walford, "Righteousness in the OT," in *The New Interpreter's Dictionary of the Bible*, ed. Sakenfeld, 4:820–21.

27. Many examples of wordplay, or paronomasia, in the Hebrew Bible and related literature are examined in Scott B. Noegel, ed., *Puns and Pundits: Word Play in the Hebrew Bible and Ancient Near Eastern Literature* (Bethesda, MD: CDL Press, 2000).

and these days many people can access it with a simple tap on their smartphone or iPad.[28] Now that it is available in so many forms and on such a variety of platforms, it would not be an exaggeration to say that the Good Book is more a part of everyday life than it has ever been.

Still, the question of its relevance persists. It might be more accessible than ever before, but studies indicate that people are reading the Bible less than they used to.[29] There are undoubtedly many reasons for that decline in readership, but one that is likely near the top of the list is its age. Because it is an ancient text from a world very different from our own there is a perception that the Bible does not address most of the things that modern people are concerned about. There is a certain truth to that claim because much that is in the Bible does not have a direct bearing on many of the burning issues of our day.

Another possible reason why the Bible does not have the cachet it once enjoyed is that we live in a society that celebrates and lionizes whatever is new and fresh. We are always on the lookout for The Next Big Thing, and when it arrives we embrace it and make the most of it until The Next Next Big Thing comes along. There is nothing wrong with taking advantage of progress and innovation, but sometimes it can have

> What are some other possible explanations for why people are reading the Bible less these days?

the unintended consequence of devaluing what came before. The Bible does not convey a sense of novelty for one obvious reason: it has been around forever. Consequently, there is a tendency to view it as a quaint relic from the past containing some useful teachings that can come in handy on occasion, but for the most part it is as relevant in today's world as an eight-track tape player.

This chapter presents a credible counter-argument to the view that the Bible really does not matter much today. An underlying assumption of this entire book is that the biblical literature, or at least significant portions of it, can have a direct bearing on how modern people live and think. Nowhere else in the biblical corpus is this more apparent than in the prophetic writings, because they deal with social concerns that are as important for us as they were for the prophets and the people of their time centuries ago. As was mentioned earlier, their words were intimately tied to the contexts that Amos and his fellow prophets lived in and responded to, and one aspect of those contexts that caught their attention and raised their hackles was the presence of various forms of social injustice. It is no secret that this is a problem that plagues modern society as well, and so

---

28. The iTunes website boasts that its top-rated Bible app is found on more than 180 million devices around the world (*https://itunes.apple.com/us/app/bible/id282935706?mt=8*). That is just one app out of the thousands that are out there.

29. See, for example, the results of this Gallup poll, Alec Gallup and Wendy W. Simmons, "Six in Ten Americans Read the Bible at Least Occasionally," Gallup, *http://www.gallup.com/poll/2416 /six-ten-americans-read-bible-least-occasionally.aspx*.

there is a clear link between our context and that of ancient Israel. That shared experience raises the question of what we can learn from our forebears, who long before us wrestled with one of the hot-button topics of our time. How might the biblical critique of social injustice inform our own efforts to address the issue in the twenty-first century?

Those who study the phenomenon of prophecy maintain that prophets typically come along during times of social upheaval when the winds of change are in the air. As the status quo is being challenged, prophets enter the fray to confront the powers that be and point to a way forward, a way that can transform society. They are not always successful in that effort, but even if they fail they sometimes plant seeds that will lead to future change down the line. Amos was a good example of how prophets play this role. Israel was experiencing both internal and external upheaval when he left his job as a dresser of sycamore trees and took up the mantle of prophecy. The expansion and advance of the Assyrian Empire was a threat from the outside that would eventually have a significant impact on the fate of Israel. Similarly, the blind greed and rapacious way of life of the country's wealthy citizens was an internal menace that destabilized existence for the less privileged. Amos confronted this situation head-on

> What do you think of the theory that prophets are more likely to make their presence known during times of social upheaval?

by challenging the rich and powerful to come down from their high horses and calling for a new reality in which justice and righteousness would reign supreme.

Centuries later the same role was played by the Reverend Dr. Martin Luther King Jr., who, as noted earlier in this chapter, is generally held to be one of the most important prophetic voices of recent times. King lived in a period of tremendous social unrest, and he called for a new order by taking on a system that perpetuated racism and thereby denied civil rights to all people. His warning that injustice anywhere is a threat to justice everywhere, his reminder that we all share a single garment of destiny, and his observation that the long arc of the moral universe bends toward justice were rhetorical strokes of genius on a par with anything found in the writings of the biblical prophets.

Despite the efforts of King and others like him to make the world a more just place, we're not there yet. Injustice is everywhere we turn, and if you do not believe that is the case try this simple exercise that is bound to be an eye-opener. In the course of a single day, take note of and jot down every example of an injustice you come across. It could be something you see, something you read, something you hear, or perhaps even something you do. At the end of the day, you will be amazed at how long your list is. Some of the items might strike you as petty and harmless, but many of them will be serious and significant examples of injustice at work. Multiply that by how many people there are in the world, and you can begin to appreciate the enormity of the problem. King's statement could be modified to, "Injustice everywhere is a threat to justice everywhere," and it would be just as true.

Ironically, injustice is so common that it is easy to miss. That is because it can become part of the landscape that we have grown accustomed to, and so we come to accept it as the way things are supposed to be. Think about the homeless person you ignore on the street, or the food desert that is on the other side of town that you drive right

> What can one do to be more attentive to the injustice that exists in the world?

through without even noticing. Another thing that can inhibit our ability to confront injustice is that its overwhelming presence can lead to paralysis and a sense of hopelessness that nothing can be done to combat it. These can be very real hindrances, but they are not insurmountable. If we were to ask Amos and King for advice on how to overcome them, they would probably say two things: "Pay attention!" and "Choose!" They were keen observers of what was going on around them, and they undoubtedly saw much more that they could have criticized, but they chose to focus on those things they found most offensive. That is what prophets do.

Who are today's prophets, and what should their message be? The obvious answer is that it falls to all of us to speak out and confront injustice in all its many forms and manifestations because there is more than enough work to go around. Our messages will vary, depending on which cause we choose to take up and the means at our disposal. We each carry around with us our list of injustices we have observed, and its length is a painful reminder of the task before us. Nonetheless, each time an item is scratched off we move a step closer to our goal, even if we never reach it. Injustice outlived Amos, King, and the other prophets of the past, and it will outlive us. Nonetheless, we continue to move forward in our common quest to eradicate it, confident that its days are numbered.

Implications and Applications

1. How has your understanding of the Bible changed after reading this chapter?
2. How has your understanding of social justice changed after reading this chapter?
3. Should ancient texts like the Bible be used as resources to help formulate modern views on how to address social injustice?
4. What are the most egregious examples of injustice in our world?
5. Are there modern-day equivalents of the wealthy people Amos spoke out against? If so, who are they?

6. Are there modern-day equivalents of the poor people Amos tried to defend? If so, who are they?

7. What do justice and righteousness mean in the modern world?

8. Do you think every person has a duty to speak out against injustice when they see it?

9. Do the texts discussed in this chapter play a role in shaping your views about social justice? If so, how? If not, why not?

Hungering for Social Justice
Ellen White*

"Injustice anywhere is a threat to justice everywhere," is not only a mantra for Dr. Martin Luther King Jr. and the biblical prophets, it is one that is still being cried today. In the book turned movie series, *Hunger Games*, author Suzanne Collins explores how injustice indeed pollutes all elements of life, from the oppressed to the oppressors. Yet, like the Bible, the *Hunger Games* series is not univocal on the issue of justice and all is not resolved in the end. In his chapter on justice, John Kaltner ends with some reflections about how to put the biblical warnings against injustice into action in the modern world. In her novels, Collins raises similar questions through her characters and the fictional land of Panem. Like the fairytales of old, these are stories with a moral; they are designed to make you think of your own life and what lessons you can learn from the story.

Jennifer Lawrence as Katniss in *The Hunger Games*

Murray Close / © Lionsgate / Courtesy Everett Collection

   This section explores the movie as a critique of injustice. After viewing the film while paying particular attention to the role of justice, we will explore concrete examples of ways that the story integrates the biblical

continued

---

* Ellen White holds a PhD in Hebrew Bible from the University of St. Michael's College and is a former senior editor at the Biblical Archaeology Society. She has taught at five universities across the United States and Canada.

Hungering for Social Justice *continued*

philosophies regarding social justice (prophetic, Deuteronomic, and wisdom). Then we will examine what others have noted regarding justice in
the movie to gain insight from their interpretations. Then we will think
about how to apply the lessons learned to our own lives in the modern
world. Kaltner has already explored some ideas that you can use to stimu-
late your own thoughts.

Plot Summary

Panem is a nation comprising twelve (originally thirteen) districts, each of
which has a specific role to play in supporting the capitol. The districts are
poor (though there is a clear hierarchy between the districts themselves)
and the capitol is wealthy. Those in the districts want, while those in the
capitol waste.

Seventy-four years ago, after a rebellion lead by district thirteen, a
"penance" was put in place under the guise of serving justice: the Hunger
Games. Each year, one boy and one girl from every district is chosen by lottery to compete to the death in a *Survivor*-like television show. The sole survivor is named the victor and sent back to his or her district to live a life of
splendor amid neighbors who continue to live in poverty.

The protagonist in this film is the female tribute from district twelve: Katniss Everdeen. Everdeen finds herself battling for her life in the games not
because her name was drawn in the lottery but because she volunteered to
take the place of her younger sister, who actually should have had the odds
in her favor (something to think about in light of chapter 4 of this book).

Watch *The Hunger Games* (2012, time: 2:22:00), *https://xmovies8.org/
watch?v=kMjlhMWE5OT*.

When watching the movie keep the following questions in mind. If you
have watched the whole series you can pull examples and insights from
the later movies, especially as knowledge of what is to come can color your
understanding of earlier events.

- Why is it called *The Hunger Games*?
- What social justice issues are present in the movie? Identify what is
  unjust, explain why it is unjust, and indicate whether it is addressed
  as the story unfolds. Why are the district residents of Panem rising up
  against the Capitol? What are their lives like?

continued

Hungering for Social Justice   *continued*

- Think about Isaiah 5:7, "He expected justice, but saw bloodshed," and reflect on whether this accurately reflects *The Hunger Games*.
- Which characters remind you of the biblical characters discussed by Kaltner? Explain the parallels you see.
- How are the capitol and President Snow able to maintain their social injustices? What techniques do they use? Provide examples and reasons why you think these are effective tools.
- What elements represent the prophetic view of social justice? Are some things more reminiscent of Deutronomic theology? Are elements of wisdom literature present?

Below the Surface

Sometimes authors use particular characters in their work to exemplify certain philosophies, theologies, and beliefs. This is not always easy to notice, especially with main characters. Unlike a thought, position, or statement, people are complex and often contradictory, and without portraying that side of humanity, authors would end up with unrelatable characters, so such parallels are imperfect by nature. However, parallels are very prevalent in this movie.

Peeta Mellark, the male tribute from district twelve and Katniss's partner, is committed to social justice despite his circumstance. When Peeta and Katniss meet in the movie, a brief flashback shows that they had had a previous encounter, but the implications of this past meeting will not emerge until later in the film. Peeta was the son of the village baker and as such might have been better off than most in district twelve, which is not saying much. Katniss was the daughter of a miner who was killed in a work-related explosion. Her mother was left in a catatonic state by her grief and Katniss had a younger sister who required care. Her family was literally in danger of starving to death. One night in the rain the baker boy encountered the poor starving girl while he was out feeding his family's pigs. In an act that he knew would result in being beaten, Peeta threw the bread to Katniss instead—this interaction appears briefly in the movie, but is much clearer in the book. This simple act saved both the girl and her family, as it gave her just enough hope to learn to provide for herself. Here Peeta expresses the prophetic response to justice. He helps the helpless, one who has been marginalized and oppressed by the system, although his circumstances are not

continued

Hungering for Social Justice *continued*

much different from her own, and he knows he will suffer for his act. He does not turn a blind eye; he does not endure the injustice in front of him.[30]

While Peeta is a good example of the prophetic approach to justice, Effie Trinkett is almost the antitype for the wisdom perspective. At first blush she appears to express the wisdom perspective to a tee, as summed up by her statement in the luxury of the train just after they become tributes: "I think it is one of the wonderful thing about this opportunity that even though you are here . . . just for a little while, you get to enjoy all this." But in this movie, she is the embodiment of the capitol,[31] not the rulers like President Snow, but the average citizen. On the surface she appears to follow the principles of wisdom literature (one's predicaments are the result of one's own actions), but she and the average capitol citizen are in fact displaying the traits that Proverbs rails against.[32] The Careers (tributes from districts one and two who train for the games all their lives and then usually volunteer) might be a better representative of the wisdom perspective; while they might be morally reprehensible, they are not lazy and have worked hard to achieve their goals. The fact that they are largely unlikable might have more to do with the author's perspective on this view of social justice than on the wisdom perspective's theology.

Bringing in still another perspective is Cinna, the star-stylist for district twelve tributes. Cinna is part of the establishment and holds a formal role in these proceedings, which suggests a certain amount of resignation to the system, but, in keeping with Deuteronomic theology, he does everything he can to help and support Katniss. His role in the film is small, but his impact on Katniss and her circumstances is significant. Cinna is not out to change the system itself, but to have an effect on the lives of those trapped by the system. This is a Deutronomic perspective.

What additional parallels do you see? Is President Snow more like Ahab or Jezebeel? Which philosophy do the tribute sponsors hold? How does the three-fingered salute relate to the theme of justice? What type of justice does Katniss display? Does she represent more than one position? Can someone hold more than one idea regarding justice? How do you feel

continued

---

30. Peeta is complex when it comes to the issue of justice, especially in the films based on the final book. If you watch these, see if you can see elements of the puppet prophet that Kaltner discusses on page 246. In some ways, Gale is the best example of the prophetic view as he always sees the systemic injustices and fights relentlessly for system-wide change.

31. Her character evolves significantly in the rest of the series.

32. See page 250.

Hungering for Social Justice *continued*

about the characters; which character's perspective do you relate to most? How would you react to the system?

Viewers' Reactions

It is possible to recognize theological themes in the movie, despite the absence of explicit references to God. "*The Hunger Games* celebrates faith—faith in family, faith in friendship, faith in song, faith in justice," argues theologian Diana Butler Bass. "*The Hunger Games* proclaims that beyond the fences of fear built to enslave, control, and guard, there is joy, beauty, and wonder. In the end, there is true freedom, and the hard-earned hope that human beings can create a better world based not in sacrificial violence but in sacrificial love."[33] The transformative vision is that of the prophets, like Amos. This perspective sees no merit in the oppressive system, nor in the possibility of working the system for the betterment of those within it. Rather, the transformative vision seeks to replace the unjust system. It calls for social justice not at the individual level, but seeks justice for the individual as a result of a new and just system.

"The way the books and the movie are written reflects the reader's/viewer's journey from identifying with the mistreated innocent to becoming a detached onlooker," claims blogger David of The Corner Booth.[34] "As the one in the stands, you suddenly care less about the madness of the general situation and plight of each individual and much more about one tribute's success. *Your* tribute's success. . . . The revolting thought that these teens were kidnapped and *forced* to kill each other has left your mind. . . . Once we realize that we've become comfortable cheering this on from the sidelines, that's where the story points back at us. This meta-message states that not only is this situation terrible, but *we're* terrible for both watching the games and allowing them to happen." David is claiming that the author of *The Hunger Games* is using a technique similar to the oracles against the nations, which Kaltner introduced in this chapter. When the ancient Israelites first heard the pronouncements against the wickedness of the foreign nations, their enemies, they might have indulged in a moment of

continued

---

33. Diana Butler Ross, "'The Hunger Games': Spiritual, But Not Religious," *https://www.on faith.co/onfaith/2012/03/22/the-hunger-games-spiritual-but-not-religious/15570.*

34. "Social Justice and the Arena—A Review of "The Hunger Games," The Corner Booth, *https://cornerboothsocialclub.wordpress.com/2012/04/10/social-justice-and-the-arena-a-review -of-the-hunger-games/.*

Hungering for Social Justice *continued*

smugness and even cheered that their opponents would "get what they deserved." By saving Israel and Judah for the final climactic pronouncements, the prophets effectively have Israel and Judah convict themselves. David is calling for this kind of personal reflection in light of *The Hunger Games* and thus closely aligning the writers with the prophetic perspective, but he leaves the possibility open for the viewer to respond on the basis of any philosophy that rings true for them. On which philosophy would you base your response?

"It is a prophetic picture of the 1 percent and the 99 percent," states J. Ryan Parker.[35] "Our inability to see and understand the connectedness between our privileged lives and those who suffer to provide them, keep us from being poor in spirit." Parker's reference to Matthew 5:3 links him to the Deuteronomic tradition, but it also demonstrates the connectedness of us all. This is something recognized right from the beginning of the movie when Seneca Crane exudes, "It is something that knits us all together." Here the head gamemaker expresses the same sentiment that Martin Luther King Jr. does. Despite Crane's belief that this is a good thing, it demonstrates the ominous nature of this interconnectivity; change for one part of society will inevitably result in change for all.

"Movements to challenge injustice can begin when fundamental wrongs are identified and people organize to challenge power holders, institutions, and society's norms," states the Center for Healthy Teen Relationships, an initiative of the Idaho Coalition against Sexual Domestic Violence in one of their teaching documents, citing *The Hunger Games* as an object lesson.[36] "A shared passion for promoting new visions of a better world can transform the way we view our roles in society, our values and priorities, and ultimately the structure of our society and communities."

Mourning is one such shared experience, according to Julie Clawson, author of *The Hunger Games and the Gospel*:[37] "Mourning the children who are chosen on Reaping Day is exactly what the Capitol doesn't want the Districts to do. To mourn would mean tapping into the honest depth of their feelings, being truthful about how devastated they are by the Capitol's actions—honest feelings that could foster resentment and possible

continued

---

35. J. Ryan Parker, "The Hunger Games and the Gospel: A Review," Pop Theology, *http://www.patheos.com/blogs/poptheology/2012/03/the-hunger-games-and-the-gospel/*.

36. "The Hunger Games: Catching Fire for Social Justice Lesson Plan," California Partnership to End Domestic Violence, *https://www.nttac.org/tribalyouthprogram.org/resource-topics/hunger-games-catching-fire-social-justice-lesson-plan.html*.

37. Julie Clawson, *The Hunger Games and the Gospel* (Englewood, CO: Patheos Press, 2013).

rebellion."[38] Remember when Rue died. Katniss mourned her friend and sent the three-fingered salute to her family back in district eleven. Those in the district bonded with her and viewed it as a call for revolution, which they acted on immediately. Through mourning they connect to one another and move toward justice.

In June of 2014, several anti-government demonstrators in Thailand were arrested for adopting the three fingered salute used in *The Hunger Games*.[39] "In social networks, activists write that for them a gesture from 'Hunger Games' symbolizes freedom, equality and fraternity. 'You cannot stop our thoughts,' they say," explains Russian journalist, Olga Zamanskaya.[40] In the movie, this small act is one way the oppressed are able to express themselves and provide unity. That the practice was picked up by this group who believes they are oppressed by an unjust government demonstrates the power of modern media to disseminate a message.

Reel to Real

The best question that a student has ever asked me was at the end of a carefully crafted lecture that I, as a newly-minted teacher, thought was sheer perfection. The student with all sincerity asked me, "So what?" I have since come to learn that this experience is hardly unique. Teachers tend to focus on analyzing and interpreting data—important to be sure, but where is the pay off if there is no application? Muriel Spark in the *Prime of Miss Jean Brodie* said, "The word 'education' comes from the root e from ex, out, and duco, I lead. It means a leading out. To me education is a leading out of what is already there in the pupil's soul."[41] Therefore, the final step in this process is to find out what is in your "soul."

Make a list of the social justice issues that are prevalent in Panem. Are there similar issues plaguing your community? If you don't know, research the question. What examples of injustice or oppression do you see in your world? What strategies have you seen employed to combat social injustices?

continued

38. Parker, "The Hunger Games and the Gospel."

39. Seth Mydans, "Thai Protesters Are Detained after Using 'Hunger Games' Salute," *New York Times*, Nov. 20, 2014, *https://www.nytimes.com/2014/11/21/world/asia/thailand-protesters-hunger-games-salute.html?_r=0*.

40. Olga Zamanshaya, "People Arrested in Thailand for Gesture from 'Hunger Games' Film Series," *Sputnik News*, *https://sputniknews.com/voiceofrussia/news/2014_06_10/People-arrested-in-Thailand-for-gesture-from-Hunger-Games-film-series-6675/*.

41. Muriel Spark, *Prime of Miss Jean Brodie*, *http://www.obooksbooks.com/2015/4435_6.html*.

Hungering for Social Justice *continued*

Have you been involved in any activities to promote social justice—perhaps with your family, your school, your place of worship, or your community? What might you do personally to make a difference? Possibilities include writing your representative to Congress, committing to using only fair-trade products,[42] volunteering at a food bank, or organizing a food drive or a farmers' market for a food desert. As Kaltner indicated in the chapter, it is not up to individuals to fix everything, but rather to act on something. Think about what is important to you or has touched your life and then think of something concrete that you can do to make a difference.

Further Exploration

View the movie *Divergent* (2014, time: 2:19:00), paying particular attention to the theme of justice. Reflect on how the theme is expressed similarly to or differently from the biblical philosophies involving justice (prophetic, Deuteronomic, and wisdom) presented in chapter 6. Find out what others think, and evaluate their positions. Apply what you have learned to modern life and your own circumstances.

Questions to keep in mind while viewing *Divergent*:

- While both films represent the genre of dystopian literature, they are very different. Are you surprised by the choice of this film for this topic? If so, why are you surprised?
- What justice issues do you encounter in *Divergent*?
- Where do you see elements of the three biblical philosophies in this movie? Are they embodied in particular characters? Are they more prevalent in certain scenes?
- What is the main position of the writers on the issue of justice? How do you know? What do you think of this conclusion? Can you relate? Explain why or why not.

After reflecting on the film in light of justice, describe what should happen next; do not simply summarize what happens in the second and third books or movies. Analyze the film in light of the various theologies in the Bible (prophetic, Deuteronomic, and wisdom), explaining how each is found in the film. Engage in some internet research and consider perspectives you

continued

---

42. Such as Gifts with Humanity, *www.giftswithhumanity.com*.

Hungering for Social Justice   *continued*

find.[43] Think about these perspectives and evaluate them in terms of what you have learned so far. Bear in mind that something found on the internet does not necessarily represent an expert opinion. Describe how you would end the story and why, drawing on your own experience if relevant. There is no right or wrong answer to this exercise, but there are informed and uninformed answers. Make a convincing case.

---

43. A targeted search using "*Divergent*, social justice, Bible" is likely to provide more pertinent results than a search using "*Divergent* reviews."

Additional Resources

Books

Birch, Bruce C., and Walter Brueggemann. *A Theological Introduction to the Old Testament.* Nashville: Abingdon, 2011.

Carr, David M. *An Introduction to the Old Testament: Sacred Texts and Imperial Contexts of the Hebrew Bible.* New York: Wiley-Blackwell, 2011.

Collins, John J. *A Short Introduction to the Hebrew Bible.* Minneapolis: Fortress, 2014.

Coogan, Michael D., and Cynthia R. Chapman. *A Brief Introduction to the Old Testament: The Hebrew Bible in Its Context.* New York: Oxford University Press, 2015.

Gravett, Sandra L., Karla G. Bohmbach, F. V. Greifenhagen, and Donald C. Polaski. *An Introduction to the Hebrew Bible: A Thematic Approach.* Louisville: Westminster John Knox, 2008.

Lohr, Joel N., and Joel S. Kaminsky. *The Hebrew Bible for Beginners: A Jewish and Christian Introduction.* Nashville: Abingdon, 2015.

Websites

Bible Odyssey. *www.bibleodyssey.org.*

A site run by the Society of Biblical Literature where scholars present research on people, places, and passages in the Bible in an easy-to-read and accessible format. It also includes other helpful features, including a glossary, images, maps, and videos.

Enter the Bible. *http://www.enterthebible.org/.*

A site at Luther Seminary that provides information on each book of the Bible in the following categories: summary, outline, background, introductory issues, and theological themes.

Old Testament Gateway. *http://otgateway.com/.*

A comprehensive and annotated academic directory of hundreds of websites related to the Old Testament that are arranged in categories.

Oxford Biblical Studies Online. *http://www.oxfordbiblicalstudies.com/.*

A site similar to Bible Odyssey, but access to it requires the payment of a subscription fee.

Index

Note: The abbreviations *c, cap, i, s,* or *n* indicate charts, captions, illustrations, sidebars, or footnotes, respectively.